D1165696

Professional Ship Management
Marketing and strategy

PHOTIS M. PANAYIDES
Department of Shipping and Transport Logistics
The Hong Kong Polytechnic University
Kowloon, Hong Kong

Ashgate

Aldershot • Burlington USA • Singapore • Sydney

Published by
Ashgate Publishing Ltd
Gower House
Croft Road
Aldershot
Hants GU11 3HR
England

Ashgate Publishing Company
131 Main Street
Burlington, VT 05401-5600 USA

Ashgate website: http://www.ashgate.com

British Library Cataloguing in Publication Data
Panayides, Photis M.
    Professional ship management : marketing and strategy. -
    (Plymouth studies in contemporary shipping and logistics)
    1.Ships - Management 2.Shipping - Management 3.Shipping -
    Marketing 4.Ships - Marketing
    I.Title
    387.5'068

Library of Congress Control Number: 00-110604

ISBN 0 7546 1489 1

Printed and bound by Athenaeum Press, Ltd.,
Gateshead, Tyne & Wear.

Contents

List of Tables and Figures   viii
Preface   ix
Acknowledgements   xi

1 Introduction   1

2 Ship Management   6
   Introduction   6
   Ship Management Defined   6
   Ship Management: A Historical Review   7
   The Rationale for Outsourcing Ship Management   9
   The Economics of Vertical Disintegration and Outsourcing   12
   Organisational Structures   14
   Services Offered by Ship Management Companies   16
   Legal Aspects of Ship Management   25
   Ship Management Market Structure   28
   Organisational Behaviour in Ship Management   31
   Total Quality in Ship Management   37
   Information Technology and Ship Management   39
   The International Ship Managers' Association (ISMA)   41

3 Marketing Ship Management   43
   Introduction   43
   The Marketing of Ship Management Services   43
   The Ship Management Service and Service Quality   50
   Pricing Ship Management Services   52
   Location and Distribution   54
   Promotion   55
   Internal Marketing and Human Resource Management   57
   Process and Physical Evidence   60

4 Ship Manager-Client Relationships 62
Introduction 62
Marketing and Exchange Relationships 62
Relationship Marketing 64
Applying Relationship Marketing to Ship Management Services 69
Conceptual Design and Methodology 74
Elements of Ship Management Relationships 76
Strategic Relationship Groups in Ship Management 85
Profiles of Relationship Groups 89
Profiles with Client Company Characteristics 95
Frequency of Communication 99
Implications for Ship Manager-Client Relationships 101

5 Ship Manager Selection and Evaluation 111
Introduction 111
The Importance of Selection Criteria 111
Selection Criteria in Services 113
Selection Criteria in Shipping and Transport 114
Ship Manager Selection and Performance Evaluation 117
A Process Model for Decision, Selection and Evaluation 130

6 Competitive Advantage in Ship Management 139
Introduction 139
Competition in Ship Management 139
The Competitive Structure of the Ship Management Market 141
Strategies for Competitive Advantage 144
The Sustainability of Competitive Advantage 152

7 Strategy in Ship Management 160
Introduction 160
Establishing a Strategic Direction 160
Diversification in Ship Management 162
Coalitions and Competitor Alliances 169
International Market Strategy 174
Mergers and Acquisitions 178
Performance Measurement 184

8 Conclusion 187
Introduction 187
Ship Management Service Solutions 187

Markets, Location and Entry   188
Problems and Panaceas   189
Client Relationships   190
Client Needs and Expectations   191
The Sustainability of Competitiveness   192
Strategic Directions   193
Professional Ship Management: Marketing and Strategy   194

Bibliography   196

List of Tables and Figures

Table 2.1 The growth of ship management companies 1990-2000   29
Table 2.2 The growth of companies in ship management centres   30
Table 4.1 The frequency of personal contact at operational level   81
Table 4.2 The frequency of personal contact at operational level
    by location   82
Table 4.3 The frequency of personal contact at senior management
    level   83
Table 4.4 The frequency of communication at operational level   84
Table 4.5 The frequency of communication at senior management
    level   85
Table 4.6 Distinguishing relationship characteristics in each cluster   89
Table 4.7 Typical client characteristics per ship management cluster   99
Table 5.1 The importance of selection criteria: ship managers' view   121
Table 5.2 The importance of evaluation criteria: ship managers'
    view   123
Table 5.3 The importance of selection criteria: clients' view   128
Table 5.4 The importance of evaluation criteria: clients' view   129
Table 5.5 Means of importance of selection criteria   133
Table 5.6 Means of importance of evaluation criteria   136

Figure 5.1 A process model for decision, choice and evaluation   138

Preface

Professional ship management undoubtedly makes a significant contribution in the organisation of resources for the sustenance of a ship and in doing so contributes to organisational efficiency in the shipping industry at large. Professional ship managers have established themselves as strong advocates of quality and are among the first in the shipping industry to adopt and apply new techniques and technologies as they become available.

The importance of competitiveness in ship management means that interest in aspects like strategy and marketing are nowadays becoming increasingly relevant from a practical perspective. In addition, the recognition that professional ship management companies are conducive to efficiency in shipping makes this industry sector worthy of study at scientific level. This book represents an attempt to provide an analysis of the aspects identified as of importance in ship management. In doing so it is appreciated that many ship managers have been highly receptive to such analysis and what it can offer to the development of marketing and strategy within their organisations.

The purpose of this book is not to give hard and fast rules about courses of action in particular situations where marketing strategy is of the essence. It is my belief that nobody can provide, through a book of this nature, specific rules that can be wholly relied upon to yield the desired results. Hence, the purpose of this book is rather to bring issues to the forefront of a ship manager's thought process, and to provoke understanding of what is still, to a large extent, uncharted territory by many practitioners in ship management and indeed by many in the shipping industry.

The book has a role to play in shipping education and research as well. Once again, many of the issues raised can provide understanding, provoke questions and encourage the initiation of further research on many areas that have not yet been scientifically analysed. It should be invaluable to undergraduate and postgraduate students in maritime business, shipping and logistics and interested in the study of marketing and strategy. The book is unique in its nature of applying contemporary marketing and strategic management thought in the shipping industry. Most shipping business related books deal with the application of neo-classical micro-economic theory. This book brings a new perspective not just through the application of marketing and strategy but also through the implicit and at times explicit assertion that new institutional economic thought can be applied to shipping. Hence, works originating from such acclaimed economists as Schumpeter, Coase, Penrose, Williamson and Teece, provide ample opportunity for introducing another fresh perspective in this area of applied economics. This book must not by any means be construed as a completed product, for it represents a snapshot in time. It does however present some emergent ideas that are considered for the first time in such depth in a professional ship management context.

It is envisaged that the book will be a reference point and a thought-provoking medium for students, researchers and practitioners alike.

Photis M. Panayides
Hung Hom
Kowloon
Hong Kong
September 2000

"I can now rejoice even in the falsification of a cherished theory, because even this is a scientific success" John Carew Eccles

Acknowledgements

Of course, this book is by no means the fruit of my labours alone. I would like to acknowledge the direct or indirect contributions made by various people that have culminated in the development of this book in its current state. I should extend thanks to all those scholars in economics, marketing and strategy who have moved the boundaries of knowledge so that today new principles can be applied to business that improve productivity and efficiency, and ultimately yield economic prosperity. Their works are referred to in the text. Appreciation is also extended to the professionals who responded to the surveys conducted during the process of research.

I would also like to thank many people with whom I had the honour and pleasure of co-operating. The contribution of Dr. Richard Gray, of the Institute of Marine Studies, University of Plymouth, to this book and to my personal educational and professional development has been immense and invaluable. It is a blessing that the research and educational shipping and logistics community is served by a person with his wisdom and integrity of character.

I am grateful to Dr. Harry Heijveld, Professor Michael S. Roe and Mr. Sydney T. Harley of the Institute of Marine Studies, University of Plymouth, for their influence on my educational development as teachers and colleagues.

Further thanks are due to Prof. Kevin P. B. Cullinane, Head, Department of Shipping and Transport Logistics, The Hong Kong Polytechnic University for his encouragement and belief in me. It is a pleasure and an honour to work with somebody having his credentials and capabilities in shipping and logistics academia. My colleagues and friends at the Department of Shipping and Transport Logistics are gratefully acknowledged for their co-operative attitude.

My former students at the Institute of Marine Studies, University of Plymouth (September 1995-July 1999) also deserve to be mentioned, for I have probably gained much from the challenges they posed in the process of lecturing and thesis supervision. Many of them remain my good friends.

I would also like to specifically mention a few names as a measure of my appreciation towards them. They include Marie Bendell, Rachael Burbidge, Lynn Stott, Josephine Hobbs of the Institute of Marine Studies and my Hong Kong Chinese friend Man-Lai Chan (Elley). Thanks are extended to Lai-Mui (Teresa), Shirley, Joyce and Szeto of the General Office, Jasmine Lam, my research assistant and Kathryn Mennier for meticulous proof-reading.

Last but not least I thank my family for their investments, encouragement and belief in me. My tireless father and mother, Michael and Evridiki, my sister Chryso and my brother Mario.

1 Introduction

The provision of ship management services by third parties is a relatively new type of service in international shipping when compared to the time period during which ships have been managed by their owners. Professional ship management also represents a major structural change in the maritime industry. Sletmo (1989) argued that shipping developed in 'four waves'. The first wave was the early use of water transport by man, followed by the quest for maritime power occurring in the 17th to 19th centuries. The third wave began after the Second World War and culminated in the transnationalisation of shipping with the greatly increased dependence on manpower from developing countries and flagging out. According to Sletmo (1989) professional ship management may represent the fourth wave in international shipping.

The growth of third party ship management in recent years led to a number of people characterising the sector as an industry in its own right. The strides towards growth and the importance of ship management have been recognised since the early 1970s. This is documented in the report prepared by the Committee of Inquiry into Shipping chaired by Viscount Rochdale (The Rochdale Report) and presented to the British Parliament in 1970. The report recognised that:

> There is an important part to be played by good independent ship management companies to help the small owner in developing his business. There may also be special circumstances where some larger companies may benefit from their employment. We regard the existence of good independent professional management companies as conducive to efficiency in the industry (The Rochdale Report, 1970, p. 319).

Sletmo (1989, p. 298) refers to ship management firms as constituting 'an efficient organisational adjustment to the conditions of a global shipping market'. He further questions whether the optimal form of organisation in the maritime industry is that which owns and operates the ship(s). Although the latter assertion may seem to be an overstatement, there are definitely instances where it might be economically and organisationally more feasible and advantageous to have ships managed by third parties. This is because large ship management companies can offer distinct benefits to their clients that culminate in the improved efficiency of the shipping

1

market at large. Efficiency arises from the effective use of resources so as to produce the maximum output with the least input. Ship management firms can contribute to efficiency because they can achieve greatly reduced average costs by virtue of their size (economies of scale). They can also facilitate the effective organisation of resources required to maintain a ship by virtue of their professionalism.

Despite its undisputed importance in international shipping, professional ship management did not receive the attention it deserved from an academic or professional point of view until the 1990s. The most notable attempts to address aspects of the ship management industry included some contributions by Sletmo (1986; 1989), books by Spruyt (1990; 1994) and Willingale (1998) and various contributions by Panayides and Gray (1997a; 1997b; 1999a; 1999b) and Panayides (1999).

This particular book emanates from research carried out over the last seven years and aims to address contemporary issues and current and future developments in professional ship management that are worthy of rigorous scholarly attention and practitioner consideration. At the forefront of managing a professional ship management firm are issues of growth, expansion and profitability. The achievement of these objectives rests on the ability of management to prescribe and implement courses of action that will yield the desired results. It also rests on the ability of management to instil a corporate culture that will empower employees to work towards the achievement of the firm's objectives. Issues of delivering a service that is both of high quality and differentiated from competition are imperative in the competitive environment that ship management firms are now operating in. It is increasingly recognised in ship management that in order to achieve growth, it is not enough to offer the basic service well, engage in traditional cost-reduction and seafarer training and recruitment tactics, and monitor changes through accounting measures. The ambitious ship management firm should be able to engage in practices that yield additional value to the firm. Such practices can be learned by recognising where the company is and where it wants to go, analysing market opportunities and competitive threats, and taking proactive steps to retain clients and create markets. It would seem that such practices and actions could be methodically applied by learning from past practices and appropriately applying contemporary aspects of marketing and strategy. Hence, the theme of this book.

As it is a professional service, the marketing and strategic management principles that apply to professional services in general also apply to ship management. This is reflected in the book, where principles of marketing and strategy that have been empirically examined in a professional ship management context are presented. In addition, a great deal can be inferred and many implications of practical value can be deduced from the conceptual application of such principles to ship management.

The need for this approach arises from the fact that the application of well-established principles, particularly in theory but also, to a large extent, in practice, seems to be somewhat limited in the professional ship management context. This is despite the importance of ship management in efficiently organising the allocation of resources required for the sustenance of a ship and despite the contribution of ship management to the efficient organisation of the shipping industry at large.

This book is made up of eight chapters including the introduction. All chapters deal with marketing and strategy issues that are at the forefront of scholarly thought and are also imperative for addressing the needs and achieving the objectives of the modern ship management firm.

Chapter 2 provides an overview of the ship management industry. This is accomplished through reviews of past literature and informal external inquiry with practising ship managers. The chapter details the nature and practices of ship management companies in addition to examining organisational behaviour and other characteristics of the industry. It identifies the issues at the forefront of managerial practices in ship management. This provides an early indication of the approaches that may be applied for their thorough study with the potential for making valuable recommendations.

The following chapter (chapter 3) deals specifically with the marketing practices of professional ship management firms. It also identifies and places into context the major issues and challenges faced by contemporary ship management companies. This is accomplished through a thorough study of the marketing practices and systematic application of established marketing concepts. In addition, ways in which such practices may be improved are also highlighted in this chapter.

One of the approaches that were identified to have enormous applicability in the context of professional ship management is the concept of relationship marketing. Relationship marketing has been at the forefront of academic marketing thought and professional practice since the early 1990s and its applicability to services, and professional services in particular, has been very well documented. The concept is examined in the context of professional ship management through an empirical investigation detailed in chapter 4. Chapter 4 initially provides justification of the applicability and usefulness of applying relationship marketing to ship management. This is followed by a review of the relationship marketing literature that identifies the major issues in buyer-seller relationships. An empirical investigation is then undertaken that culminates in the identification of the relationship marketing elements present in ship manager-shipowner relationships. A typology of ship management relationships is developed and the implications thereof are discussed.

One of the most important issues for professional ship management firms is to possess knowledge and understanding of the factors that will be considered by potential clients in deciding whether and which ship manager to select. In addition, the criteria used by current clients in establishing an assessment and evaluation of the performance of the ship manager are also of critical importance, particularly for client retention. Recognising the importance of the issues, chapter 5 provides a detailed analysis, which includes an empirical investigation revealing the criteria both from the ship manager's and from the client's point of view.

Competition may be regarded as an economist's dream, but for practising ship managers competition in the industry requires action that will ensure sustainable competitiveness for the companies. Chapter 6 addresses the issues of competition and achieving a sustainable competitive advantage in professional ship management. Following an evaluation of competitive conduct in ship management, the chapter considers the potential of applying the generic strategies for competitive advantage as well as the application of contemporary thought as exposed in the resource-based view and the competence-based competition perspectives.

A fundamental question for business organisations and their management is why do some companies succeed whereas others fail. It is a fact that some organisations achieve profits and growth whereas others stagnate and decline or even never take off. To examine these issues, chapter 7 will address why companies produce what, and how and for whom they produce it. In addition, there will be an examination of how companies go about organising their activities in terms of internal organisation and in their relationships with other organisations. Finally, the chapter explores how companies adapt and change to accommodate changing environmental tendencies and take advantage of arising opportunities. These are fundamental issues in the agenda of strategy for professional ship management firms.

The last chapter provides the concluding remarks to the aspects scrutinised throughout the book. The chapter highlights a number of fundamental implications for marketing and strategy in professional ship management emanating from the theoretical, conceptual and empirical examinations of the issues as depicted in the text. It provides a discussion and extension of the major issues with particular emphasis given to managerial implications and the direction of professional ship management as deduced from a thorough study of marketing and strategy in the industry.

2 Ship Management

Introduction

Ship management is a professional service available to companies or individuals owning ships. To some, professional ship management has developed into an industry in its own right within the maritime sector. This chapter aims to describe and analyse all major issues associated with this professional service. The description will utilise a commercial and economic perspective with particular focus on marketing and strategic practices. This is essential, as the focus of this book is commercial viability, growth, competitive advantage and profit for professional ship management firms.

The rapid growth and the complexity of ship management (Underwood, 1989; Spruyt, 1994) require an analysis of both the firm and industry perspective in order to accomplish a comprehensive understanding. Hence, the aim of this chapter is to provide a description and evaluation of firm- and industry-specific factors including such issues as range of services offered, organisational behaviour, market structure and other legal, economic and commercial issues that have shaped the contemporary ship management sector.

Ship Management Defined

A prerequisite for understanding the analysis is a definition of ship management. The wide range of activities comprising ship management have given rise to differing definitions by practitioners. For instance, Downward (1987, p. xi) gives the following definition:

> The functions of taking care of a ship, i.e. responsibility for manning, maintaining, supplying and insuring the ship, and ensuring that the ship is available to the operators for the maximum amount of time possible. In other words, all the activities not carried out by the operators.

Rodger (1993, p. 3) stated that ship management means 'the management and sustenance of the ship itself rather than of the trade in which it is engaged'. Spruyt (1994, p. 1) defines ship management as:

The contracted and professional supply of all on-board services, together with their shore supervision, which would normally enhance a vessel from a bareboat into a time charter description, by a management company usually separate from the vessel's ownership.

A definition is also given in the Code of Ship Management Standards (CSS) developed by the International Ship Managers' Association (ISMA). Section 1.1.5 of Part 3 of the ISMA Code states: 'ship management means the rendering of services for ship operation and associated services'.

Although the above definitions are not taken lightly, they do represent the views of the aforementioned and may be incorrect in the strict legal or economic sense (Rodger, 1993; Spruyt, 1994). In addition, Spruyt's definition seems to be vague and does not seem either simple or complete. Willingale (1998) in the revised edition of the book recognised this and departed from it by defining ship management as 'the professional supply of a single or range of services by a management company separate from the vessel's ownership in support of the primary objectives of the shipowner' (Willingale, 1998, p. 13). In an attempt to close this gap even further, a mere generalisation would give a more acceptable conceptualisation of ship management. Hence, professional ship management may be defined as the rendering of services under contract related to the systematic organisation of economic resources and transactions required for the sustenance of a ship as a revenue-earning entity. The advantage of this definition is that it recognises that ship management involves the organisation of economic resources and not the mere supply of services.

Although this systematic organisation of resources has traditionally been the task of the shipowner, nowadays it may be carried out by third parties. Hence the growth of the professional, independent ship management companies. A brief review of the evolution of ship management would serve as the key to a better appreciation of the company's functions and the current state of the industry.

Ship Management: A Historical Review

Independent ship management as we know it today has a fairly recent origin if we consider that '...man discovered water transport long before he saddled a horse' (Heyerdahl, 1978, p. 19). However, to state that the basic ship management functions are of recent origin would be a misconception.

Leeson (1983) suggests that primarily the master of the ship performed the basic ship management functions in the early days of shipping. The master not only sailed and navigated the ship, but also procured cargo, fixed freight and received payment, engaged and disengaged the crew, directed maintenance and generally carried out all the necessary day-to-day operations for the sustenance of the vessel.

With the further commercialisation of shipping, the increasing legislative and administrative demands and the advancement of technology, it was impossible for the ship's master to carry out the management functions. Those functions were transferred to the shore-based office of the shipowner and the master's role was restricted to navigation and on-board administration. This type of organisation may be considered as the traditional way of running a vessel.

According to Underwood (1989), the practice of having an independent entity or person running a vessel for the owner has been part of the shipping industry since medieval times. The practice continued (with the manager usually being a retired master) until the 19th century. At that time, the introduction of limited liability companies encouraged the merger of entities owning and managing vessels, forming the traditional shipping company. Independent management companies were primarily formed after World War II, but in insignificant numbers in order to serve niche markets.

It was not until the late 1960s that developments in the shipping industry triggered the formation of a new type of organisation. Sletmo (1989) described this as the shipping industry's fourth wave. It may be argued that the evolution of third party ship management was begun by organisations not directly related to operating ships - principally by the oil majors and to a lesser extent by banks and other financial institutions. The traditional way of transporting oil was by time-chartering vessels suited to the particular trade operation. However, with the increasing availability of tax breaks on ship investment, the oil majors seized advantage of the opportunity by making capital investments to acquire ships. They then delegated the management of those ships to specialised managers. Banks, on the other hand, at times wished to make investments in ship purchase (when trends and conditions were favourable) and delegated the task of running the ships to third parties. A significant number of vessels fell into the hands of bankers during and after the 1973 oil crisis. At the time, poor conditions in the shipping markets (low freight rates and poor sale and purchase market values) made it impossible for shipowners to repay debts. Stokes (1992, p. 35) notes that 'between 1973 and 1974 the average value of a 1972/73-built 250,000 dwt tanker fell from US$65 million to US$28 million and the following year it slumped further to US$16 million'. It was virtually impossible for many shipowners to survive these poor conditions, with the result that many went into liquidation and abandoned their vessels to their creditors - the banks. The bankers again entrusted these vessels to the hands of ship managers. This initial demand for third party ship management services encouraged experts from within the shipping industry to form offices and limited liability companies and tender for contracts. The fact that the formation of such companies was an easy task since it required little capital investment encouraged their further development. Ship managers were not required to have an equity stake in the ship and hence faced little risk as they were not directly affected by the vagaries of freight rates and shipping markets. Further boosts for ship management business came from emerging national shipping companies seeking assistance in establishing merchant fleets and new entrants to the shipping sector (Gilbert, 1994). Additionally, the fact that many shipowners viewed vessels as asset plays, and were more interested in sale and purchase rather than ship operation, was another reason for the growth of ship management.

Nevertheless, the ship management industry would have never grown to what it is today, if many of the traditional shipowners themselves had not recognised the opportunities offered by ship managers and handed over their own vessels for management. This came about not only because of the recognition that third party management offered obvious financial and administrative advantages but also because of the increasingly regulated environment the shipping arena had grown to be. To overcome national and international legal, ecological, public and trade union pressures and to enjoy the fiscal advantages of economies of scale, many owners decided to entrust their vessels to third party experts - the ship managers.

The Rationale for Outsourcing Ship Management

Over the years there have been many arguments made for and against the use of third party ship managers. It is obvious that third party ship management undoubtedly offers significant advantages to those choosing to outsource and also contributes to efficiency in shipping operation and the shipping industry at large. It is also true that third party ship management does not appeal to many types of shipowners with various size and type fleets and based in various countries. The reasons for the choice not to entrust vessels to third party ship management may be very well justifiable in the context of the particular owner's circumstances. What is important, however, is for the owners to consider the potential for outsourcing and for managers to seek ways in which to satisfy the needs and wants of those, as yet untapped, market segments. Although the latter is reflected in numerous occasions throughout this book, it is justifiable at this point to consider the various advantages for outsourcing ship management.

The major arguments advocating the outsourcing of ship management to third party professionals include improvement in efficiency, reduction in costs and professionalism. For a traditional shipowning company that decides to outsource, the primary considerations will be efficiency and cost reduction. For other companies like oil majors or banks, outsourcing to professionals is a logical option bearing in mind that shipping, and to that extent ship management, is not their primary activity. Efficiency arises from the competency and ability of professional ship management firms in performing the ship management functions. It also arises from the global presence and networks of ship management firms that facilitate the capability to source crew from any of the various low cost supply centres throughout the world. In the increasingly tighter labour market, particularly for competent and qualified seafarers, the ship manager's expertise in this respect can be invaluable. In addition, through their global networks ship managers can obtain low cost crews, thus contributing to the shipowner's quest for cost reduction. Porter (1985) has advocated cost leadership as one of the strategies to be pursued for achieving competitive advantage. Cost reduction is particularly important in shipping, mainly due to the volatility of the markets and possible concurrent oversupply of tonnage that can lead to depressed freight rates and an erosion of operating margins. This can be exploited by ship managers who can achieve low operating costs by reaping the benefits of scale economies and bargaining power by virtue of the number of vessels under their management. Bargaining power is used in the purchase of supplies for a large number of vessels and culminates in the achievement of large discounts. The prices that can be obtained by big ship management companies cannot be matched by small shipowners. By achieving the right balance between the benefits to accrue to the company and those passed to the clients, ship managers can assure profitability and competitiveness, and increase the attractiveness of outsourcing ship management.

If an owner needs to expand its fleet, the ship management company can provide crews at short notice, thus contributing to efficiency through operational flexibility. Ship management companies have a greater pool of managed vessels and in case of divestment by shipowners they are able to employ seafarers elsewhere, thus reducing externalities or social costs. The ship manager also relieves the owning company from the need to maintain a ship management department. Hence, the owner may concentrate on other aspects of the shipping business like sale and purchase or chartering, which are the two functions that are most often not entrusted to third party managers from traditional shipowning companies. In other instances it has been noted that many owners, being captains and engineers, are very good on the technical side of the business and prefer to concentrate on that and outsource commercial management. According to the managing director of the Danish third party management company Wind Shipping Aps, which provides commercial management to smaller owners, shipowners prefer the company in order to avoid the cost of having to set up an operations department, a chartering department and so on. By outsourcing these parts of their business the owners are saving money.

Efficiency and cost reduction are also aspects related to the adherence to international shipping regulations that are becoming increasingly stringent. Implementing and adhering to the specifications of regulations like the International Safety Management (ISM) Code requires additional staff that are technically competent. Bearing in mind the overwhelming need for cost reduction in order to remain competitive, it would seem almost impossible for smaller companies to employ additional staff to oversee the implementation of the Code and adherence to the increasingly regulated shipping environment. Professional ship management firms are able to do this because they can achieve economies of scale by virtue of the size of their managed fleet.

Apart from the purchasing power from managing a bigger fleet that culminates into achieving discounts in the open market, certain ship managers have pointed out that larger fleets can even assist them in raising finance for the owner-client at competitive rates. According to one particular ship manager (Anon, 2000a, p. 37):

> We can obtain finance because we have a good credit rating and many smaller owners cannot do that. We can also market vessels world-wide, whereas many owners know only their local markets. By using us, they have but one broker instead of having to hire their own people and I am sure that, in this respect, we are much more efficient because we are specialists.

The Economics of Vertical Disintegration and Outsourcing

Apart from the above practical arguments advocating the potential benefits of outsourcing ship management, there is a body of economic theory mainly built around the transaction cost approach (Williamson, 1975; 1981) which provides a framework for understanding the outsourcing decision. The strategic objective of outsourcing should be to minimise the total costs of receiving the given services at a given quality. Such costs include the costs of production, bargaining costs and opportunism costs. Production costs are either the costs of in-house management or the third party management fee. Bargaining costs include:

- the costs arising from negotiating the contract details;
- the costs of negotiating changes to the contract after it has been agreed due to unforeseen circumstances;
- the costs of performance measurement of the third party;
- the costs of disputes in case of disagreement in contract termination.

Opportunism costs arise when one party acts with self-interest in bad faith, for instance in attempting to change the terms of the contract to his favour. Bargaining and opportunism costs can also exist within organisations, therefore it is the incremental bargaining and opportunism costs of outsourcing that are relevant (Alchian and Demsetz, 1972).

Production costs are directly generated by the opportunity costs of the resources – land, labour, capital – actually used in production. As stated earlier in this chapter, ship management may be defined as the systematic organisation of these resources for the sustenance of the ship. If a third party carries out this organisation, the production costs may be lower for a number of reasons.

First, in-house production of the good or activity often entails production at too low levels to achieve minimum efficient scale (McFetridge and Smith, 1998; Lyons, 1995). Hence, smaller owners may not be able to achieve the same economies of scale in ship operation as a larger ship management company. In addition, according to Muris, Scheffman and Spiller (1992) the most significant economies of scale may be in intangible factors such as administrative and information systems, knowledge and learning, access to capital markets and marketing. Hence, it is not just economies of scale in purchasing supplies that may be of importance in deciding whether or not to outsource ship management, but also scale economies in the efficiency of producing all inputs associated with ship management.

Second, economists have argued that internal production units have a tendency to act like monopolists, thereby reducing efficiency incentives (Crozier, 1964; Alles, Newman and Noel, 1998). This arises due to the reduction of comparative performance benchmarks for internal customers or the monopolistic pricing of the good produced (Reichelstein, 1995) that may be created by the lack of incentives to achieve minimum production costs that are technically feasible (Leibenstein, 1976). As stated by Vining and Globerman (1999, p. 649):

> Market competition is normally the crucial driver in forcing down production costs to their lowest level. Profit-maximising firms in a competitive market will be forced to price at the lowest possible marginal cost, thus eliminating inefficient practices. Internal production units are not normally subject to this same level of competition.

Third, firms can experience diseconomies of scope in managing multiple firm activities or diseconomies of scale in producing a single activity. It might be better for some activities to be given to third parties for an organisation to concentrate on its core competencies (Cross, 1995; McFarlan and Nolan, 1995).

Finally, internal production of an input may generate significant negative externalities that can be reduced or eliminated by outsourcing. This might be the case when a distinct corporate culture may be needed which is dysfunctional with the rest of the organisation (Camerer and Vepsalainen, 1988). Negative externalities may arise in companies whose primary function is not shipping/ship operation as such but who may, nevertheless, own/charter ships for their transport requirements.

On the basis of the above economic arguments it may be inferred that there should exist cases where outsourcing ship management to a third party can lower production costs. However, there is no empirical evidence in a ship management context that scientifically affirms this assertion. There is evidence from a variety of other sources that outsourcing can lower production costs (e.g. Ang, 1998) and evidence to suggest that such a finding is generalisable (Benson and Ieronimo, 1996; Lyons, 1995; Walker and Weber, 1987). In short, a shipowning firm should seek the regime that minimises the costs of production, bargaining and opportunism by comparing internal production versus outsourcing.

Having discussed the major issues supporting the case for outsourcing ship management it must be mentioned that a number of owners are still not convinced by the potentially beneficial effects of outsourcing and prefer in-house ship management. The reasons for such behaviour and attitudes have been recognised as challenges to the ship management industry and will be discussed in more detail in the following chapter.

Organisational Structures

The ship management functions are performed by organisations that may have different forms of organisational structure. The particular differences in organisational structure reflect the evolution of traditional shipowning firms, the establishment of new entrants into ship management, and the changes they have undergone over time in the effort to achieve their organisational objectives. Five such organisational structures have been identified, a brief outline of which is given below.

In-House

In this type of ship management company, management functions are carried out by a separate, in-house department of the traditional ship owning company. The ship management functions are performed under the auspices of the owning company, which controls the day-to-day operations of the company's vessels. It must be noted that this type of organisation does not manage third party vessels.

Independent

This structure refers to the professional ship management companies managing vessels for third parties and having no equity stake in the vessels or having any vessels of their own. Their function is to offer the ship management service to their clients. These clients vary from traditional owners to owning organisations (e.g. charterers, banks, investors) who, having little or no knowledge of ship operation, entrust their vessels to the independents.

Owner-Managing

Some owners have diversified into performing ship management functions for third parties, i.e. other owners. These owners operate under a hybrid arrangement, managing vessels for other owners in addition to their own ships. However, the performance of ship management services is still carried out by an in-house department of the traditional owning company. An example of this arrangement is the family-owned Malaysian company Halim Mazmin, which expanded its in-house ship management arm in 1995 to undertake full, technical and commercial management for Japanese shipowners (Ion, 1995). The company directors believe that management of the owned fleet has contributed to the build-up of expertise that could be applied to the management of ships for third party owners.

Manager-Owning

This type of hybrid structure is one of the latest developments in ship management company structures. It was brought about by the increase in size and financial capacity of independent ship management companies who decided to invest in ship purchase and, of course, manage the acquired vessels and trade them for profit. Their main function, however, is still the provision of third party services.

Subsidiary

Many large shipping companies have formed subsidiary companies that will principally undertake the management of the owned fleet of the parent company. These subsidiaries may or may not undertake third party business. Examples include Unicom Management Co. in Cyprus, which manages a large fleet for its Russian parent company and does not undertake third party management. Another example is Safman in the Isle of Man, which was created to undertake all crewing arrangements for its parent company Safmarine; any third party business will normally be conducted through joint ventures (Anon, 1995a). Of course, with the increasing propensity for forming joint ventures, other organisational structures that undertake ship management have emerged, albeit in less significant numbers.

Services Offered by Ship Management Companies

The services that may be offered by ship managers have grown to include virtually anything required to run a ship profitably but excluding, however, the provision of equity finance (Spruyt, 1994). The services on offer can be easily ascertained from the BIMCO (Baltic and International Maritime Council) SHIPMAN Standard Ship Management Agreement. The SHIPMAN is a standard contract that may be used by the ship manager and his client, for legally agreeing their respective rights, responsibilities and liabilities. The services specified in the contract include crewing, technical management, insurance, freight management, accounting, chartering, sale or purchase of vessel, provisions, bunkering and operation. The list may, however, be stretched further and it is at the owner's discretion to sub-contract ship management companies to provide other services, mainly comprising newbuilding supervision, payrolling services, vessel inspection both for purchase and condition audit services, claims handling, supervision of major damage repairs and conversion projects, and planned maintenance and inventory control systems. Ship management companies may also offer advice on the choice of flag and ship registration procedures.

The range of services on offer may continue to grow as the larger ship management companies have already demonstrated a response to the international marketplace. For example, Columbia Shipmanagement has specifically targeted newbuilding supervision projects (Anon, 1996a), whereas V. Ships has been reported to be involved in the conversion of a newbuilding hull into a cruise vessel (Anon, 1995b). A number of companies have also diversified into the provision of various types of accounting related and information technology services.

Considering the services on offer in more detail will reveal the actual functions undertaken and performed by ship management companies.

Crewing

Crewing is a service offered by most, if not all, of the existing ship management companies. Indeed, many of these companies came into being as ship managers by initially offering this service alone. The responsibilities of the ship manager include selection and supply of qualified crew for the vessel(s) under management. They also include paying, insuring and overseeing all the necessary administrative procedures that must be fulfilled for proper employment according to national and international regulations. A more detailed consideration of the ship manager's obligations may be ascertained from Clause 3 of the BIMCO CREWMAN Standard Crew Management Agreement. The CREWMAN is another contract of standard form developed by BIMCO, which determines the rights, responsibilities and liabilities of ship manager and client with regard to crew management specifically.

The ship manager will need to have knowledge of the employment laws of the seafarers' country of domicile and the related flag state regulations. He must also be aware of up-to-date trade union and International Transport Workers' Federation (ITF) demands and requirements. Apart from the basic pay, the ship manager must negotiate and arrange for associated costs such as overtime, leave, bonuses, social security, travel expenses, medical expenses, manning agency fees, levies, cadet costs, study leave, superannuation and recruitment costs (Downard, 1981). It will also be the manager's responsibility to present to the owner a budget (as agreed in their individual contract) which should include costs and expenses with regard to crewing. The manager, being a professional, is also expected to provide a service with a view to promoting the interests of the owner-client (SHIPMAN clause 2.2, CREWMAN clause 2.3). Therefore, one of his major concerns for cost-effective crewing will be the manning source. Tolofari (1989, p. 26) states that 'the nationality of a ship's crew can be extremely varied and it is this more than anything else which accounts for the wide disparities in wages'. It has been possible to engage crew from a variety of sources depending on flag state regulations. Thus, if a ship is registered under an open registry system or in a second international ship register (see Ready, 1994), it may be possible for the ship manager to work out cost-effective crewing options.

However, performing the crewing service is not limited to the aforementioned obligations. Since ship managers are expected to provide competent crew, they are among the first in the shipping industry to be concerned with the shortage of qualified labour the industry is now faced with. Mitas (1992), quoting an ISF/BIMCO report published in 1990, revealed that the shipping industry as a whole was at that time short of 50,000 qualified officers with the figure likely to increase to 400,000 by the year 2000. The study showed that a surplus of ratings of approximately 200,000 in 1990 would become a shortage of 360,000 by the year 2000, if current trends were to continue. Training requirements are high on a ship managers' agenda and many spend a substantial part of their budget on training. For example, Hanseatic Shipping Co. established an in-house marine training school in order to achieve the continued availability of qualified staff (Meyer, 1992). Columbia Ship Management is also one of the few ship management companies that actually funds its own training programme by injecting up to US$400,000 annually into various training institutions for training the company's supply of crew members (Anon, 1996b).

Technical Management

Technical management is integrated with the supply of spare parts and includes all those functions necessary for maintaining the mechanical efficiency of the vessel. Thus, the mechanical efficiency is maintained by engaging competent personnel, both on board and ashore, to carry out, oversee and administer the technical requirements and operations. Depending on the type of ship under management, the company has to employ qualified personnel that will be well acquainted with the specific shipboard operations. Technical management also includes negotiating and arranging for drydockings, surveys, alterations and temporary or permanent repairs. It will be the ship manager's job to supervise the aforementioned functions. The ship manager will also be responsible for supplying the spare parts, lubricant oil and general stores necessary for the upkeep of the vessel. A prudent shipowner will normally require a vessel to be maintained up to a certain standard, stated in the company's policy and dictated by international regulations and classification society requirements. It is the ship manager's task to ensure that the vessel never falls short of that standard.

Technical management may also include overseeing the operational capabilities of ship-to-shore communication equipment. It will be the manager's task to install and maintain an efficient and cost-effective communication system. Thus, a satellite communication system may handle ship performance data, inventory control, planned maintenance, personnel records and cargo loading information at considerably less cost than a conventional telex system (Hughes, 1989). It will be the ship manager's responsibility to offer advice on the installation of a system that will serve the best interest of his client. The ship manager is also obliged to furnish the owner with reports regarding the technical efficiency of equipment and operational procedures as well as related budgets. According to Verma (1993, p. 111):

> In order to evaluate the performance, the owner requires feedback from the ship of various data which will be indicative of the expenses incurred for the fixed and variable costs, time gained or lost, cargo loaded and deadweight

reports, cargo loading and discharging operations and the performance of the vessel vis-à-vis stipulated speed and fuel consumption.

It might be possible for technical-only management to be agreed by the ship management and owning company. Whether this is the case or not, the usual practice of handing over the vessel will be by conducting an overall survey by a mutually appointed independent surveyor. A similar survey will be carried out when the vessel is redelivered to the owners. The technical condition of the vessel should be the same at the time of delivery and redelivery.

Throughout the technical management period the ship manager must serve the owner with utmost good faith and use his best endeavours to promote his interests while maintaining discretion with regard to his client's business secrets.

Insurance Provision

The manager may undertake the task of insuring the vessel under management in accordance with the owner's instructions. This may include taking out cover for Hull and Machinery (H&M) as well as mutual Protection and Indemnity (P&I) insurance. The owner's instructions should be specific as far as insured value, deductibles and premia are concerned. The manager may, however, arrange for an independent estimation of the vessel's value for insurance purposes. All money paid by the manager will be charged to the owner's account.

The issue of P&I insurance is very important since the manager may find himself exposed to liability if, for example, the owner becomes insolvent. He must, therefore, pursue joint P&I insurance with the owner. However, Martyr (1994) notes that in case the owner becomes insolvent, the manager may be liable to pay overdue P&I calls irrespective of the contracting out of such liability in agreement with the owner. This is true provided the P&I club does not concede and be party to such an agreement.

Freight Management

This service, being minor in itself, is usually carried out in conjunction with the other functions of the chartering department within the ship management company. Preparation of voyage estimates, i.e. 'calculating the return a ship will make after deducting from the income the expenses of a particular voyage' (Packard, 1978, p. 9), is among the primary functions.

This involves comparing the perceived costs with the expected hire or freight and calculating the net profit. It is of vital importance for the profitable trading of the ship and provides the level for accepting or rejecting offers for chartering. However, with the advent of computer technology, it has become possible for ship managers (and owners) to carry out sophisticated analyses of voyage estimates quickly and at least cost (Kendall and Buckley, 1994).

When the vessel is under charter, the ship manager will have to carry out calculations regarding *laytime* (see Packard, 1979) and possible *demurrage* that may be owed by the charterer or *despatch* due to the charterer in accordance with the terms of the charterparty. He will also arrange payment of any monies due as well as the receipt of hire and/or freight on behalf of the owner. The requirements of discretion, utmost good faith and commitment to the owner's interests are, once again, imperative.

Accounting

A requirement for the provision of prudent ship management services is establishing a detailed accounting system. This will facilitate the prompt despatch to the owner of costs and expenditures associated with ship management and also assist the manager in the preparation of budgets and reports with which he will have to furnish the owner from time to time. A system for keeping account records will be an additional bonus when strategic decisions for different operations have to be made.

Chartering

The business of chartering is a very complex process upon which depend the trading viability of the vessel and the business sustenance of the owner. As it is the lifeline of the shipowning business, traditional owners have been reluctant to entrust this function to the hands of third party managers. Consequently, managers have underplayed the formation of chartering departments. Where such departments are present, they merely perform associated functions rather than actually fixing the vessel. However, as noted earlier, shipping business investors and banks owning vessels and not having the expertise of ship operation will delegate the responsibility of chartering the vessel to the ship manager.

A vessel may be chartered for a single voyage, a period of time (time charter) or under a contract of affreightment (COA). The type of charter will depend upon the owner's instructions and thus involves close liaison between manager and owner. The manager must be aware of the trading intentions of the owner, the economic feasibility of particular charters, current market conditions and the changing political regulations enforced by governments (Gorton, Ihre and Sandevärn, 1990).

It is a prerequisite for ship managers operating a large chartering department to directly employ their own brokers specialising in seeking employment for the vessels. However, as Packard (1986, p. 10) suggests, 'smaller organisations will probably rely on the services of perhaps one competent shipbroking company to seek and to secure profitable cargoes for their vessel(s)'.

Depending on the type of charter, the ship manager will assume the responsibilities and functions the owner would have assumed, although any ultimate liability will lie with the owner. Obviously, more responsibilities are assumed if the vessel is voyage-chartered. Packard (1980) notes that the owner - and hence the manager - would be responsible for the running expenses as well as the incidental voyage expenses incurred. The latter costs include port charges, light dues, special voyage insurance, bunkers, canal tolls, tugs and pilotage, which would have been assumed by the charterers had the vessel been time-chartered. The expenses incurred by the manager during the charter period will be for the owner's account in addition to the ship management fee that will be charged for the service.

Sale or Purchase of Vessel

It is highly unlikely that traditional shipowners will assign to the ship manager the responsibility for negotiating the sale or purchase of a vessel. Shipowning entrepreneurs will have the last word before a sale or purchase agreement is concluded, even if the managers are assigned the task of supervising the process. As sale and purchase is usually conducted through S&P brokers (Packard, 1988), it might seem inappropriate to engage another middleman (the ship manager) in the process. Where this is done, the assignment of the ship manager is merely to supervise an independent market valuation of the vessel and carry out the administrative aspects of the process. This means he would arrange for the vessel to be inspected and surveyed and probably engage an expert S&P broker to carry out the valuation. To this end, Clause 9 of the SHIPMAN agreement is illustrative: 'The managers shall, in accordance with the owners' instructions, supervise the sale or purchase of the vessel including performance of any sale or purchase agreement, but not negotiation of the same'.

Acquiring a vessel, however, may also mean building a new one rather than engaging in the second-hand market. If this is the case, the ship management company has the newbuilding supervision service to offer to the shipowner.

> Right from the arrival on site of the first batch of materials put aside for the commencement of construction of the new vessel, it is essential that a construction engineer/surveyor representing the purchaser should be on hand to protect his employer's interest (Packard, 1988, p. 39).

Ship management companies having the 'in-house' expertise of competent surveyors will readily furnish the owner with such services.

Provisions

The supply of consumables for ship operation is another function undertaken by managers. Consumables include victuals, cleaning materials, paint, brushes and electrical supplies. It might be in the best interests of the shipowner to assign this service to a manager because he can take advantage of economies of scale. Obviously, a ship manager providing supplies for a fleet of one hundred vessels or more will be able to purchase these from ship chandlers at competitive prices.

Operation

Ship operation involves functions associated with the day-to-day running of the ship. Thus, when the ship is approaching a port of call, the shipowner's agents at the particular port have to be informed. Personnel have to be engaged to carry out cargo inspection and stevedores must be employed to facilitate the loading or discharging of the vessel. If the vessel has to begin on another voyage, the ship manager will issue the appropriate instructions, i.e. the date, time and place at which the next cargo is available and sailing times and schedules. In order to ensure the efficient and most economical sailing schedules, the ship manager has to review passage times in light of operating and voyage expenses.

   If a fleet of liner ships is being managed, the ship manager may also undertake the task of marketing space availability and concluding cargo bookings. In marketing the service, the ship manager will have to draw up a plan for the liner tariff rates, ensuring profitability, and at the same time carry out advertising campaigns.

Bunkering

The supply of bunker fuel for the vessel is one of the most important services offered by ship managers. The significance of this service lies primarily with the considerable cost of fuel oil and the probable sudden price variations. The ship manager must possess the knowledge of where to buy bunkers from at any particular time, so that the cost is minimised whilst bunker quality is maintained. While the vessel is sailing on a particular voyage, the ship manager undertakes a continuous review of potential bunkering ports to ensure that the most favourable prices are obtained (Branch, 1989). It is not uncommon to see vessels deviating from their original route in order to obtain cheaper bunkers from a particular port.

It is also very important for bunkers to be supplied in accordance with the specifications for the particular ship engine. Especially when a vessel is voyage-chartered. it would be the owner's (and hence the manager's) responsibility to supply bunkers. If bunkers of incorrect quality are supplied, the vessel's seaworthiness may be at risk and the charterers may take legal action against the owner. Such disputes are very common and it is the operator's responsibility to 'ensure that samples of fuel from each bunkering are properly collected, labelled and retained on board so as to provide important evidence in the event of a dispute involving fuel quality' (Ewart, 1982, p. 14).

Commercial Management

Spruyt (1994) includes in the term 'commercial management' functions like voyage operation service (estimates, accounting etc.), marketing, chartering and technical operating service. However, following the BIMCO SHIPMAN notation, it is evident that such functions form services in their own right or are included under the term 'operation'. Hence, it would seem more appropriate to include under the more general term 'commercial management' services offered by ship managers and related to the general 'commercial' sustenance of the vessel or the owning company. Such services definitely include advice on flagging strategies, ship registration, medium to long-term financial strategy and research on market trends on behalf of the owner.

The wide availability of ship registers enables managers to offer the service of providing feasibility studies to owners wishing to take advantage of more economical flag options. The provision of this service is made possible by the advantages of flagging-out, encouraged by the higher level of marginal cost of output under traditional high-cost flags (Tolofari, 1989), beneficial ownership anonymity, freedom to trade world-wide and avoidance of protectionist measures under an open registry flag (Ready, 1992). To the aforementioned, the political factor may also be added (Franco, 1992). Shipowners have, nowadays, more than 143 different flags to choose from (Chapman, 1992) and the ship manager's expertise may be employed for such choice.

After the choice is made, ship managers may provide expert advice on ship registration in the particular country. This is necessary since ship registration is subject to statutory control (Gaskell, Debattista and Swatton, 1994; Hill, 1995) and different countries have different maritime law requirements. Thus, ship managers will have to know not only the registration procedures but also the legal requirements.

Ship managers have been around long enough to be able to provide advice on financial and investment aspects of ship ownership. Managers may also provide financial services to shipping investors despite the fact that the investing public is not very receptive to shipping shares (Gaunt and Morgan, 1994). Financial advice services by ship management companies may be more applicable in various European countries that organise shipping ownership through various schemes. For instance, the Norwegian K/S financing system has attracted investors from a variety of backgrounds to shipping (Vikoren, 1992, p. 42), although more recently the system has been cancelled and replaced by tax incentives attributable directly to corporate shipowners rather than individual limited partnership investors (Drewry, 1996). Similar tax incentives for shipping investment operate in Denmark, Holland and Germany, and the potential of niche markets in financial services for ship management companies may be exploited.

Other Services

The wide range of services on offer by the largest ship management companies may include supervision of major damage repairs and conversion projects (technical and administrative), handling of claims and administrative services. Advice on maintenance and lay-up planning may also be available.

Legal Aspects of Ship Management

The legal relationship between the ship manager and the shipowner commences at the time the ship management contract is agreed and signed. The contract will specify such things as the services to be performed, the duties, responsibilities and liabilities of the parties, and the fees to be paid, and will state potential events that will lead to termination of the contract. It will also state the law governing the agreement and the procedures to be followed for resolution of disputes. The law of contract, thus, governs the relationship. In cases where the ship manager fails to carry out his obligations under the contract, there is a breach of contract and he may be liable to the payment of damages. Further, he will have no claim to his agreed fee and the owner will be free to terminate the contract. The same, of course, applies to the manager in case the owner fails to perform a term in the contract. As has already been mentioned, in an attempt to provide a balanced apportionment of liability and responsibility in contractual terms, BIMCO has developed two standard form contracts that can be used by managers: the SHIPMAN Standard Ship Management Agreement for ship management and the CREWMAN Standard Crew Management Agreement for crew management (see also Panayides, 2000).

Although the terms of the ship management contract are conclusive, there is more to the duty of the ship manager than the responsibilities specified in the contract. A ship manager is deemed to be a professional, i.e. someone who a reasonable person would expect to demonstrate his tasks with a higher degree of care and special skill. Hence, whether in contract or in tort, the manager owes the shipowner the duty to take reasonable care and skill in carrying out the ship management tasks. The law of agency is also central to the relationship. Agency is 'the fiduciary relationship which exists between two persons, one of whom expressly or impliedly consents that the other should act on his behalf, and the other of whom similarly consents so to act or so acts' (Reynolds, 1985, p. 1).

The ship manager acts 'as an agent' or 'for and on behalf' of the shipowner. This must be clearly indicated in the agreement. The owner will be bound by any agreement entered into by the manager who will have the power to affect his principal's legal status. This is subject to the condition that the owner has given the manager the authority to make such agreement or has effectively indicated to the third party that the manager has such authority (Bundock, 1989). The manager owes a duty of loyalty to his principal, he must protect the principal's interests and, where he has many principals, he must treat them equally. In case the manager has been negligent in performing his duties he will be held liable. This liability is strict and cannot be excluded or restricted contractually unless it satisfies the requirement of reasonableness as held in Flamar Interocean Ltd v. Denmac Ltd (formerly Denholm Maclay Co. Ltd) The Flamar Pride [1990] 1 Lloyd's Rep. 434. The attitudes of the courts to exclusion clauses are notable in that they are construed *contra proferentem*, against the party relying on the clause. Thus, in Glafki Shipping Co. S.A. v. Pinios Shipping Co., The Maira [1986] 2 Lloyd's Law Rep. 12, the managers agreed to place the ship's insurances 'in accordance with the insurance clauses of the mortgage bank', but failed to do so. When an action was brought against them by the owners, they tried to rely on clause 10 of the agreement which provided, *inter alia,* 'that the managers should not be responsible for any act or omission involving any error of judgement...in performance of the managers' duties under the agreement'. The court held that the omission was not an error of judgement and the clause could not go wider and exclude liability for breach of earlier clauses of the agreement.

Failure to comply with the contractual terms, negligence or wilful default are the most common reasons for which a ship manager may be found liable for claims from three directions, viz., his principal, second parties and third parties. As far as claims from second and third parties are concerned, the ship manager will only be liable if he contracts with such parties as a principal, or loses his agency status or breaches his warranty of authority. Such cases are rare, as it is extremely unwise for managers to contract in their own names when acting for somebody else. As from 11th May 2000, any contracts entered into between managers and owners under English law are subject to the Contracts (Rights of Third Parties) Act 1999. The Act enables a person who is not a party to the contract to take action under English law to enforce a term of the contract, either if the term says he can, or if it purports to confer a benefit upon him. The 'Himalaya' clause (11.4) in the SHIPMAN 98 contract provides an example of a clause intended to confer a benefit on third parties. The benefit is the right of the employees, agents or subcontractors of the managers to limit their liability. Managers must also ensure that they are co-assured on the owner's P&I policy so that they are insured in case they are held liable. This happened in the case of The Marion [1984] 2 Lloyd's Law Rep. 1, where both the owner and the manager were co-assured on the owner's P&I policy, so the P&I club was unable to bring a recourse action against the manager for what had been found to be the result of his negligence (Lawford, 1989).

More recently, the liability of the managers has been made statutory. Under sections 30 and 31 of the Merchant Shipping Act 1988, re-enacted in sections 94, 98 and 100 of the Merchant Shipping Act 1995, the managers may be held liable if found responsible for sending an unseaworthy vessel to sea or failing to take all reasonable steps to secure that the ship is operated in a safe manner. However, managers are granted the advantage of being able to limit their liability. According to Lawford (1992, p. 10):

> A ship manager is quite unable to bear the same degree of exposure to risk as the shipowner and must limit his exposure either by fixing a specific monetary limit on the amount of his liability, or set the gauge for the degree of negligence for which he is prepared to accept liability at a high level.

The liability of ship managers is limited in the standard agreements to ten times the annual management fee in the SHIPMAN agreement and six times the monthly lump sum fee received by crew managers in the CREWMAN contract. Limitation of liability is also available to ship managers under the 1976 Convention on Limitation of Liability for Maritime Claims, incorporated into English law by the Merchant Shipping Act 1979 (Schedule 4). The only situation where ship managers may incur unlimited liability is under the United States Oil Pollution Act of 1990 (OPA 90), where they may be found jointly and severally liable with the owners.

Considering the case where an owner does not honour his contractual obligations, a manager may terminate the contract and be awarded damages. However, it will be very difficult to obtain any security for any monies due. Managers may have a lien in respect of goods or materials supplied to a ship for her operation or maintenance. However, a manager's lien is not a maritime lien. Therefore, their claims will rank after those of a mortgagee or holders of maritime liens. As far as arresting the ship is concerned, according to Section 20(2) of the Supreme Court Act 1981 (giving effect to the Arrest Convention 1952 in English law) the applicable claims for the purposes of arrest by a ship manager are: (a) any claim in respect of goods or materials supplied to the ship for her operation or maintenance, and/or (b) any claim in respect of disbursements made on account of the ship (The Westport No.3 [1966] 1 Lloyd's Rep. 342). The management fee itself is not capable of supporting an arrest under English law. It is not a claim made by an agent in respect of disbursements made on account of a ship, it is simply a fee paid for a service (The Borag [1980] 1 Lloyd's Rep. 111).

The increasingly regulated relationship will ultimately give rise to more disputes between managers and owners. Thus, it is imperative for the parties to have a close understanding of each other's needs in order to avoid costly litigation procedures.

Ship Management Market Structure

It has been identified earlier that there can be five types of organisations involved in the management of ships. This fact has been detrimental in the identification of the actual number of existing ship management companies attempted by various researchers. The problem arising is which companies to include as performing management services and which to leave out. For example, an owning company may separate - in legal terms - its management department, thus adding one more company in the list of operators whilst only performing in-house management. Other companies may only offer the manning service and thus not be eligible for inclusion in the list of ship managers offering full management but still may be considered as ship management companies. It follows that whatever statistics of the ship management industry are considered, some assumptions have to be kept in mind. Table 2.1 illustrates the growth in the number of ship management companies over the period 1990-2000.

The Shipmanagers' Register (1994) includes 395 companies offering ship management services. Rodger (1989) estimated that there were around 300 companies at the time, increasing by about 9 per cent per annum, whilst he assumed the number of total ships under management to be around 3,400, with 2,200 managed by independent companies. Hackett (1989) stated that there were 500 companies on the consultancy's database, many of which were owner- or operator-managers. He suggested the number of ships under management to be in the region of 3,000, with 1,200-1,300 being managed by ten leading companies. Dorey (1989) suggested that there were only 250 companies with 4,000-5,000 vessels under management. Spruyt (1990), after consulting Lloyd's Confidential Index, revealed that 3,000 ships are under management, with 25 per cent of those managed by six leading companies. Unsurprisingly, all researchers stressed the difficulty of obtaining any form of statistics regarding ship management and the greater difficulty of making any absolute quantification.

Table 2.1 The growth of ship management companies 1990-2000

Year	Number of Companies
1990/91	226
1991/92	412
1992/93	504
1993/94	504
1994/95	499
1995/96	515
1996/97	614
1997/98	631
1998/99	643
1999/00	667

Source: World Fairplay Shipping Directory (various issues)

Williams (1993) revealed the findings of research conducted between 1985 and 1987. He stated that the number of companies existing at the time was above the 200 mark, with 31 per cent providing in-house and third party services and 69 per cent providing services solely to third parties. The number of ships under management was around 2,200, with 28 per cent being bulk carriers, 26 per cent cargo ships, 16 per cent tankers and 30 per cent other types of vessels. He also revealed that the research identified over 450 owners entrusting their vessels to third party management.

Current statistics retrieved from maritime directories indicate the presence of around 600 ship management companies world-wide, although this includes all types of companies including some manning agencies and companies offering services ancillary to ship management. It was not possible to retrieve the total number of vessels currently under management due to the unavailability of updated secondary data. It must be noted that during this study maritime directories were found to be inconsistent in their reporting of ship management companies.

There are a number of factors affecting the establishment of a ship management company in a particular geographical location. Of the countries listed in various maritime directories, it may be claimed that eight are established ship management centres. These are Cyprus, Germany, Greece, Hong Kong, Norway, Singapore, the United Kingdom and the

United States of America. Table 2.2 shows the increase in the number of companies at the particular ship management centres between 1994 and 1999.

There are different reasons for the establishment of ship management companies in the above countries. For example, countries like the United Kingdom, Norway, Greece and Germany are traditional maritime centres. Companies have traditionally existed at these locations and the good maritime and ancillary services infrastructure of London, Oslo, Piraeus and Hamburg provide advantageous characteristics encouraging establishment in these places. However, it must be noted that establishment at the aforementioned locations also entails significant disadvantages. For instance, the cost of renting office space in London or Oslo is considerable. In addition, companies and individuals will generally incur higher costs in taxation (both corporate and personal), wages and telecommunication expenses in the traditional maritime centres. It must be noted that ship managers offer a service and the company's profitability depends significantly on balancing the costs against a generally fixed management fee. The recent changes in shipping policy in the United Kingdom aimed at attracting more vessels under the British flag may assist in attracting more companies to London.

Table 2.2 The growth of companies in ship management centres

Ship management centre	Number of companies	
	1994	1999
United Kingdom	45	108
Germany	29	76
Hong Kong	25	76
United States of America	47	75
Greece	35	63
Singapore	29	61
Norway	30	54
Cyprus	20	36

Source: The Shipmanagers' Register (various issues)

The mushrooming of open registries, concomitant with South-East Asia becoming the major source for crews, has led a number of companies to compare benefits with costs and seriously consider relocation. Among those who have benefited are Singapore, Hong Kong, the Isle of Man and Cyprus. Ship management companies moved to Singapore and Hong Kong primarily to be close to the labour recruitment areas of Korea and the Philippines but also to be close to suppliers of ships' spare parts. Since these countries also offered favourable living conditions as well as cheaper state-of-the-art office equipment and telecommunication facilities, the choice was not a hard one to make. On the other hand, Cyprus and the Isle of Man have lately been favourable locations for the establishment of ship management companies. Perry (1994) discusses a number of favourable conditions for the establishment of ship management companies and both locations seem to fulfil the most demanding prerequisites. Both countries may be considered as tax havens, offering low corporate as well as employment taxes in line with relaxed employment regulations for non-citizens. They are also open registries, which may equate to increased ship management business. Furthermore, the Cypriot government in particular has demonstrated clear support for the shipping industry and the offshore sector. The availability of good telecommunication facilities, office equipment and low rents, coupled with cheap local labour and a good source of accountants and lawyers, have made the two islands attractive ship management locations in recent years. Further aspects with respect to location for marketing and cost-effectiveness will be discussed in the following chapter.

Organisational Behaviour in Ship Management

This section will provide a review of the past and present organisational and strategic behaviour of ship management companies in the industry. The major strategic behaviour characteristics of companies in the industry include the formation of subsidiary companies by the large ship management groups, joint ventures and expansion of the service offering through diversification. The ship management industry is also driven by an eagerness to reduce costs, apply quality management principles and adopt information technology systems. The last two issues will be discussed further on in this chapter.

Corporate Structures

A study of Lloyd's Maritime Directory (1995) reveals that the large ship management companies have become international, with established offices in maritime centres around the globe. For example, Denholm Ship Management (Holdings) Ltd operate from offices in Glasgow, the Isle of Man, Oslo, Singapore, Hong Kong, Bermuda and Houston. Similarly, V. Ships operate offices in London, Southampton, Bombay, Genoa, Limassol, New York and Oslo, whereas Barber International Ltd is established in Malaysia with offices in Oslo, Bombay, Hong Kong, New Orleans, Twickenham and Singapore. Whereas this is a standard pattern for the large ship management companies, it is not the only structure adopted by parent organisations. For instance, the Hamburg-based Bernhard Schulte Group also controls six self-sustained ship management companies. The companies are established in Cyprus (two), Germany, Hong Kong, Bermuda and the Isle of Man, and while all fall under the auspices of the Schulte Group, decentralisation has been stated to be the strength of the Group (Anon, 1989a). Probably one of the prime reasons for ship management company formation is provided by Navigo Management Co., which is established in Cyprus and controlled by the Schulte Group. With the other Cyprus-established member of the Group (Hanseatic Shipping Co.) managing more than 100 vessels, Navigo was established 'to meet the demand of a number of shipowners who prefer to put their vessels under the management of a smaller company' (Anon, 1989b, p.10). It follows that the size of the company is an important factor as far as restructuring is concerned.

Joint Ventures

Joint ventures are another characteristic of the ship management industry and can take a variety of forms. For instance, ship managers may engage in joint ventures as intermediaries between two investors with the benefit of managing the vessels of the resulting entity or for a commission (Morel, 1994). On the other hand, two ship management companies may decide to co-operate by forming a joint venture if they can recognise an opportunity, as 'joint ventures will in many cases boost the business potential of both partners in other fields' (Muller, 1994, p. 68). This is a type of joint venture of growing importance in ship management. The ship management group Acomarit is one of the companies most actively engaged in joint venture activities in ship management. The company engaged in three joint ventures in 1994, with Osprey Ship Management in the United States, LPL Shipping S.A. in Piraeus and Black Sea Shipping Co. forming Blasco Ship Management (Cyprus) Ltd, while withdrawing from another one with Unicom in Cyprus (Gunton, 1995). The company formed another joint venture with Orient Ship Management in 1995 (Gunton, 1995). Acomarit also formed a Dubai-based joint venture with a Kuwaiti oil services company to sell third party management to Arab shipping (Guest, 1995a), and another in 1996 with the National Shipping Corporation of Saudi Arabia (Thorpe, 1996). This prime example of joint venture activity is by no means unique in the ship management industry. The reasons may be summarised in a statement made by Airey (1995, p. 27):

> As the market for ship management services reaches saturation, the number of joint ventures, co-operation agreements and perhaps buy-outs will increase. Smaller companies with compatible services or specific geographical markets will see the advantages of combining forces to achieve further economies of scale.

Another example is the formation of a joint venture between the Scandinavian shipowning group Ugland and US-based company Interocean Management to operate from the UK (Richardson, 1995a) and concentrate on tanker management (Anon, 1995c). The Hong Kong-based Univan Ship Management set up a joint venture ship management company with the Rams Corporation, a Japanese trading house. Chadha (1996, p. 3) reports on this latter joint venture:

> The new company, Uniram Ship Management, will offer management and other technical services to owners and operators of ocean-going ships from offices in Hong Kong and Japan. It will also provide ancillary services, such as crewing, arranging insurance, claims handling and investigation, accounting, surveys and advice and drydocking and newbuildings supervision.

Interorient Navigation expanded its ship ownership and operation sector by forming a joint venture with the Latvian Shipping Company, and also joined forces with Baltic Shipping to form Baltinter to specialise in recruiting seamen for its parent operators and third parties (Anon, 1996c). Hopson (1995) reports on a joint venture company formed by the UK's Vanguard Floating Production and Cyprus' ship management company Navigo to provide an integrated project management and operational capability for the offshore floating production market. Bibby-Harrison Management Services was formed in order to attract more third party business through the credibility provided by the complementary nature of the parent companies (Osler, 1997), whereas competition forced two Japanese ship management companies to join forces (Anon, 1997a). Ship management companies may also be involved in joint ventures with national carriers (Dickey, 1995) or shipowners (Ion, 1995) to offer third party services. The formation of joint ventures in ship management may be considered as one of the most important aspects in contemporary strategic direction. Therefore, it is dealt with in much more detail in chapter 7, where collaborative ventures and alliances are depicted as fundamental strategic issues in the quest for competitiveness and growth for ship management companies.

Diversification

Another characteristic of ship management companies is that of diversification into business investments which are either related or even unrelated to ship management. For example, Hanseatic Shipping Co. has formed subsidiaries offering insurance broking, telecommunication, accounting, and travel and tourism, whereas the group that controls Columbia Shipmanagement in Cyprus has also invested in hotels on the island as well as a plant-growing company (Spruyt, 1994). The example of an in-house subsidiary travel agency is a favourite with many ship management firms, as these services can be used in conjunction with manning and form an indispensable part of it. Wallem Ship Management, for instance, has its own travel business group known as Wallem Travel in its headquarters in Hong Kong (Anon, 1996d). However, many other companies seem to have different views and prefer quotes from outside agents (Anon, 1995d). Another example of diversification and service expansion is the growing involvement of V. Ships in the management of cruise ships (Anon, 1996e) and the entry into new markets by the same company (Anon, 1997b).

The ship management market is definitely one where fierce competition predominates with the result that companies either form partnerships or consider diversification, or alternatively face the risk of being pushed out of the market. The dynamic nature of the sector does not allow for definite answers regarding its future behaviour. Underwood (1988) made the prediction that six or seven dominant players would exist together with a number of smaller companies serving niche markets. The medium-sized companies will thus be placed under great pressure and will face the decision of corporate restructuring. However, such behaviour still remains to be seen. The major issues emanating from the above are that companies are strongly pursuing the attraction of more clients by forming subsidiaries, engaging in joint ventures and diversifying into the provision of other services, mostly ancillary to ship management, but also sometimes completely unrelated. Current trends in ship management are indicative of the importance of corporate diversification as a strategy for achieving growth and profitability. Hence, further consideration of the concept including the application of established theoretical principles is justified. This will be carried out in chapter 7.

Cost Reduction

The reduction of costs for ship management companies has been of prime importance, mostly because of their inability to charge high fees and reap greater profits. For example, Acomarit (UK), the Glasgow-based subsidiary of a leading ship management group, recorded a profit of £38,092 on a turnover of £4.1 million in 1994, after staff costs, depreciation, operating expenses and tax (Guest, 1995b). Another Glasgow-based company, Norbulk Shipping (UK), reported an after tax profit of £5,331 on turnover of £953,678 in 1994 (Guest, 1995b). The meagre profits made by companies over the years led to the adoption of various strategies for cost reduction.

Such strategies include relocation to areas offering tax incentives for offshore companies and low real estate costs, as well as consolidation of the service offering. For instance, Barber International transferred its top and middle management together with its technical operations from Hong Kong to Malaysia due to the high rental costs and the need to consolidate crewing and technical operations under one office structure in an efficient environment (Anon, 1995e; Richardson, 1995b). The aspect of location in a ship management context is discussed in more detail below. Another strategy aimed towards achieving a reduction in costs is investment in information technology and communication systems that will improve efficiency and minimise clerical tasks (Anon, 1996f). Barber International managed to double its net income without changing the level of fees charged by relocating its headquarters and introducing information technology so that purchasing and requisition could be done from the ship (Anon, 1997c).

Despite these attempts to reduce costs, it is becoming increasingly difficult for ship management companies to do so as the stringent regulatory shipping environment requires adherence to higher safety standards and the implementation of quality management standards, which require additional investments. Additionally, implementation of cost reduction strategies such as employing low-paid crews may not be the best route to ship management viability, because absolute crew cost savings are not in the best long-term interests of the owner (Anon, 1995f).

Implications of the ISM Code

It has been suggested that the demand for ship management services will grow due to the introduction of the ISM Code. This is certainly true to a point, because many shipowners may have recognised that it is not economic to implement and maintain the requirements of the ISM Code. Hence they might have turned to managers that have the ability and expertise to implement the requirements of the Code. Nevertheless, this is only true for small shipowning companies. If companies own very few vessels, then maintaining an additional department or employing additional personnel for overseeing the requirements of the Code is not a viable option. For companies with a large number of vessels, however, the decision is much easier because economies of scale will be achieved by implementing the Code over a large fleet. In fact, this is one of the reasons that ship management companies are able to offer this service and obtain ISM Code certification at a relatively lower average cost. Hence, although business has been set to increase prior to the implementation of the first phase of the Code, there has not been a major boom for the ship management industry. Benefits that have accrued to some ship managers are only for the short term as the increase in business will only be a short-term phenomenon, and problems of competition will again arise as new companies enter the market. Ship managers should not, therefore, view the ISM Code as a long-term solution to their problems. Long-term solutions must be sought by concentrating on clients' needs. The predictions made on the basis of this study just before the introduction of the Code were supported one year later. Specifically, Osler (1999, p. 8) stated:

> Whatever the manifold merits of the International Safety Management Code...it did not spark the widespread flight to third party management many pundits were predicting just over a year ago.

Similarly, a number of managers are expecting a surge in business with the implementation of the second phase of the Code (2002). This is because it is believed that owners of general cargo and break bulk vessels are not as well prepared as the tanker and dry bulk owners of phase 1. Nevertheless, it must be pointed out that such types of increase in business, despite being welcome, are not enough to sustain competitiveness and growth.

Total Quality in Ship Management

Probably one of the most often-quoted words in ship management in the 1990s has been that of quality. Since the Second World War, quality management has been implemented in product industries, mainly in Japan. The achievements of Japanese companies have inspired modern approaches to quality management epitomised by what has become known as total quality management or TQM (Redmand and Mathews, 1998). The Americans followed suit and quality management has gradually attained wider popularity and has also been implemented in many service industries. Wilkinson et al. (1992) found through a survey that the term TQM is often used loosely. This may have been the case in ship management as well, where it would seem that certain companies may have equated the accreditation to a particular standard as evidence of operating TQM or delivering a high quality service. It is therefore important to consider in more detail what quality and TQM mean.

Quality, according to document 8402 of the International Standards Organisation (ISO), means 'the totality of features and characteristics of a product that bear upon its ability to satisfy stated or implied needs'. Quality management is, thus, the performance of all those functions and activities that will ensure strict adherence to specifications and conformance with pre-determined standards.

Total quality management is often seen as a general business management philosophy, which is about the attainment of continuously improving customer satisfaction by quality-led, company-wide management. According to Dean and Bowen (1994), the TQM literature suggests that its key principles are customer focus, continuous improvement and teamwork. Feedback from customers, employees and processes in the organisational setting are imperative for the achievement of these key principles. Total quality management also requires employee involvement, commitment from the top and pervasive customer orientation. Wilkinson and Witcher (1991) note that quality becomes a way of life that permeates every part and aspect of the organisation.

The era of quality management inevitably swept across the ship management industry in the late 1980s and has been the major 'talk' of the industry in the 1990s. The requirement of quality management was inevitable because it is 'the most efficient, user-acceptable and cost-effective way of running a vessel, while ensuring compliance with all statutory requirements in a safe and environmentally friendly way' (Cochran, 1995, p. 6). The different pressures on ship managers and the wide-ranging number of direct and indirect benefits that may accrue from quality management and certification has led most, if not all, ship management companies to seek and achieve accreditation to a particular standard. The pressures on ship operators, which may also reflect some of the benefits to be derived, include the increasingly regulated shipping environment and the move towards tighter port state control inspections and measures. For instance, during 1994, 16,964 inspections of 10,694 different vessels registered in 112 different flag states were carried out by states that are signatories to the Paris Memorandum of Understanding (MOU) on Port State Control, and 1,597 ships were detained or delayed because of deficiencies (MOU, 1994). With similar measures to the Paris MOU being taken by virtually all of the countries in the developed world, the pressure on operators is immense. Surely the last thing a management company would like is a ship under its management to be detained. On the other hand, the image of the individual companies and the ship management industry in general may be at risk if safety and quality in operations are not maintained. Accidents and injuries may also cost dearly in financial terms as well, while it is certain that a poor track record will be reflected in higher premiums for P&I and H&M cover.

A survey reported in Lloyd's Shipping Economist (Anon, 1995g) revealed some of the most important benefits derived from quality management. Twenty ship-operating companies were asked to give their impression of quality management benefits in seven specified key areas. The most important benefit cited was that of improvement in internal communication and co-operation. Market standing (access and share), productivity and risk management (reduction in personal accidents, pollution prevention and mitigation of spills) were the areas that followed. However, companies were still waiting to see any significant benefits with regard to lower operating costs and insurance premiums (both P&I and H&M), as well as improved personnel motivation and morale, and customer relations. The latter is significant as it was cited by a company with the longest experience in quality management and with certificates held for over five years (Anon, 1995g). Whereas such a finding cannot be taken to reflect the opinion of the whole industry, it does at least show that quality management may not be the most effective way of improving customer relations, at least in the way practised by certain ship management companies.

The standards available to the ship manager for implementation are wide-ranging. They include the ISO 9000 series - with ISO 9002 being the most applicable to service industries and hence ship management - the International Maritime Organisation's (IMO) International Safety Management Code (ISM Code), the ISMA Code and various standards developed by classification societies such as Det Norske Veritas' Safety and Environmental Protection (SEP) rules. In order to implement a standard, both shoreside and on-board safety and quality systems have to be developed in accordance with the requirements of the standard and the company's specific functions. After implementation, auditing by qualified assessors will take place. Auditing will include inspections of a technical nature as well as assessment of management procedures to confirm compliance with the requirements. A document of compliance will then be issued by the auditing body and a shipboard management certificate for the particular vessel. Achieving quality is, however, a never-ending process and in order to ensure continuous improvement and compliance, both internal and external audits should be carried out regularly.

According to Cooney (1992), the cost of implementation and final accreditation for a medium-sized to large ship management company lies in the range between US$150,000 and US$250,000. In the long term however, the costs of non-conformance may be much higher than the initial conformance costs, indicative of the reasons why quality and safety management have thrived within the ship management industry.

It has been suggested that the compulsory obligation for conformance with the ISM Code of the IMO for most ships in July 1998 (it has been incorporated into Chapter IX of the SOLAS 1974 Convention) will increase ship management business. This is because many owners will not have the ability to comply alone, or because it will be more economically viable to entrust a small fleet to a ship manager rather than set up a quality management department. Although some increase in business has been reported, a surge for third party ship managers has definitely not occurred prior to or since the implementation of phase 1 of the Code.

Information Technology and Ship Management

The introduction and implementation of information technology (IT) systems in ship management companies undoubtedly represents a major task that presents great challenges but at the same time can give rise to fantastic opportunities for business development and competitive advantage. It is for the latter reasons and after weighing the costs and benefits that most ship managers have warmly embraced technological innovation and developments. In fact, the question for ship managers nowadays is not whether to computerise their operations but how to do it more effectively and which systems to introduce. The choice between different software programmes and systems is critical, as it will determine efficiency and good return on investment. Conversely, the choice of a system that does not fulfil or is incompatible with the company's requirements can have disastrous results. In the selection of IT solutions there are some basic rules that need to be applied. These rules can be summarised as follows:

- alternative systems should be checked and their specifications matched to the exact company requirements;
- the company should ensure that a single software covers as many of its activities as possible;
- the company should choose widely adopted modular systems developed under open platform technology to facilitate portability as technology changes;
- the software must be designed to serve the user, who should be able to operate it without extensive training. The system should reflect the latest available technology and be enhanced with time;
- the vendor of the software and the relationship it develops with the company is of utmost importance. The vendor must have a good reputation, expertise with ship management systems, a long-term outlook and the ability to keep the system technologically alive with frequent updates.

The recent history of technological advancements and applications strongly suggests that companies should be quick in applying new concepts. This is because information technology is nowadays a strategic and not a mere operational concern. Ship managers should view information technology as a tool for providing value-added services and as an instrument to use in the quest for achieving a competitive advantage. The aim is not the mere transfer of information but the most efficient transfer and storage of valuable information. In addition, the advent of electronic commerce strongly suggests that technology can be used for improving efficiency in market exchanges and transactions, something of crucial value to the ship management sector. Information technology and computerised systems will be instrumental in achieving higher efficiencies in the production and provision of ship management services. This issue has wide implications for ship management companies. Companies that cannot afford to move forward with technological advances will limit their growth potential. On the other hand, companies that make investments in technology will be able to become more competitive by providing a higher quality service at a lower price, resulting from the achievement of improved efficiencies and scale economies.

The International Ship Managers' Association (ISMA)

The dramatic growth of the ship management sector over recent years made the formation of a ship managers' association feasible. The development of a professional body was also seen as a move by ship managers to establish their involvement and have a say in international shipping affairs.

Founded in 1991 by five of the largest ship management companies, viz. Barber International (Norway), Columbia Shipmanagement (Cyprus), Denholm Ship Management (Scotland), Hanseatic Shipping Co. (Cyprus) and Wallem Ship Management (Hong Kong), the Association has grown to include some 32 members. Lately, however, there has been a decline to 20 ISMA Code-compliant members. The Association is a company limited by guarantee, established in Cyprus and with a secretariat based in London. Membership and organisational regulations are set out in the 'Articles of Association of the ISMA'. The Association is governed by an executive committee of between seven and ten members elected at the annual general meeting every two years. The Association has set itself 23 aims, enumerated in the 'Memorandum of the Association of the ISMA'. In general, the objectives of the ISMA are to promote the interests of members at all levels and liaise with other bodies for the solution of the problems confronting the shipping industry, including training, safety and environmental protection.

Probably the most notable achievement of this professional body was the development of the ISMA Code of Ship Management Standards (CSS). The objective of this code, which is mandatory for members, is to set standards to be applied to ship operation and personnel both at sea and ashore (Anon, 1994a). The Code is very comprehensive (covering 22 different subjects) and may be applied by ship managers, crew managers and traditional shipowners. Members are audited by an independent body formed by three leading classification societies (Det Norske Veritas', Germanischer Lloyd and Lloyd's Register) and 'if compliance is achieved, a certificate is issued and signed by the three classification societies jointly' (Anon, 1994b, p. 9).

The ISMA Code is seen by many ship managers as a means of quality assurance (Anon, 1995h). This may be ascertained by the number of leading companies applying for certification and the belief that compliance with the ISMA Code will assist in complying with the ISM Code. This belief is not an unsubstantiated one as the ISMA Code takes into account the IMO resolutions A.647[16] and A.680[17] (predecessor of the ISM Code) as well as ISO standard 9002, and has also been revised to reflect changes in both the ISO 9002 and the final wording of the ISM Code as embodied in IMO resolution A.741[18] (Anon, 1995i). In 1996, the ISMA achieved new benefits for its members following an agreement by which an ISM Code document of compliance will be issued on request by any of the classification societies involved in a successful ISMA office audit (Anon, 1996g).

Reservations have been expressed, however, by many other leading ship managers and shipowners about the Code (Anon, 1991; Anon, 1992). For instance, the management of Acomarit expressed reservations about the effectiveness of the Code with regard to the timing of surveys on-board ships (Anon, 1995j). The management of Dorchester Maritime accepts that ISMA did a fantastic job in raising safety standards, but felt it inappropriate to join ISMA and impose on its clients an additional burden on top of the quality standards already adhered to (Anon, 1995k). Two of the biggest ship management companies, V. Ships and Acomarit, are not among the ISMA membership list. The extra expenses involved in ensuring compliance with the ISMA Code (which is a prerequisite for membership) mean that the association does not enjoy widespread membership and only a small proportion of the total number of ship management companies are currently ISMA members. Despite this, the Association is striving to achieve many worthwhile objectives (Anon, 1995l) and has a very important role to play in the international ship management scene.

Having discussed the major issues related to ship management, the next chapter aims to provide a review of marketing practices in ship management and apply principles of importance for achieving the marketing and organisational objectives of the companies.

3 Marketing Ship Management

Introduction

Corporate objectives cannot be achieved without marketplace interaction and the facilitation of continuous exchanges. The core concepts of marketing rest on the issue of exchange and the transactions that take place in the market. To facilitate such continuous transactions and exchanges, ship managers need to be proactive in their approach, with the aim of actively engaging in the attraction and retention of clients by offering a service that, depending on their objectives, at least conforms to fundamental specifications or exceeds requirements. The aim of this chapter is to lay down the foundations for successful marketing of the professional ship management service.

The Marketing of Ship Management Services

It has been recognised both in academic and business circles that marketing services is different from marketing physical goods. The differences may be attributed to some extent to the distinct characteristics of services that culminate into specific marketing implications. The marketing of ship management services in particular entails certain characteristics and poses certain problems that need to be evaluated in the process of identifying marketing implications.

Characteristics of the Ship Management Service

In the process of effectively marketing services, various writers (e.g. Kotler, 1980; Lovelock, 1980; Shostack, 1977) have recognised the importance of providing a classification of services in order to identify marketing implications. Lovelock (1983) proposed five such classification schemes, each representing one of five significant issues that need to be addressed. The first issue concerns understanding the nature of the service act. The ship management service may be classified as a series of intangible actions directed principally at a physical asset (the ship). Of course, with the continuous expansion of the range of services offered by ship management companies, the nature of the ship management service act is to a large extent much more complex. Secondly, ship management involves the continuous delivery of the (virtually 24-hour) service on the basis of a formal relationship with clients. The third classification scheme involves the extent to which personnel involved in direct customer contact can exercise judgement in meeting individual customer needs and the extent to which service characteristics are customised. It must be stated that competent and qualified personnel such as superintendents can and should be able to exercise their own judgement in order to meet the needs of individual clients. The extent to which the ship management service can be customised depends on the ability of management in balancing the benefits and costs of customisation according to particular circumstances. Certainly there exists ample opportunity for customisation and catering to individual customers' needs. Equally, however, the higher the degree of customisation, the higher the cost in terms of the resources which need to be employed. The fourth classification scheme proposed by Lovelock (1983) involves the nature of demand for the service relative to supply. For ship management in particular there is no evidence to suggest that any company cannot meet peak demand without a major delay. In any case demand fluctuations over time are quite narrow as far as ship management is concerned. As to the last classification scheme, it is suggested that the service should be classified on the basis of the nature of the interaction between customer and organisation and the availability of service outlets. In the case of the ship management service, clients and ship management companies chiefly transact at arm's length. This means that personal interaction is limited compared to communication via other media. The availability of ship management service outlets is primarily through a single site at the location of the company's headquarters. However, with proper networking and the establishment of agents and subsidiaries, companies may be able to deliver part of the service from various locations.

Challenges in Marketing Ship Management

The major challenges faced by contemporary ship management organisations as far as marketing is concerned include the propensity of clients to shop around or take management in-house. This behaviour may come about as a result of uncertainty and dissatisfaction that may arise due to poor communication, weak relationships and the complexity of the ship management service itself.

The fact that the management of ships is a very complex process has been widely recognised in the past (Spruyt, 1994). The shipping environment itself is extremely dynamic in nature, characterised by economic booms and busts (e.g. Stokes, 1997) and market volatility (Stopford, 1997). These characteristics of the external environment are indicative of the uncertainty faced by shipowners in handing over their high value assets for management. Duncan (1972) argues that environmental complexity and dynamism are positively related to uncertainty. Additionally, according to Wittreich (1966), buyers of professional services are faced with uncertainty because of the difficulty of evaluating service performance characteristics before and even after purchase and use. In his Harvard Business Review paper he contended that the professional service organisation promises to introduce more certainty in a particular area in which the client feels uncertain. Such uncertainty mainly arises from three sources. First there is the basic uncertainty of not knowing with whom to deal and on whom to rely. Shipowners have a number of alternatives in their quest for obtaining the ship management service. This issue has implications for the process of choice criteria in ship management, which will be discussed in chapter 5. Secondly, there is uncertainty in the purchase of the services themselves, especially where large sums of money are involved. The amount of money involved in ship operation and management is certainly large, and this is therefore an obvious source of uncertainty for clients. Thirdly, there is uncertainty over the problem itself, in this case how to perform ship operation. This may be the case where the shipowner has not been involved in ship operation, for instance, banks and oil majors whose major business activity does not involve ship management.

The wide availability of ship management companies has also resulted in an increasing propensity among shipowners to 'shop around' and consider different options when contracts come up for renewal. This indicates that clients are uncertain of the level of service quality that they receive. In consequence, they are inclined to try something different that may result in greater benefits at a lower price. The managing director of a ship management company was quoted in the trade press saying that there has been a trend by shipowners to take management back in-house, in order to be able to exercise better control and to limit the risks. The problem of contracts being on a shorter time cycle has been reported since the late 1980s (Anon, 1987; Williams, 1993).

Another problem reported in the trade press is the reluctance of charterers and mainly oil majors to charter vessels that are operated by third party ship managers (Guest, 1994). Oil majors used to be major clients for the third party ship management business. Lately, however, they have argued that they prefer communicating with an owner directly rather than through the owner's agent, i.e. the ship manager. It seems that this attitude may be attributed to problems of communication, both between owner and managers, and also between manager and charterer. A chief executive of a ship management company stated that the reluctance of owners and charterers to accept ship management as a service could be a real threat to the industry. He also added that such trends may culminate in ship managers losing their most prestigious and lucrative contracts. The loss of many contracts can also be attributed to the uncertain nature of the shipping environment itself. During the 1970s and 1980s, major oil companies formed a substantial sector of the clientele of ship management companies. However, in recent years the fleets of these companies have been decreasing dramatically. Prescott (1995) identified a fall of 48 per cent in the period 1984-1994. The vessels are replaced through investments made by independent owners, who also tend to manage and operate their vessels.

Communication between ship manager and client has also been identified as a major challenge posing potential problems for ship managers. Grey (1995, p. 5) states, for instance:

> One of the inherent difficulties of third party ship management has traditionally been that of communications between the manager who takes over the day-to-day husbandry of the vessel, and the owner who finds himself provided with reports from the manager from time to time. Strain on the relationship has come from the owner being provided with insufficient information about the operation of the vessel, caused by the manager being too selective or secretive, or being too busy to provide the owner with what he regards as adequate reports.

Poor communication and the complexity of ship management gives rise to conflicts and disagreements that may occur between the ship management company and the client's organisation. Minor disagreements tend to occur frequently at all levels of the organisational hierarchy. It is inevitable that even the smallest of errors may result in client dissatisfaction in ship management. Client dissatisfaction leads to conflict that may give rise to expensive litigation procedures and the potential termination of ship management contracts (Bundock, 1989). Mulrenan (1994, p. 1) reported the following in a Lloyd's List issue:

> Leading tanker owner Vela will end its reliance on commercial ship management by taking full control of its 6 million deadweight fleet. The Saudi

Arabian controlled shipowner will establish a ship operating centre in Dubai within three months as a first step to moving to in-house management.

Two ship management companies based in the United Kingdom managed the fleet of this company. The companies obviously lost one of their major clients in terms of revenue-earning capacity.

Client uncertainty and dissatisfaction with the service and the ship manager-shipowner inter-organisational relationship may result in the inclination to take ship management in-house. This is reflected in the case of American Automar. The president of the company stated that the problems of managing US-flag vessels through a third party ship manager were so great that the company was forced to bring the operation back in-house. In his words: 'we were not getting the level of integration on a technical and engineering level from a third party ship manager' (Anon, 2000b, p. 31). In 1993, the company set up Osprey Ship Management (OSM) a subsidiary that would undertake improvements in asset maintenance and heighten the focus on crew continuity, training and safety, as well as integrating the financial, engineering and operating decision-making process. To this effect, the president stated (Anon, 2000b, p. 32):

> This is a very litigious society, especially for personal injury, so you need top-notch safety and a proactive risk management system, which we were not getting with third party management. We had a high rate of machine casualty which seemed to be related to the human factor and our P&I loss ratio was higher than we wanted. We have saved in both of those areas now.

The problems of intense competition, client uncertainty and dissatisfaction, and the lack of coherent marketing practices aimed towards retaining current clients is reflected in the loss of more than 1.5 million deadweight of tanker tonnage by Wallem Ship Management to a newly formed entity. A report in Lloyd's List indicates:

> Wallem obviously fought hard to keep the four large tankers, but at the end of the day it was the vastly smaller Ugland/Interocean grouping – which Argonaut executives say offered a more personal service because of its size – that won through (Anon, 1995m).

The quote is indicative of the problems faced in ship management and of the importance of close relationships, personal service and service delivery according to requirements.

On the issue of client uncertainty and dissatisfaction, the comments made by the technical director of Laurin Maritime are also notable:

> We used to have a third party manager, but it was not an overall happy experience. I should point out that we had a good relationship with the management company, which had been set up by a former crew member. He was contracted to manage four vessels, but I do not consider the results to have been positive. This is for two main reasons. Firstly, he was simply too expensive. Secondly, we did not feel that we had complete control over the running of our vessels. So, the contract was allowed to end and now we undertake all vessel management in-house (Anon, 2000a, p. 37).

The amount of differentiation that can be achieved among ship management service providers is quite limited as far as the core service is concerned. Differentiation is essential in the provision of professional services such as ship management. An organisation should pay close attention to the aspects in which it possesses a differential advantage in order to gain competitiveness. Kotler and Bloom (1984) suggest that the innate differentiability of professional services is quite limited. The amount of variation in the way ship management services can be offered is minimal. Although ship managers frequently refer to their accreditation to particular quality standards as a means to imply service differentiation, this cannot be considered as an effective strategy. The reason is that accreditation to industry standards such as the International Safety Management Code is expected from clients and quality management has been practised before the implementation of the Code by virtually all reputable ship management companies (Panayides, 1996). Additionally, even if the service is provided differently from competing services, it may be difficult to get clients, who are confronted with uncertainty, to perceive and recognise the real differences. Some ship management companies have tried to combat the problem of limited differentiability by expanding into non-shipping businesses (Kerr, 1996). This is indicative of the difficulty in achieving differentiation in the ship management market and is hardly a strategy to be adopted for effective ship management. In addition, diversification in new lines of business activity is not without dangers itself. Such a strategy will be termed unrelated diversification, where a company expands into new lines of activity that have nothing in common with its current line of business. In fact, it has been found that unrelated diversifiers seem to under-perform related diversifiers in the general industry (Rumelt, 1982).

Ship Management Marketing Implications

The challenges faced by contemporary ship management organisations have important marketing implications. For instance, issues of complexity, client uncertainty and dissatisfaction can be effectively tackled by the adoption of the service quality philosophy that should transcend the delivery of the ship management service. The problems faced in ship management are indicative of the importance of close client relationships, personalised service and service delivery according to requirements. The achievement of such objectives entails the entrenchment of an organisational culture of service that can be achieved through the adoption of human resource and internal marketing policies as well as specification of processes of service delivery and contingency approaches. Uncertainty as to the level of cost and fees that clients are required to incur should be tackled with proper pricing policies and detailed budgeting procedures. Location and distribution can assist in the development of closer client relationships and the facilitation of improved inter-organisational communication. Finally, effective methods of promotion supported by tangible aspects of physical evidence illustrative of the strengths of the ship management organisation can be supportive in facing the challenges. These implications are discussed in more detail below through the application of conventional marketing principles to ship management.

As stated earlier, ship management is a fairly new service in the shipping industry. Consequently, advanced marketing strategies for the companies have been underplayed, as managers had first to establish themselves in the marketplace. The marketing strategies adopted were mainly intended to attract clients. A conventional and long-standing approach to marketing analysis is the marketing mix (McCarthy, 1981). The marketing mix has been defined by Kotler (1994, p. 98) as the 'set of marketing tools that the firm uses to pursue its marketing objectives in the target market', these tools being classified under the four main headings of product, price, place and promotion. In services marketing in particular, Booms and Bitner (1981) extended the marketing mix by adding participants, physical evidence and process to reflect the idiosyncratic nature of services marketing. The marketing mix elements have been utilised to some extent by professional ship managers in their quest for client attraction, cost reduction and improvement in service quality. There is a need, however, to apply such principles in a co-ordinated and systematic manner that will involve input from all departments making up the internal organisation and not only from the marketing or the so-called business development unit.

The Ship Management Service and Service Quality

In the ship management context, the first aspect of the marketing mix (product) entails the offering of the ship management service and the implications for value and quality. The actual service is made up of various components. Gronroos (1990a) identified a basic service package as consisting of the core service, facilitating services (and goods) and supporting services (and goods). The core service is, in essence, the management of the ship with facilitating and supporting services being the operational and technical aspects of management as well as the land, labour and capital (not equity finance) that is provided by the ship manager. The core service may be turned into a generic form, an expected form, or may be augmented (Kotler, 1994; Christopher, Payne and Ballantyne, 1993). The generic form consists of the basic ship management service in its most plain version, i.e. an office with basic equipment and personnel with some expertise in the management of ships. Spruyt (1994, p. 138) puts it frankly: 'any competent ex-mariner with a telex and some pals can tender for a contract'. In its expected form, the service actually consists of what the customer expects from it. For instance, the customer will expect the basics of the generic form but also prudent management of the ship according to the terms of the contract. The augmented service would consist of additional features in the ship management service provision that individual companies may employ and offer. For example, a ship management company may adopt a total quality management system that will differentiate it from other companies, it may offer additional services to its clients and a measure of adaptation to personal requirements. Competition among ship management firms nowadays takes place at this level of service development. Another level has been identified: that of the potential product, which ultimately means all the augmentations to the service that might take place in the future in the competitive ship management environment. Companies that are innovators and strive to make use of new technologies and processes in their service delivery are more likely to offer an augmented service that may lead to a competitive advantage.

Of significant importance in professional ship management is the delivery of a high quality service. High service quality will culminate in a series of benefits. Empirical research by Parasuraman, Berry and Zeithaml

(1990) indicates that delivering high service quality produces measurable benefits in profit, cost saving and market share. In addition, retaining customers through service quality raises profit through increase repurchases and referrals. Parasurman, Zeithaml and Berry (1993) contend that firms providing a service above the level considered adequate will gain a competitive advantage that will ensure customer loyalty. Heskett et al. (1994) found a link between profitability in service industries and customer loyalty. One other aspect, that of internal service quality, is also of importance in services marketing. Internal service quality is the term used to denote employee expectations and satisfaction. It is based on tangible elements like workplace design, job design, employee selection and rewards, and intangible elements like recognition, support and development. When properly implemented, internal service quality leads to employees' satisfaction, loyalty and improved productivity.

Ship management companies operate in a competitive market where clients have the right to compare, select and enjoy the value of services available. The ship manager should be able to enhance the value and the perceived quality of the service from the perspective of the client. It is not enough to adhere to the specifications of a quality management system and claim that the service offered is of high quality. It is the needs and perceptions of individual clients that dictate high service quality. A service is different from perceptions of quality of service. According to Groth and Dye (1999), the perceived value of the service and the quality of the service are determined by some key variables in the customer's mind, which collectively influence:

- the perceived certainty of service delivery;
- expectations about the characteristics of the service;
- *ex ante* perceptions of need or desire for the service.

It is important for ship managers to actively pursue the enhancement of the perception of the client as to the value of the service/quality delivered. Differences between expectations and perceived service quality may result in a perceived shortfall of service quality. Ship managers should foster the formation of realistic expectations, permit the customer to recognise the variables of greatest importance in fulfilling the required needs, and aim to reduce bad service experiences. Ship managers must give increasing attention to the time spent with the client, either on a personal level or when communicating by various media. The aim should be to deliver customer satisfaction at every encounter. To achieve this there must exist contingency plans in case of service failure. Ship managers must foster a culture of adaptability and flexibility within their organisations, encourage spontaneity, particularly by people that interact with the client directly, and help employees to cope with problem customers.

The importance of service quality in services marketing means that a significant body of research has been carried out to identify what determines service quality. Bitner (1993) contends that service quality is the single most researched area in services marketing. Gronroos (1984) defined two dimensions of service quality namely, technical quality or what the customer receives, and functional quality or how the service is provided. Service quality perception is a multi-dimensional concept. This means that customers' assessments of quality include perceptions of multiple factors. Research by Parasuraman, Zeithaml and Berry (1988) and Parasuraman, Berry and Zeithaml (1991) indicated five dimensions that can be used to measure service quality. These dimensions are referred to as 'tangibles', 'reliability', 'responsiveness', 'assurance' and 'empathy'. Although the dimensions were originally intended to apply to consumer services, their application to professional services or ship management services to that extent may be equally important. Reliability refers to the ability of the service provider to perform the promised service dependably and accurately. Responsiveness is the willingness to assist the customer and provide prompt service. The employees' knowledge and courtesy and their ability to inspire trust and confidence has been termed assurance. Empathy refers to the caring and individualised attention given to customers, whereas tangibles are the physical facilities, materials, equipment and personnel. It is logical to assert that the presence of such characteristics in the delivery of the ship management service will improve clients' perceptions of service quality.

Pricing Ship Management Services

The price charged for the provision of services can be an important determinant of client attraction. In the case of ship management, however, the ship management fee can be an important variable if everything else remains the same. The complex nature of the service renders the fee itself a less important determinant that has to be viewed in the context of service quality and associated cost advantages that may be passed on to clients. Price as a determinant of selection of a particular ship management company as opposed to competitors will be considered in more detail in chapter 5. At this stage the importance of price lies in its use in the price-service quality relationship. Price can be an important variable in the quest for influencing perceptions of service quality.

With respect to the fees earned by ship management companies, it is fair to say that the rates charged are fixed and only vary by a small margin from company to company. Chapman (1994) notes that an annual turnover in fee income for crewing and technical management of a fleet of ten to 12 vessels would be in the region of US$800,000-US$1.2 million. Guest (1995c) indicates that ship managers receive between US$5,000-US$7,000 per month per ship, which for ship managers with large fleets (over 150 vessels) would mean an annual income of above US$10 million. Ship managers have over the years been claiming that the level of management fees has remained low and static while costs have been rising. The vice-president of a major ship management company was reported saying that the level of ship management fees has basically been the same for the last ten years (Gray, 1997).

The management fee levied is typically between five and ten per cent of the total vessel running costs, largely depending on vessel type (Fry, 1993; Willingale, 1992). In setting the management fee, ship managers must place importance on the positioning of the service relative to competitors, and not base the fee calculation on a mere cost-plus basis. Price is a powerful influence on customer expectations, and many shipowners are prepared to pay a higher price for higher service quality. The actual price will be agreed between ship manager and shipowner after a series of negotiations. If the shipowner is price-sensitive, the ship manager may be willing to bend a little in order to secure a contract. The actual price set by a company will also be determined by the cost-effectiveness of its operations. As most companies try to achieve tight cost control, however, variations in prices are relatively small and differentiation cannot be achieved through the isolated use of the price variable alone. The standard methods used in pricing, the relatively low fees charged and the small variations in prices between companies suggest that a pricing marketing strategy based on fees alone has limited effectiveness in ship management unless used in conjunction with the other variables in ship management service delivery.

Location and Distribution

Ship management companies must strive to make their service offering easily accessible and widely available. The companies can achieve these goals through establishment in key geographical locations, market entry strategies and marketing channel configurations.

The location of the ship management company is important, not only as a means of marketing but also for associated advantages. Thus, ship management companies have increasingly fled from traditional shipping and ship management centres to locations which provide cost-effectiveness in terms of operation, taxation, and cheap land and labour (Anon, 1997d; Perry, 1994). The location of customers and the degree of customer contact often determine the location of a service organisation's facilities (Mersha and Adlakha, 1991), hence, ship management companies have been inclined to relocate or establish subsidiaries at places in close proximity to clients.

Various maritime directories report the United Kingdom to be the leading ship management centre. Companies are principally located in London and Glasgow. The Isle of Man also attracts a number of companies due to its offshore status. London is preferred because it is an established commercial centre (Anon, 1995n), whereas Glasgow offers excellent communications and office personnel with special skill in managing ships (Anon, 1995o). In addition, both accommodation and staff costs in Glasgow are much cheaper than, say, in London. Many big players among the ship management fraternity are based in Glasgow, including Denholm Ship Management, Acomarit and Northern Marine Management. It has been estimated that more than 265 ships of 14 million deadweight are managed from Glasgow (Anon, 1999a).

In the Mediterranean area, ship management companies are centred in Cyprus, Malta and Monaco because:

> Fiscal incentives offered by local legislation, communication networks, vastly improved air links on a global level, ideal infrastructure, and an awareness by governments of the importance of certain maritime industries are all criteria that these countries satisfy (Anon, 1995p, p. 11).

For Cyprus in particular, it is estimated that more than 75 per cent of the companies involved in third party ship management are located on the island which is the home to the big names in the industry.

Another consideration for relocating (mainly to East Asia) is the fact that seafarers are increasingly recruited from the relocation area and provide the companies with the advantage of being close to manning sources (Anon, 1997e). They later used this advantage, provided by their geographic proximity to manpower, as a means of marketing their service. A further aspect that has been used for marketing is the fact that managers relocate closer to suppliers or shipbuilding yards. Perry (1994) states that, with the majority of ships in the world being built in either Europe or the Far East, managers in these locations perhaps have a slight advantage.

Hong Kong and Singapore are the most prominent ship management centres in Asia. Hong Kong provides excellent shipping-related infrastructure and geographical proximity to Japanese clients in particular. Local staff in Hong Kong are extremely hard-working and well-educated, and basic infrastructure and support services like air travel, telecommunications, banking and insurance are top class. The drawback for establishment in Hong Kong is the high cost of property, but for many managers this is outweighed by the numerous advantages that arguably make Hong Kong the best location in Asia to operate a ship management company (Anon, 1999b). Lately, however, Singapore has emerged as a prominent competitor to Hong Kong's ship management status. This has been brought about not least by the uncertainty created due to the hand-over of Hong Kong to China (although any fears must have been alleviated by now). In addition, Singapore provides comparable infrastructure and support services to Hong Kong, and its strategic position is suited for serving Asian clients. The city-state of Singapore has also provided a challenge to Hong Kong's status as the Asian ship management centre, primarily through the introduction of tax breaks (Lim, 1999).

Promotion

The promotional marketing mix of a ship management company may take various forms, including advertising, entry in directories, production of literature, participation at exhibitions and public relations (PR).

Despite the fact that there is no evidence to support that advertising directly generates enquiries in a ship management context, it does take a significant sector of the promotional mix in terms of monetary investment. This is despite evidence that tends to suggest that consumer reaction toward comparative advertisements in professional services is significantly lower than consumer reaction toward all other types of advertisements (Donthu,

1993). Whether advertising is effective in changing the desires of potential clients in a ship management context remains largely an empirically untested proposition because of the wide range of influences on client preferences. Traditional economic analysis has tended to the conclusion that the primary effect of advertising is to raise prices to consumers and to lead to the creation and maintenance of monopoly power (Comaner and Wilson, 1974). Stansell, Harper and Wilder (1984) conclude that advertising significantly increases sales for many, but not all, firms. In addition, empirical research carried out in a ship management context has revealed that advertising is probably the least important criterion upon which shipowners will select a professional ship manager. This seems to be the perception of both ship managers and their clients. More details regarding choice criteria in ship management can be found in chapter 5. The largest ship management companies advertise heavily in a number of widely circulated maritime newspapers and periodicals, such as Lloyd's List, Lloyd's Ship Manager, Seatrade and Fairplay. It is also a fact that the bulk of advertisements place emphasis on the ability of companies to offer a service of high quality, followed by international coverage and an adequately trained crew. Entry in maritime directories has become usual practice for ship management firms. Directories such as Fairplay World Shipping Directory, Lloyd's Maritime Directory and Ocean Shipmanagers' Register are among the best known.

Another method of promotion used by ship management companies is that of production and distribution of marketing literature (brochures). The contents includes description of the functions of the company and a basic departmental structure, accompanied by colourful pictures of vessels under management, the company's premises and staff. The brochures are distributed among prospective clients and people that visit the company's premises.

Participation in exhibitions is a method of promotion widely adopted by companies in the maritime industry, but to a lesser extent by ship managers as ship management involves the provision of an intangible service.

Public Relations (PR) has been defined as 'any area of communication that reflects the public image of a company' (Peterson and Porges, 1991, p. 355). Although all methods of the promotional mix may be perceived to be embraced within the PR context, PR actually goes a step further than mere advertising. PR involves methods of communicating the image of the company in a more authoritative way by, for example, a speech in a conference or seminar, or a press release. Ship management companies adopt such methods, and representatives of the companies very often appear as speakers in maritime conferences throughout the world. In this way they appeal directly to an audience of prospective clients.

Internal Marketing and Human Resource Management

The expanded marketing mix for services as articulated by Booms and Bitner (1981) makes reference to the importance of people in delivering a high quality service. The term 'participants', as referred to in a marketing context, would incorporate the persons involved in the production, delivery and consumption of the service. In a ship management context, this would include personnel ashore and on-board the vessels, as well as customers. There is no evidence to indicate whether ship management companies actually implement this variable in marketing their service offering. Of course, ship management companies strive to recruit competent personnel both ashore and on-board. However, it is extremely doubtful whether personnel are trained to become 'part-time' marketers (e.g. Gummesson, 1991), i.e. there is no evidence to suggest that internal marketing (e.g. Judd, 1987) is actually taking place in ship management companies. Furthermore, the limited evidence (e.g. Gunton, 1994) suggests that few companies actually implement customer surveys systematically.

Whereas interactive marketing is concerned with the interactions between employees and the firm's customers in services marketing organisations, internal marketing deals with the relationship between the company and its employees. Internal marketing entails viewing employees as internal customers and striving to satisfy their requirements so that they can better satisfy the requirements of external customers through interactive marketing.

Integral to the concept of internal marketing and human resources is the concept of service quality. The importance of quality to a firm's success has been well-documented (Deming, 1993; Juran, 1992; Feigenbaum, 1991). As indicated in the previous chapter, quality may be viewed as 'meeting customer requirements accurately and precisely'. Juran (1988) defined customers as all persons who are influenced and/or interact with an organisation's processes and products. In consequence, this definition would include not only the organisation's external clients, but also its internal employees. To capture the market and stay in business, Deming (1986; 1993) suggests that managers of any organisation need to help their employees to understand the interdependence between various departments and people within the organisation. In addition, they must see themselves as components in a system, and work in co-operation with preceding and subsequent stages (Kuei, 1999). These issues have given rise to the concept of internal service quality and the view that employees should be provided with the training and appropriate tools, and a supportive managerial environment in order to improve quality and efficiency, and potentially achieve a competitive advantage (Pfau, Detzel and Geller, 1991). It follows that there is a key role to be played by human resource management practices in the quest to improve service quality. In this context, Redman and Mathews (1998) specify that the key issues would include recruitment, retention, teamwork, training and development, appraisal, rewarding quality, job security, and employee involvement and relations.

The starting point for a high quality ship management service must be a qualified and competent staff that is able to produce and deliver the service. This is also reflected in the preferences of clients regarding ship manager choice criteria and service evaluation referred to in chapter 5. Both clients and ship managers believe that technically competent and qualified seafarers and personnel are among the most important criteria for success in client attraction and retention. It must be pointed out, however, that under TQM regimes workers are expected to be highly flexible, and selection often focuses on attitudes to flexibility and customer service rather than skill or qualification levels (Beaumont, 1992). Selection methods should also be designed to test for aptitudes in problem-solving and team-working as well (Bowen and Lawler, 1992).

Turbin and Rosse (1990) assert that retention of key strategic employees, especially managers and professionals, can have a major impact on the success or failure of an organisation. The retention of employees has numerous positive effects on an organisation. Among others, it increases the reputation and image of the organisation and thus increases selection attractiveness, which in turn enhances the firm's ability to recruit high-performing staff. Equally, a decline in employee loyalty and retention is costly to the organisation because it might result in lower productivity (Withley and Cooper, 1989) and the development of a turnover culture (Iverson and Deery, 1997). Turnover refers to the outflow of skilled labour from an organisation and a high turnover rate may result in decreasing, standards of customer care. Reichold (1993) views retention of selected employees as the key to customer retention. Hence, customer retention and employee retention feed one another and this results in quality improvement. As Cole (1993, p. 14) stated:

In the end a customer's contact with a company is through employees. It is with employees that customers build bonds of trust and expectations. When these employees leave, the bonds break as well.

Employee retention is of particular importance in the ship operation industry, especially with regard to retention of officers and ratings on board ships. The sense of belonging and loyalty as a means for improving safety on board has been well established in the maritime literature. Safety and accident minimisation are among the most important factors considered by shipowners in evaluating ship manager performance.

Another key aspect in the quest for high service quality is the entrenchment of a culture of teamwork among employees. In fact, Berry, Parasuraman and Zeithaml (1994) characterise teamwork as one of the 'essential lessons' America's service industries have learned in the quest for high service quality. In ship management, teamwork is of equal importance on-board and ashore. On-board teamwork can assist in overcoming cultural differences and language barriers, which play such a crucial role in safe ship operation. Ashore, it can assist in overcoming boundaries across departments, which are a major contributor to service failure (Schonberger, 1994). Redmand and Mathews (1998) note that there is a real danger that effective development of teamwork in many service organisations is being left to chance. The implications of this statement in the ship management context is that managers must take a proactive stance and expedite the systematic planning of programmes that can facilitate and encourage teamwork.

It goes without saying that training is imperative in ship operation. This aspect is stressed on a continuing basis among shipping practitioners, shipping regulators and ship managers in particular. Hence, there is no need to reiterate the benefits that would result from training in safe ship operation. It is fundamental to acknowledge, however, that training and development should not just include training of seafarers on the technical aspects of ship operation and safety. It is equally important that training and development is also carried out to support the implementation of TQM. Service quality will suffer without training and continuous improvements in service delivery. In addition, performance appraisal should focus on the quality goals of the organisation, and evidence of achievement of quality by employees should be rewarded. A high level of job security and employee involvement in the understanding of the quality process and how they can contribute towards it are crucial elements for achieving high service quality through internal marketing.

Process and Physical Evidence

Process refers to the way the service is produced and delivered (Cowell, 1984). Regarding the production and delivery process of the ship management service, it has been mentioned already that most, if not all ship management companies nowadays implement quality management in their operations. This has been discussed earlier, where it was revealed, however, that this process on its own might not be effective for improving customer relations and offering differentiation.

Physical evidence includes elements like the physical environment and facilitating goods that enable the service to be provided (Cowell, 1984). In a ship management context, physical evidence includes the building (and internal decoration) from where the company operates, as well as the quality of tangible goods supplied (e.g. bunkers, spare parts, provisions, etc.). Ship management companies seem to attach importance to the external and internal physical working environment. Physical evidence also includes the various deliverables such as the reports and documentation with which the ship manager frequently furnishes the client. The presentation and, in particular, conduct of personnel also plays a role in the client's perception of the quality of service that the ship management company is able to offer.

The importance of conventional marketing mix elements in marketing the ship management service is evident. There is however evidence to suggest that, in practice, marketing in ship management revolves around some of the marketing mix elements, some of which are not even systematically implemented. It has been recognised that service businesses are more difficult to manage using a traditional marketing approach (Kotler, 1994). The variables of the marketing mix concentrate on customer attraction rather than retention. The development of academic marketing theories and models suggests that marketing nowadays is moving away from the traditional approach of the marketing mix paradigm towards a relationship approach (Gronroos, 1994). Gunton (1993, p. 34) made an important prediction regarding ship management: 'relations with customers will become increasingly important in the future...'. Reporting on a 'listening to customers' programme set up by Ocean Fleets in 1991, he revealed the first signs of proper marketing research within the ship management industry. Although there are no indications to show that this move has been followed by others, ship management companies will inevitably come to realise that the most precious asset in their possession is the customer itself. On this premise, and recognising the importance of customer retention and satisfaction, the following chapter is devoted entirely to the aspect of developing ship manager-client relationships. Aspects of managing such relationships, including the elements that should comprise them, are discussed in the context of an empirical investigation carried out.

4 Ship Manager-Client Relationships

Introduction

Marketing thought has recognised that the retention of existing customers may be much more important than the attraction of new ones, particularly for service firms. By establishing the concept of exchange as being at the core of marketing, empirical and conceptual developments formulated a new body of scientific interest, termed relationship marketing. This concept, which is shown to be particularly applicable to the practice of ship management, is discussed in this chapter at a theoretical and empirical level. The chapter attempts to establish a classification of the relationships that ship management companies have with their clients, and to discuss the resulting marketing implications. This is done through an empirical investigation. The chapter begins with the theoretical depiction of relationship marketing, and its applicability and importance in services and ship management in particular.

Marketing and Exchange Relationships

The fundamental concept of marketing is deeply rooted in the concept of exchange. In fact, exchange is so pivotal to marketing theory and practice that contemporary marketing thought and practice treats it as the basis for the development of future marketing strategies. It is also regarded as the linchpin of marketing theory and the foundation of what has been regarded by many as a new marketing paradigm – relationship marketing.

Exchange has been widely accepted by marketing scholars as the core concept of marketing (Alderson and Martin, 1965; Bagozzi, 1974; 1975; 1979; Houston and Gassenheimer, 1987; Hunt, 1976). For instance, Bagozzi (1975, p. 39) states that marketing 'is the discipline of exchange behaviour, and it deals with problems related to this behaviour'. The official definition of marketing, approved by the American Marketing Association, indicates that exchange is at the centre of marketing:

Marketing is the process of planning and executing the conception, pricing, promotion, and distribution of ideas, goods, and services to create exchanges that satisfy individual and organisational objectives (Anon, 1985, p. 1).

In an examination of the fundamental explananda of marketing from a philosophy of science perspective, Hunt (1983, p.13) stated: 'marketing science is the behavioural science that seeks to explain exchange relationships'. Given this perspective of marketing science, Hunt (1983) proposed that a general theory of marketing should aim to explain the behaviour of buyers and sellers directed at consummating exchanges, the institutional framework directed at consummating and/or facilitating exchanges, and the consequences of the above phenomena on society. Exchange between two parties may take the form of a discrete transaction characterised by a distinct beginning and end, and lacking any relationship elements. On the other hand, exchange may facilitate a long-term interaction characterised by the development of relationship attributes between the participants. The latter is indicative of the belief that the development of relationships should be a central aspect in marketing thought and practice.

The relationship marketing approach is in line with the paradigm of dyadic exchanges. It has been argued that, since marketing is an inherently social activity, concentration upon individuals as the unit of analysis is not sufficient (Bagozzi, 1978). Instead, complex relationships in the market place should be modelled in the form of systems of dyadic exchanges (Bonoma, Bagozzi and Zaltman, 1978). Bagozzi (1978) proposes a formal theory of exchange, which is represented as a dynamic social process, functioning under both economic and psychological constraints.

An important consideration in exchange theory is how the exchange and behaviour of the actors might be influenced by past and prospective exchanges. The introduction of the exchange relationship (Dwyer, Schurr and Oh, 1987; Spekman and Johnston, 1986) or relational exchange (Frazier, Spekman and O'Neal, 1988) aims to take this situation into account. Exchange relationships are distinguished from discrete exchanges. For instance, MacNeil (1980, p. 60) states:

> Discreteness is the separating of a transaction from all else between the participants at the same time and before and after. Its pure form, never achieved in life, occurs when there is nothing else between the parties, never has been and never will be.

Hence, relational exchanges can be distinguished from discrete exchanges (MacNeil, 1978; 1980) by:

- having a history and expected future;
- possible implicit and explicit assumptions, trust and planning;
- participants perhaps deriving complex, personal, non-economic satisfactions during the social exchange;
- increased interdependence;
- obligations being customised, detailed and administered within the relationship.

Although research on exchange relationships has been carried out, it is not considered conclusive. Exchange relationships and consequently relationship marketing may still be considered to be at a relatively young stage in marketing theory. Various research attempts have been made in different contexts (e.g. industrial marketing, channels of distribution, etc.), and a framework of buyer-seller relationships has been developed. Moreover, scholars have attempted to explain exchange relationships by the application of theories such as the political economy perspective (Achrol, Reve and Stern, 1983; Arndt, 1983; Stern and Reve, 1980).

Relationship Marketing

The emergence of the relationship concept in the marketing arena stems from the marketing reality that the acquisition of new customers is much more expensive than the retention of existing customers (Stone and Woodcock, 1995). This has important implications for ship management companies that, as indicated in chapter 3, concentrate merely on customer attraction rather than customer retention. In fact, Congram (1991) suggests that acquiring a new customer may cost at least six times as much as retaining an existing one. The cost of establishing contact with a potential customer and achieving the first sale may be so high that the returns from the sale are minimal or even negative (Gronroos, 1989). It is only when the customer keeps buying that the sought benefits will be achieved. Relationship marketing provides an effective approach to customer retention over the long term. It involves the development of bonds that will tie the customer to the particular product/service supplier and ensure continuing exchanges. To this end, relationship marketing has been defined as 'encompassing all marketing activities directed towards establishing, developing and maintaining successful relational exchanges' (Morgan and Hunt, 1994, p. 22). Since client defections to competitors, or switching to in-house management are major problems in ship management, the application of relationship marketing in order to ensure client retention seems to be an attractive proposition.

The advantages accruing from relationship management between the buyer and seller dictate the need for serious consideration of this new marketing approach by both academia and practitioners. Levitt (1983) states that the nature of services requiring repeat negotiations and technological complexity necessitate long-term and involved relationships between buyers and sellers. Repeat orders will go to those sellers who have done the best job of nurturing relationships with their buyers. A long-term relationship will definitely enable the parties to develop an acquaintance with complex products and hence master their efficient use. In a services context, the clients' processes and practices will be known within a few encounters. It will also reduce transaction costs (see Williamson, 1979) in cases where contracts have to be re-negotiated, as is very often the case in ship management.

Apart from customer retention, Congram (1991) enumerates a series of relationship-associated advantages. Existing customers are easier to serve and constitute a continuous revenue stream. When customers are lost and are not replaced immediately, there will be a revenue gap for the firm. Customers will ultimately become advocates and hence marketers of the organisation, and help it identify new services or improve current ones. By doing so, they will also improve their own situation. Relationship management is also cost-effective because time is spent only on those accounts where the potential for success is greatest (Sonnenberg, 1988). Berry and Parasuraman (1991) suggest that relationship marketing entails benefits that are not just important to customers but also difficult for competitors to duplicate. They posit that the stronger the relationship, the greater the opportunity to deliver those benefits. It follows that relationship marketing probably offers the best available opportunity for product (service) differentiation and the achievement of competitiveness. It has been recognised in chapter 2 that limited differentiability and difficulty in achieving a competitive advantage are major issues with which ship management is confronted. Hence, the relevance and potential contribution of applying relationship marketing are established.

Relationship Marketing as the New Marketing Paradigm

Scholars have seen the relationship marketing approach as a possible paradigm shift in established marketing theories. A paradigm is an accepted model or pattern which underlies scientific achievements (Dixon and Wilkinson, 1989), and inspires theory building as distinct from being mere theory itself (Arndt, 1983). Iacobucci (1994) notes that relationship marketing is currently enjoying popularity as a paradigm. Gronroos (1990a, p. 138; 1990b, p. 5) for example, gives a relationship approach definition to marketing:

> Marketing is to establish, maintain, enhance and commercialise customer relationships (usually but not necessarily always long term) so that the objectives of the parties involved are met. This is done by a mutual exchange and fulfilment of promises.

This definition provides an obvious diversion from the more conventional view of marketing as identifying, anticipating and satisfying customer requirements profitably (Kotler, 1994), and in line with definitions of marketing considered previously, underpins the view of relationship marketing as a paradigm.

Clark, Peck, Payne and Christopher (1995, p. 278) indicate that 'relationship marketing reflects an emerging paradigm of marketing that is cross-functional, relationship driven and focuses upon processes as well as functions in achieving long-term customer satisfaction'. Parvatiyar and Sheth (1994) speak of 'the emergence of a relationship orientation in marketing'. Ambler (1994) discusses the evolution of the 'relational paradigm' but expressly states that it is, in a broad sense, the same as relationship marketing. Gronroos (1996) strongly argues that the underlying philosophy of relationship marketing, with the transition from a product-based to a resource-based and competencies-related perspective (see also Gronroos, 1997), means that relationship marketing is a new paradigm. Fisk (1994) asserts that relationship marketing is an emerging new paradigm, whereas the relationship marketing process is 'an adaptive learning process innovation rather than a new paradigm'. The view of relationship marketing as a paradigm is also illustrated in the advocacy for its inclusion in undergraduate courses (Gentry, Macintosh and Stoltman, 1993; Palmer, 1994).

The view of relationship marketing as the new marketing paradigm also arises from the recognition that the traditional marketing mix paradigm is too simplistic and far from satisfactory nowadays. Kent (1986) posits a series of issues rendering the marketing mix of the 4 Ps unsatisfactory. He states that research has revealed that what counts as marketing by the 4 Ps is rarely followed in practice, either on a departmental or managerial level. Further, the separation of the 'product' variable from the other Ps implies the erroneous assumption that 'price', 'place' and 'promotion' are not product-related, and tends to isolate decisions about a single product without due consideration of other products the firm might produce. The concept is seen as a handy classification rather than a theory. Kent (1986) suggests that a more useful approach would be to follow the sociologists' approach of viewing individual, everyday interactions as the construct of a reality of meanings that exist in the world, and building upon those. The latter implies the adoption of a relationship approach.

Enthusiastic advocates of the new relationship marketing paradigm include Gummesson (1987), Gronroos (1991; 1994) and Christopher, Payne and Ballantyne (1993). Gummesson (1987) calls for renewal of what he refers to as the 'old marketing concept' by consideration of long-term interactive relationships between suppliers and customers both at the corporate and marketing level. Gronroos (1991) views the relationship paradigm as an alternative and complement to the marketing mix approach, which is inapplicable to situations other than discrete transactions or single exchanges. Gummesson (1994) goes a step further and considers it justifiable to call relationship marketing a new paradigm that marks the beginning of a new marketing-oriented management theory.

Despite the widespread acceptance of relationship marketing as the marketing concept of the 1990s (Christopher, Payne and Ballantyne, 1993), the concept has also had its critics. The criticism stems not from a question over the importance of relationship marketing as such (which is undisputed) but on its applicability in different buyer-seller situations. Blois (1996a, p. 172) argues that although relationship marketing may encompass a broad range of ways of organising the buyer-seller interaction, 'the appropriateness of relationship marketing to all buyer-seller relationships is open to question'. Despite the acceptance that relationship marketing can be beneficial to interacting organisations, Blois (1996b) suggests that the costs and benefits must be assessed before implementing a relationship marketing strategy. By applying an economic perspective, he suggests that suppliers must assess whether relationships are going to result in a higher level of profits than a series of discrete transactions with customers. Low (1996) argues that in certain industrial environments it might not be feasible or ideal for long-term relationships to be sought, especially where short-term opportunistic relationships are favoured. Oliver

(1990) suggests six critical contingencies, viz. asymmetry, stability, legitimacy, necessity, reciprocity and efficiency, which affect the probability of a relationship developing. Awareness of the contingencies that will make the development of a relationship with customers more feasible, will assist towards the implementation of a relationship marketing programme.

Berry (1995, p. 236) suggests that relationship marketing 'is an old idea but a new focus now at the forefront of services marketing practice and academic research'. Iacobucci (1994) argues that relationship marketing has been defined too broadly and is in danger of becoming a 'fad' rather than a new marketing paradigm. Buttle (1996) reviews the wide-ranging definitions and concludes that relationship marketing has yet to acquire uncontested status and meaning. Iacobucci (1994) goes on to demonstrate that the wide-ranging use of the term 'relationship marketing', is nothing more than traditional marketing 'done better', with a simple re-focus to the customer.

Barnes (1994) also questions the acceptance of relationship marketing simply on the basis of long-term profitability. He argues that research needs to be carried out on how and with whom relationships are to be established and the form they should take. He also puts forward the controversial issue of customer retention by stating that customers may come back simply on a repeat purchase decision and not because they are tied to a relationship. He, like others, states that relationship establishment requires the formation of bonds on a business basis, as well as on a more personal one.

Hogg, Long, Hartley and Angold (1993) have also questioned the authenticity of relationships. They raise the question of how special certain customers should be treated compared to other customers, and the need to consider the effects of relationships on third parties who are not recipients of the service but passive participants. Most of their arguments, however, (for example that of privacy) are based on relationship formation in consumer marketing and are not applicable to business marketing.

Brodie, Coviello, Brookes and Little (1997) examined empirically, using four case studies and a survey of 134 firms, whether relationship marketing constitutes a 'paradigm shift' or whether transactional marketing is still predominant. They found that the notion of a 'complete paradigm shift' could not be supported as for many firms transactional marketing was relevant and practised in conjunction with various types of relational marketing.

Indeed, the concept of relationship marketing requires extensive research and detailed consideration before it can be successfully applied to particular buyer-seller situations. However, although relationship marketing can be a difficult challenge for the marketer (Jackson, 1985), its importance and perceived advantages cannot be underestimated.

Applying Relationship Marketing to Ship Management Services

This section will provide justification of the importance and potentially beneficial effects that may accrue from the adoption of relationship marketing policies and programmes in ship management companies. Prior to discussing specifically the application of relationship marketing to ship management, there will be consideration of the applicability of relationship marketing to services, ship management being itself a professional service.

Applying Relationship Marketing to Services

Research in relationship marketing has mainly concentrated on the area of industrial marketing (e.g. Hakansson, 1982; Ford, 1990; Wilson and Mummalaneni, 1986; 1988). More recently conceptual applications of relationship models in the services marketing context have been considered (Beaton and Beaton, 1995; Palmer and Bejou, 1994). The applicability of relationship marketing to services stems from some unique characteristics of services. Gronroos (1990a, p. 27) states:

> A service is an activity or series of activities of more or less intangible nature that normally, but not necessarily, take place in interactions between the customer and service employees and/or physical resources or goods and/or systems of the service provider, which are provided as solutions to customer problems.

Services are characterised by their intangibility (in contrast to goods) and the fact that they are consumed at the moment they are produced (Berry, 1981). Grove and Fisk (1996), quoting Lovelock (1981) and Berry (1981), suggest that these characteristics of services necessitate an awareness of the social and physical context of the marketing exchange in order to deliver customer satisfaction. The direct outcome of an interactive and exchange process in marketing is the relational approach (Perrien, Filiatrault and Ricard, 1993). The criticality of the service encounter (the period of time when the customer interacts directly with the firm) as a means for delivering customer satisfaction was also advocated by Parasuraman, Zeithaml and Berry (1985), Shostack (1984; 1987), Solomon, Surprenant,

Czepiel and Gutman (1985), and Surprenant and Solomon (1987). Since the pivotal issue for services marketing effectiveness requires investigation of the service encounter, and relationships tend to form during the service encounter, it follows that relationship marketing is an applicable, if not critical, approach to services marketing.

Within the services context, relationship marketing has received particular attention in the marketing of corporate banking. Banks have decided to emphasise relationship marketing because of the pressures imposed on them by competitive and environmental developments (Moriarty, Kimball and Gay, 1983). When competition is intensified, the basic strategy is to increase the retention rate of clients (Perrien, Filiatrault and Ricard, 1992). Client retention is the outcome of relationship marketing (Congram, 1991). Once again, this is in line with the issues encountered in the ship management industry and establishes the applicability of relationship marketing in this context. Apart from competitiveness, Perrien, Filiatrault and Ricard (1992) discuss other reasons that have forced banks to implement relationship management. The advancement of technology, for example, has enabled them to widen their product portfolio, thus requiring more detailed knowledge of the buying centre (i.e. their clientele). Deregulation, technological innovation and increased competition among banks have shortened the expected lifetime of most banking products (Turnbull and Gibbs, 1987). Such problems could be combated by developing close, long-term relationships with clients. Relationship banking has been defined by Moriarty, Kimball and Gay (1983, p. 4) as 'a recognition that the bank can increase its earnings by maximising the profitability of the total customer relationship over time, rather than by seeking to extract the most profit from any individual product or transaction'.

Berry and Thompson (1982, p. 72) state that 'relationship banking concerns turning customers into loyal clients'. Watson (1986) describes in detail a ten-stage process by which relationships can be built in corporate banking. The process is in line with other traditional relationship marketing approaches, being initiated by market research and establishing contact, to nurturing the relationship. Exchange of information, fulfilment of promises and ensuring client satisfaction are again stressed. The work concentrates around the responsibilities of the account manager as a builder and manager of relationships, thus emphasising the importance of interpersonal relations. It is interesting to note that the problems faced by banks are in many ways similar to the problems that are encountered by professional ship management companies.

Relationship marketing represents a new concept now at the forefront of services marketing practice and academic research (Berry, 1995). This reality is paradoxical given that there are few conceptual applications of relationship marketing constructs in the services marketing literature and even fewer operationalisations and empirical investigations. Notwithstanding this constraint, a review of the current relationship marketing models in services will be carried out in an attempt to reveal the key variables that are applicable to services and, hence, the ship management context.

Relationship Marketing in Consumer Services

Palmer and Bejou (1994) use previous relationship marketing models as starting points to identify six variables that lead to relationship quality. The variables are operationalised to provide cross-sectional empirical evidence of the existence of a buyer-seller relationship life-cycle in the investment services sector. The six relationship quality components are conceptualised to be: relationship satisfaction, sellers' trustworthiness, sellers' customer orientation/empathy, selling orientation/salesperson's pressure, sellers' expertise and sellers' ethics. Relationship satisfaction refers to whether the perceived outcome of a service encounter meets customer expectations. It includes satisfaction with the core service, personnel and the organisation at large. The importance of trust in buyer-seller relationships is also acknowledged in this study. Trust forms the second component of relationship quality. Sellers' customer orientation and empathy refer to the ability of the salesperson to identify and satisfy customer needs and at the same time build trust and co-operation to enhance the development of a long-term relationship. Unlike the aforementioned variables, which are positively related to relationship formation, the fourth component (selling orientation/salesperson's pressure) may have a positive or negative effect on the formation of a relationship. If there is insufficient pressure from the salesperson, the relationship may not even begin. On the other hand, if the salesperson is perceived to be more sales-oriented than customer-oriented, it is highly unlikely that a relationship will be formed. The sellers' expertise is the fifth variable of relationship quality. Expertise reflects competence, with credibility, reliability, responsiveness and an ability to provide solutions being its most important determinants. Last, the ethical behaviour of sales personnel is seen as an important variable in complex, intangible and high credence services, i.e. services whose quality is difficult to evaluate before consumption.

The hypothesis that buyer-seller relationships go through a life-cycle has been validated by the study. It was also found that empathy increases as the relationship develops, whereas at the same time sales orientation/selling pressure decreases, enhancing the relationship even further. Ethical credibility and trust have a positive effect on relationship development as well.

Shemwell, Cronin and Bullard (1994) investigated constructs specific to relationship marketing in three consumer-to-business areas, viz. physicians, car mechanics and hairstylists. Unsurprisingly, the variables on which the research hypotheses were based were trust, commitment and perceived risk. It was found that increasing the level of trust results in greater commitment to the continuation of the relationship (this hypothesis was not supported in the hairstylists' area). Also, increasing the level of trust results in lower levels of perceived risk (this hypothesis was not supported in the physicians' area). Strong support in all areas was found, however, for the hypothesis that an emotional or affective commitment results in greater intentions to continue the relationship (continuance commitment). The fourth hypothesis, that affective commitment is negatively related to perceived risk, was not supported by the results. Although an introductory and illustrative study, it makes a significant contribution to relationship marketing in consumer services: the fact that commitment and trust are very well applicable to consumer-service provider relationships.

Relationship Marketing in Professional Services

Beaton and Beaton (1995) made a significant conceptual contribution to relationship marketing in professional services by treating the concept of commitment as the central variable in such buyer-seller relationships. They posit that commitment is not only the primary concern, but actually overtakes quality and value in a services context. Service value and quality are actually treated as commitment determinants. They state (at p. 57):

> Commitment has come to represent the continued stability of a relationship at the conceptual level, and its manifestations serve as surrogate measures of the likely longevity of the marriage between buyer and seller, service provider and client.

The Wilson and Mummalaneni (1986) framework of commitment is expressly adopted in their study. Courtship, bonding and forsaking others are viewed to be the major commitment determinants. Courtship refers to the satisfaction outcome of the parties from their rewards v. costs assessment during their interactions and exchanges. Because satisfaction is not easily quantified, service quality (reward) and monetary price (cost) may be equated to give a measure of service value and, hence, satisfaction. Despite adoption of this definition, there has been research (Bolton and Drew, 1991) which suggests that satisfaction is actually an antecedent and not a consequence of service quality. Also, service value perceptions may change once the client becomes committed to the organisation, rendering the construct sufficient only as a determining variable of commitment. Bonding is the second construct of commitment that is utilised in this research. Bonding (structural and social) is again described in the form of investments and adaptations in procedures, policies and people made by the service provider and his client. The third construct of forsaking others refers to the availability of alternative service providers and their comparison level in terms of service quality and price. The negative impact of alternatives on structural bonding and commitment is discussed. The variables put forward are discussed in the context of the legal services sector but are not operationalised.

Ship Management Services

Relationship marketing theory is directly applicable to ship management because the latter is a professional service offered to shipowners. Gummesson (1978) puts forward a criterion for identifying professional services. He suggests that the service should be provided by qualified personnel, be advisory and focus on solving problems. The professional should be identifiable in the market, independent of suppliers of other goods or services and have specialist know-how of the tasks (the service) assigned by the buyer. It can be easily deduced that this criterion applies wholly to the professional ship management service.

Other reasons, however, not only prove the applicability of relationship marketing to ship management, but also necessitate the application of such an approach for effective marketing. Following the classification of services due to Lovelock (1983), it might be suggested that ship management falls into the category of an intangible service directed to a tangible asset (the ship). Relationship marketing is recommended by Berry (1983) as an appropriate strategy to overcome service intangibility. Furthermore, evaluation of the quality of the ship management service offered may not be easy for the shipowner, even after he has entrusted his vessel(s) to a particular company. This is especially true when the shipowner has no shipping background himself. Relationship marketing has been identified as appropriate for complex and 'credence' services, that is services that are difficult for customers to fully evaluate even after purchase and use (Zeithaml, 1981).

A lot of hard work has been done towards improving the ship management service. For example, the majority of companies now operate in accordance with high industry standards, hold quality certificates or are under the process of obtaining such certificates. However, improving the service alone may not be the best marketing method in the increasingly competitive ship management environment. Palmer (1994) states, that in competitive marketplaces, good products and service alone are increasingly inadequate for a company to gain competitive advantage. This suggests that a point is reached where ship management companies will need to differentiate themselves in order to gain a competitive advantage. It is at this point that marketing and relationship marketing in particular come into play. Applications of relationship marketing will not only ensure client retention, but will also assist towards achieving differentiation and competitiveness.

Conceptual Design and Methodology

Following the identification of the applicability and practical importance of developing client relationships in ship management, and the key issues involved in relationship marketing, it seems justifiable to perform further investigation of the concepts in a ship management context. The empirical investigation will seek to determine the major factors or characteristics of ship manager-shipowner relationships and explore the possibility of relationship classification.

In order to facilitate empirical investigation of ship manager-shipowner relationships, there is a need to specify and delimit the issues that need to be examined. This can be done through the development of a model that will be intended to represent the real-life situation under scrutiny. Models are of extreme important in science as they are used to delineate constructs that can be manipulated and tested empirically, something that could not have been achieved otherwise, bearing in mind the complexity of real-life situations. Buzzell (1964) purports that a model is anything used to represent something else, whereas Naert and Leeflang (1978, p. 9) state that 'a model is a representation of the most important elements of a perceived real world system'. In developing an adequate model to describe aspects of the ship manager-shipowner relationship, one has to have in mind the inherent problems and limitations. The aim should be to develop a model that adequately describes the real situation, and is general enough to permit exploration but focused enough to delimit the study. The model that will be developed for the ship manager-shipowner relationship would initially fall into the conceptual models category of Lilien (1975). The conceptual model should permit exploration of ship manager-shipowner relationships and conceptual links between the explored issues. The empirical testing of the model will identify its validity in the real world and permit the description of real-life situations in a ship management context.

The model developed initially permits exploration of the ship manager-client relationship and identification of the underlying characteristics of this relationship. It is conceptualised that not all relationships between the ship management companies and their clients are exactly the same, and that many of these relationships may share similar characteristics. On this basis, relationships may be broadly assembled into clusters, with ship management companies in the same cluster having similar relationship characteristics in the interaction with their major client and different ones from companies in other clusters. The model also permits exploration of the existence of an association between the hypothesised relationship clusters and the organisational characteristics of the ship management and client companies. Further, it allows the exploration of this association by initially profiling the clusters with the characteristics of the entities independently, and by permitting subsequently a combination of the profiles to reveal an underlying typology. Hence, the model aims at classifying ship management organisations on the basis of client relationships and the characteristics of the interacting entities. Rich (1992) notes that classification provides the basis for strong research by breaking the continuous world of organisations into discrete and collective categories. Classification permits parsimony without simplicity, the ability to recognise fundamental structure and relationship (McKinney, 1966), and a basis for theory development (Haas, Hall and Johnson, 1966).

The methodology for the empirical investigation was structured so as to address the following issues:

- identification of the data required in order to connect empirical materials to the conceptual model;
- identification of the most appropriate source for data collection;
- strategies of research inquiry;

- methods and research tools that will be used for collecting and analysing empirical materials.

The required data included the relationship and organisational characteristics of the interacting organisations. Having identified the eligible respondents after a sampling procedure, telephone interviews and a mail survey were employed to collect the data. The telephone interviews assisted in retrieving the dimensions of ship manager-shipowner relationships from the practitioners themselves. These dimensions were later used in the mail questionnaire sent to the sample participating in the study. The sample included eligible companies from two major ship management centres, the UK and Cyprus. A total of 98 companies were retrieved from the maritime directories; 50 companies were found to be eligible for interviews, and 45 agreed to participate. After two mailings of the questionnaire, an overall response rate of about 87 per cent yielded 34 useable questionnaires.

Elements of Ship Management Relationships

The results reported in this section are based on descriptive inference. Description and explanation are the basis of scientific inquiry. Description comes first: 'It is hard to develop explanations before we know something about the world and what needs to be explained on the basis of what characteristics' (King, Keohane and Verba, 1994, p. 34). It is also important to acknowledge that responses are not analysed by consideration of the number of ship managers giving a particular response. Because a non-probability sample was assumed, any attempt to assign numbers to particular responses will be fundamentally flawed. Instead, the value of this analysis lies in the type of responses, rather than the number of ship managers giving a particular response. As already mentioned, the objective of this part of the study is to reveal the dimensionality of the ship managers' perceptions concerning the relationship with the major client.

At the beginning of the interview, ship managers were asked to comment upon some preliminary questions. This assisted in the build-up of rapport and acquaintance with the process of respondent-researcher interaction over the telephone. Of course, the preliminary questions were relevant to the subject matter of the study.

Ship managers were asked to comment on the importance of marketing in the management of their company. Managers responded to this question in two ways. For the bigger companies, marketing was more important. However, there was a diversity of opinion as to what marketing is. Many managers thought that marketing is advertising and the quest for attracting clients. Hence, the aforementioned aspects are important in ship management, although they are very restrictive to the definition of the term 'marketing'. Managers also thought that there is a fair deal of competition in terms of attracting clients from competitors. None of the managers has accepted that his/her company is engaged in such activities. The fact that many managers thought that this type of competition exists justifies the problems in ship management discussed in chapter 3. The vast majority of managers stressed the importance of retaining clients. However, this was done only when they were asked directly. None of the managers indicated that client retention forms part of their marketing activities.

The brainstorming technique outlined in the methodology section proved very effective for the elicitation of relationship attributes from chief executives among the ship management fraternity. A number of variables that form the central tenets of relationship marketing research were elicited. In particular, ship managers mentioned the following issues during the interviews.

Nature of Ship Management Relationships

The maritime business is largely based on acquaintances and personal relationships. This is also the case in ship management, and this has been ascertained during the course of this research. Many ship managers indicated that they have known important personnel from within the major client's company for many years. These acquaintances resulted in the formation of a personal/friendship relationship, rather than one governed by a contractual agreement. It was also revealed that a business relationship began on the basis of a prior friendship between key members of the two organisations.

Trust

Trust is an essential element in business relationships where buyers and sellers rely on each other for the achievement of their individual objectives (Pruit, 1981). Many ship managers have indicated that the relationship with their major client is based on mutual trust. Ship managers that avoided mentioning trust during the elicitation procedure were asked to comment on this aspect. The range of responses included 'we would trust the client to a fair degree', 'we cannot always trust the client' and 'trust is not a word that I would use to describe this relationship'.

Commitment

Commitment has been defined as 'an enduring desire to maintain a valued relationship' (Moorman, Zaltman and Deshpande, 1992, p. 316). Commitment is viewed as the most advanced phase in buyer-seller relationships (Dwyer, Schur and Oh, 1987). The ship manager's degree of commitment in the relationship with a client may determine the longevity of that relationship. Managers' views on commitment varied. The great majority of managers pledged their strong dedication to their major client. Fewer managers indicated that the nature of ship management, with many ships being managed for many owners, makes it difficult for the manager to give individual attention and dedication to any one client.

Co-operation

Co-operation is imperative in the ship manager–shipowner relationship, as it reflects the companies' ability to collaborate and work together toward their respective goals, as well as the joint striving towards mutual goals (Skinner, Gassenheimer and Kelley, 1992). For the ship manager, co-operation with the client is the means of achieving greater efficiency in delivering the ship management service. Because of the personal nature of certain ship management relationships, co-operation between the ship management and shipowning entities is high. Managers specified that they would be willing to help and co-operate with the client, even if that required performance of tasks beyond those stipulated in contractual agreements. The growth of many ship management companies was associated with a willingness to make investments in ships. Some ship managers have indicated that their company has co-operated with the major client to the extent of making joint financial investments in ships.

Conflict

The nature of ship operation is such that conflicts and disagreements between ship manager and shipowner are inherent. Most ship managers indicated that the company had had several minor disagreements with the client's company. Disagreements arise mainly in the area of presentation of financial reports. They stressed, however, that such disagreements are never of a nature that could disturb the relationship, and that they are resolved through negotiation. Mutual solutions are often reached amicably. Only a few companies indicated major problems with the client. This type of conflict present in ship management relationships is comparable to conflict in channels of distribution classified by Robicheaux and El-Ansary (1976) into functional and dysfunctional. Functional conflict is a healthy phenomenon and occurs when the parties reach amicable solutions.

Investments

In the transaction-cost approach, Williamson (1979) identifies the importance of idiosyncratic investments in an exchange relationship. Idiosyncratic investments are specific to a particular relationship and thus non-marketable. Transaction-specific investments render the investing party committed to the relationship. Many ship managers seem to make investments as a matter of being in business and not for specific clients. A number of managers indicated that they have made investments in the particular relationship with the major client. Such investments included the setting up of an office close to that of the client, in order to facilitate better communication. Other ship managers indicated that investments had been made at the beginning of the relationship with the client, but no particular investments from there on. This seems to be the case when specialised vessels are taken up for management. Ship managers have to make investments in order to facilitate the special requirements for the operation of such vessels. Such investments, however, are in a sense compulsory and represent only a one-off case – certainly not the kind of investments discussed in the relationship marketing literature. Such investments may be viewed as initial transaction costs.

Adaptations

The adaptation of business processes and administrative procedures is an important aspect of long-term business relationships. This is because business relationships are based on some kind of match between the operations of two companies (Hallen, Johanson and Seyed-Mohamed, 1991). Owing to the complexity of ship management, it is almost inevitable that ship managers will have to adapt their business processes or administrative routines. Most managers indicated, however, that they make minor adaptations in their business processes in order to accommodate the special needs of their client. Such adaptations are mostly in the area of accounting reporting procedures. Other managers indicated that it is hard to make any changes to their tailor-made offering because they operate under a quality management system, which specifies strict procedures that must be adhered to. Even if quality management does specify rules and procedures, however, showing flexibility and adaptation to clients' needs does not necessarily impede the application of quality management standards. Managers presented with this statement still believed that, because of the standard nature of their service offering, major individual needs could not be accommodated.

Communication

Communication has been defined as 'the formal as well as informal sharing of meaningful information between firms' (Anderson and Narus, 1990, p. 44). The exchange and sharing of information is a critical factor in inter-organisational relationships. Dwyer, Schurr and Oh (1987, p. 17) state: '...a relationship seems unlikely to form without bilateral communication of wants, issues, inputs and priorities'. Communication facilitates mutual participation in goal setting, adaptability of behaviour through feedback, and co-ordination of efforts to achieve objectives (Anderson, Lodish and Weitz, 1987).

In resource dependence theory, organisational uncertainty and interdependence are two critical variables (Pfeffer and Salancik, 1978). In order to reduce uncertainty and alter their interdependence, members of organisations engage in interaction and information exchange. Communication is seen, therefore, as a medium for coping with and reducing dependency (Euske and Roberts, 1987). Therefore, the greater the dependency, the greater the willingness to engage in communication.

Various dimensions are used in the literature (e.g. Mohr and Nevin, 1990) to describe inter-organisational communication. Such dimensions include frequency, direction, modality and content. Frequency is used as an indicator of the amount of communication between the parties. Communication may be formal or informal (Stohl and Redding, 1987). Formal communication refers to the structured, routinised manner of conveying day-to-day information, whereas informal modes are more spontaneous and personalised ways of communicating and may occur outside the organisational boundaries. Informal modes tend to contribute to the build-up of trust. Content of the transmitted communication refers to what is included in the message that is transmitted. Content has been categorised in the literature on the basis of the type of information exchanged and the influence strategy embedded in the exchanged information (Frazier and Summers, 1984; Mohr and Nevin, 1990).

Communication is an important aspect of relationships in general and the ship manager–shipowner relationship in particular. Communication between ship manager and shipowner is both formal and informal. It takes place very often at departmental or operational level, and less often at senior management level. Meetings of an informal and social nature also take place, particularly with smaller companies whose managers have developed a personal/friendship type relationship. The modality of communication is also important, with most ship managers preferring the telephone and fax.

Personal Contact at Operational Level

Table 4.1 indicates that personal contact at operational level is not very frequent, with representatives of 56 per cent of the companies meeting once every three months at the most. At operational level, meetings can be arranged on board a ship when representatives from the manager's and client's offices plan to visit.

Table 4.1 The frequency of personal contact at operational level

Frequency	Companies (%)
Once/week	14.7
Once/fortnight	8.8
Once/month	20.6
Once/three months	29.5
Twice/year	17.6
Once/year	8.8

It is possible that face-to-face contact at operational level will be hampered by the location of the ship management company. To explore this possibility, a cross-tabulation between meetings at operational level and location of ship management companies was performed (Table 4.2).

It is evident that personal contact at operational level occurs more frequently for UK-based companies. This may be attributed to the distance between the companies and the client's headquarters. Most UK-based ship management companies manage vessels for UK-based clients, unlike Cyprus-based companies, which mostly serve German clients. The frequency of meetings may be further increased by vessels visiting UK and European ports, where it will be easier for UK-based personnel to visit.

Table 4.2 The frequency of personal contact at operational level by location

	Ship management company's headquarters	
Frequency	UK companies (%)	Cyprus companies (%)
Once/week	22	0
Once/fortnight	9	9
Once/month	22	18
Once/three months	34	18
Twice/year	4	46
Once/year	9	9
Total	23	11

Personal Contact at Senior Management Level

Table 4.3 indicates that the vast majority of senior personnel meet their counterparts from their major client company about once every three months. This is true for both UK companies (ten companies) and companies based in Cyprus (eight companies). Senior managers from UK-based companies, however, also meet senior managers from their major client company quite frequently (eight companies reporting meetings of once a month or more, compared to one Cyprus-based company indicating a meeting once a month). This may be attributed to the close distance between the premises of the ship management company and the client in the UK. UK-based companies, however, also reported less frequent meetings – two companies reporting meetings once a year and three companies twice a year. Again, this may be attributed to physical distance, with some UK-based companies serving the needs of clients based in the US and the Far East.

Table 4.3 The frequency of personal contact at senior management level

Frequency	Companies (%)
Once/week	5.9
Once/fortnight	8.8
Once/month	11.8
Once/three months	52.9
Once/year	5.9
Twice/year	14.7
Total	100.0

The number of vessels entrusted to the manager may also account for the frequency of meetings at senior management level. Frequent meetings with clients entrusting small fleets to the manager were reported, although two companies reported annual meetings with clients entrusting one to three ships to the company. None of the companies managing more than three ships reported annual meetings. Some companies reported meetings of twice a year for fleets of up to 21 vessels. Companies that manage more than 21 vessels reported quarterly meetings at senior management level. Hence, it can be claimed that the larger the fleet managed for the client, the more frequent the meetings at senior management level. This may be due to the importance attributed to the particular client by the senior managers of the ship management companies. A cross-tabulation between meetings at senior management level and the percentage of annual revenue generated by the client confirms the above assertion. The higher the annual revenue generated by the client, the more frequent are the meetings at senior management level. Of course, other factors, such as proximity to the major client's offices may account for the frequency of face-to-face communication.

Communication at Operational Level

Communication between the ship management company and the client's company at operational level is of the utmost importance. Gray and Panayides (1997) note that once the manager assumes management responsibilities he must keep close contact with the owners in order to receive instructions and supply reports on all aspects relating to the management of the ship(s).

Table 4.4 illustrates the frequency of communication of any sort at operational level, as reported by the companies participating in this study.

Table 4.4 The frequency of communication at operational level

Frequency	Companies (%)
Every day	67.6
Twice/week	14.7
Once/week	11.8
Once/month	5.9
Total	100.0

The importance of communication at operational level is clearly illustrated in the table. The majority of the companies are in daily contact with their major client's company, and five companies communicate twice a week with the client's company. Nevertheless, six companies reported communicating with their major client only once a week or even once a month. This may be attributed to the business of the client, but also to the main business activity of the ship management company. For instance, if the financial owner of the vessel is not engaged in shipping as such (e.g. banks, investors), then communication may be less frequent. Indeed, a cross-tabulation indicates that one of the clients of the six companies is a banker and another is engaged in waste disposal. However, two other companies are engaged in container liner shipping and two in tramp shipping.

Communication at Senior Management Level

The relationship marketing literature indicates that communication at senior management level is a prerequisite for the development of long-term relationships with clients. Table 4.5 illustrates the frequency of communication between the ship management and major client companies at senior management level. The majority of senior managers seem to maintain close contact with senior management at the major client's office, with nearly 60 per cent of the companies communicating with the major client company at least once a week.

Table 4.5 The frequency of communication at senior management level

Frequency	Companies (%)
Every day	20.6
Twice/week	11.8
Once/week	26.4
Once/fortnight	11.8
Once/month	23.5
Once/three months	5.9
Total	100.0

Both ship management companies reporting communication of once every three months at senior management level, manage one ship for their major client and receive 1 per cent and 1.3 per cent of annual revenue from the particular client. This indicates that the number of ships managed for the client and the percentage of revenue generated by the client may influence the level of communication at senior management level. A cross-tabulation between frequency of communication at senior management level and both number of ships managed for the client and percentage of revenue generated by the client confirms the above.

The major client's main business activity also seems to influence communication at senior management level. The two clients referred to above are engaged in banking and fish farming. Hence, shipping is not the major business activity of either of these companies. Two companies whose clients are primarily engaged in manufacturing and transportation of their own oil requirements also reported communication frequency of once a month at senior management level. Three companies whose clients are engaged in tramp shipping, two whose clients are engaged in container liner shipping and one whose client owns a combination of different vessel types reported similar communication frequency.

Strategic Relationship Groups in Ship Management

The aim of this section is to explore the perceptions of ship managers with regard to the relationship with their major client. The objectives of this endeavour include the identification of particular segments or strategic groups of ship management companies whose executives have reported specific relationship perceptions, and the drawing of inferences based on the above.

Strategic groups is a term used to denote the existence of segments of companies within industries that follow similar strategies or are similar in certain characteristics and different from other segments of companies within the same industry (e.g. Lu and Marlow, 1999; Mehra, 1994). In referring to these configurations, Miller (1981) used the term 'gestalts' and stated that they represent 'tightly integrated and mutually supportive parts, the significance of which can best be understood by making reference to the whole' (Miller, 1981, p. 3). The strategic groups approach can assist in identifying differences among competing firms in the marketplace. The identification of strategic differences will lead firms to a better understanding of the competitors' approach and can induce the adoption of strategies for achieving a sustainable competitive advantage.

In order to identify the existence of strategic relationship groups in the sample under scrutiny, and to develop a typology of relationship segments, cluster analysis procedures were utilised. In addition, the data were subjected to further scrutiny using multivariate techniques such as multiple correspondence analysis and multiple discriminant analysis. The statistical analyses resulted in the identification of four distinct groups of ship management companies that share particular characteristics. The four identified clusters or segments of ship management companies were distinct in terms of the relationship that they have with their clients. Hence, particular groups of companies have similar relationships with their clients, which at the same time are different from the relationships other groups of companies have with their own clients. The identification of this typology or classification of ship manager-client relationships has important implications, not least for marketing and client retention in professional ship management firms. The four identified groups of companies that have distinct client relationships will be discussed. To facilitate interpretation, the groups were assigned names that reflect the distinguishing characteristics associated with the particular group. The groups were thus named 'investors', 'friendship', 'rigid' and 'reactive'.

The Investors Cluster

The first group of companies was assigned this particular name to reflect the fact that these companies make major investments in their relationship with their major client. In addition, companies in this group do not seem to have conflicts of a serious nature with their clients, and demonstrate a highly trusting relationship. The relationship between investments and trust is justified in the literature. For instance, Lorenz (1988, p. 209) states:

> Trust is crucial when contracting parties invest in specific assets, locking them into a relationship. Limited rationality means that efforts to protect ourselves from opportunism through comprehensive contracting will inevitably be deficient. Rational comprehensive contracting is impossible. Trust is expedient.

Young and Wilkinson (1989) cite the work by Twomey (1974), who found a positive association between trust and the resolution of conflicts. It has also been ascertained in the marketing channels literature that communication may substantially reduce the amount of conflict between two parties (Etgar, 1979). Communication at operational level between the interacting organisations in the 'investors' cluster is extremely high. The majority of companies (91 per cent) indicate communication on a daily basis (unlike companies in the three other clusters). Most disagreements and conflicts in shipping will be related to operational procedures on-board and in the company. The high level of communication at operational level within the 'investors' cluster suggests the reduction of conflict among the interacting organisations. Hence the low level of conflict associated with companies in this cluster.

Companies in the 'investors' cluster make both major and minor adaptations in the relationship with the major client. Adaptations may be regarded as an investment in the relationship. For instance, Ford (1982) suggests that the more specific the adaptations, the less marketable the value of these changes, as they could be regarded as a demonstrable investment in the specific relationship. Hence, the evidence found in this cluster of companies supports a relationship between investments and major adaptations. Although the nature of the relationship is not characterised by any personal friendship bonds, companies in this cluster are willing to assist the client by taking actions that may not be within their contractual obligations.

The Friendship Cluster

The ship manager-client relationship for companies in this segment is characterised by a personal friendship nature. All companies indicated that the relationship is based on the close personal friendship of important executives in their organisations. Mumallaneni (1987) has found that formal role relationships may develop into close personal friendships in industrial marketing. The evidence from this study suggests that although this might be the case, business relationships are also initiated by previous personal friendship relationships.

Other characteristics of these particular relationships include minor conflicts, major and minor adaptations, and high trust. It seems that a relationship of close personal friendship may still involve a degree of conflict in a ship management context. Mumallaneni (1987) found that high trust is correlated with a friendship/close personal relationship. Trust in this segment is very high for 50 per cent of the companies and fairly high for 25 per cent of the companies.

It can be inferred that companies in this cluster have a strong relationship with their clients on the basis of social bonds rather than economic investments and adaptations. The strength of the relationship can be ascertained by the frequency of communication between the entities. It has been stated that relationships are strengthened by information exchange (Hallen, Johanson and Seyed-Mohamed, 1987; Hallen, Seyed-Mohamed and Johanson, 1989). The frequency of communication in this cluster is high at both senior management and operational level.

The Rigid Cluster

The third cluster of ship management companies was labelled the 'rigid' cluster. These companies make no adaptations in the relationship with their major client (indicating rigidity). The investments they make are of a general nature rather than specific to the relationship. A lack of flexibility would suggest that relationships with clients in this particular cluster are weaker than those found in other clusters. Hallen, Johanson and Seyed-Mohamed (1987) posit that relationships are partially strengthened by adaptations. The fact that certain respondents in this cluster view the relationship as being based on strict contractual terms supports the assertion that relationships are weaker due to the lack of both social and economic bonds. The lack of economic bonds is also illustrated by the fact that investments made by companies in this cluster are of a general nature and not specific to the relationship. Hence, companies in this cluster would not consider installation of a communication system or computerised safety management system to cater for the specific needs of the client (e.g. where specialised vessels are concerned). Conflicts of a minor nature are likely to arise for 40 per cent of the companies in the 'rigid' cluster. Companies in this cluster are also less likely to have a personal/friendship type relationship with their clients.

The Reactive Cluster

The fourth ship management cluster was labelled the 'reactive' cluster in order to reflect the fact that these companies are prepared to make some minor changes but do not have a proactive stance in terms of adaptations and investments. All companies comprising this cluster make minor adaptations during the relationship with their major client. Such adaptations would take the form of changes in the accounting reporting procedures of the company. The vast majority of companies also make general investments that may benefit the relationship, i.e. investments that are not directed specifically towards the particular relationship.

Investments are directly related to adaptations in the social exchange literature. For instance, companies may commit resources (investment) in order to adapt their business processes to those of the client. Therefore, the relationship between investments and adaptations found in the 'reactive' cluster supports the findings of previous research. Ship management companies in this particular cluster make investments as a matter of being in business and not for specific clients.

Personal friendship relationships are common, however, in this group of companies. Table 4.6 illustrates the distinguishing relationship characteristics of a typical company in each of the four clusters.

Table 4.6 Distinguishing relationship characteristics in each cluster

Investors	Friendship	Rigid	Reactive
Major investments	Friendship relationship	General investments	General investments
No conflict	Minor conflicts	No adaptations	Minor adaptations
High trust	Major investments	High trust	High trust
Beyond contract relationship			Friendship relationship

Profiles of Relationship Groups

Having identified the existence of four groups of ship management companies on the basis of their client relationship characteristics, it would be beneficial to determine what organisational characteristics are shared between the companies in each group. It is possible that companies with certain organisational characteristics tend to be found in a specific relationship segment. If that is the case, then this can have important implications for the development of client relationships for particular companies. The aim of this section is to explore the possibility of an association between the identified ship management groups and the characteristics of the interacting organisations within each group.

Location

The majority of companies in each of the four clusters are located in the United Kingdom. It must be restated that the companies selected for this study were located in two major ship management centres only, the United Kingdom and Cyprus. However, a greater percentage of companies in the 'investors' and 'friendship' clusters were found to be located in the UK than companies in the 'rigid' and 'reactive' clusters. The 'rigid' cluster is made up of companies more likely to be located in Cyprus than the UK when compared to the other groups of companies. This is also true for the 'reactive' cluster. Up to 75 per cent of the companies in the 'friendship' cluster, and 73 per cent of companies in the 'investors' cluster are based in the UK. Hence, it may be inferred from the statistics that there is a greater possibility for companies in the 'investors' and 'friendship' clusters to be located in the UK than in Cyprus when compared to the companies in the other two clusters. Most of the companies in the 'rigid' cluster are located in areas offering beneficial taxation arrangements (Cyprus and the Isle of Man). The fact that companies in the 'rigid' cluster pursue such a strategy indicates that these companies may be conscious of cost-reduction.

Type and Business Activity

The majority of companies in any one cluster are independent organisations. However, there is a greater number of independent companies in the 'rigid' cluster (80 per cent), whereas there is a great proportion of subsidiary companies in the 'investors' cluster (45 per cent) when compared to the other three clusters.

The 'reactive' cluster of companies is more strongly associated with those companies that offer ship management services as their primary activity. On the other hand, companies in the 'rigid' cluster are mostly associated with the operation of owned ships as their main business activity when compared to companies in any other cluster. The possibility that companies in the 'investors' cluster will operate their own ships is also high. Companies in the 'friendship' cluster are more strongly associated with offering ship management services, although own ship operation may take place. Support for the aforementioned may be provided by calculating the mean number of ships owned and operated by the companies in the four clusters. Companies in the 'friendship' cluster own the least number of ships (a mean of two ships), whereas companies in the 'rigid' cluster own the greater number of ships (a mean of six ships). Companies in the 'reactive' cluster, however, which are more strongly associated with offering ship management services rather than ship operation, also own a relatively large number of ships (a mean of five ships). Further examination of the companies in this cluster revealed the existence of a few companies owning a disproportionately large number of ships. There is a lower possibility of ship ownership by companies in the 'reactive' cluster (43 per cent of companies own ships), whereas for the 'rigid' cluster it is the highest (60 per cent of companies owning ships).

Managed Fleet Size

Companies in the 'friendship' cluster manage the smallest number of ships (a mean of 38 ships, with a mean of 15 ships under full management and 22 ships under crewing only management). Companies in the 'rigid' and 'reactive' clusters manage the largest fleets, with means of 63 and 66 ships respectively. It must be noted, however, that the majority of ships managed by the companies in these groups are under crewing only management contracts. About 60 per cent of the ships managed by companies in the 'rigid' and 'reactive' clusters are under crewing only management contracts compared with 47 per cent for the 'investors' cluster. About 56 per cent of ships managed by companies in the 'friendship' cluster are also under crewing only management. None of the companies in the 'rigid' cluster manage any vessels under technical management. This may go some way towards explaining why companies in this cluster are rigid in terms of adaptations. Ships under technical management do require adaptations and flexibility in management as failure and repair of complex equipment is an onerous task. The fact that the companies are not keen to take on ships for technical only management seems to explain in some respect the attitude towards adaptations and flexibility. Companies in the 'rigid' cluster are also the least keen to undertake commercial only management. Commercial only management mainly involves the provision of advice on ship registration etc. (see chapter 2), and the fee for the provision of such a service is relatively low.

Employees

The size of the fleets managed by the companies in each cluster is directly related to the number of personnel employed by the companies, both ashore and on-board. Companies in the 'friendship' cluster are the smallest in terms of managed fleet and employees. It is also interesting to note that the companies in this cluster do not use staff supplied by commercial manning agencies. On the other hand, companies in the 'rigid' cluster tend to use commercial manning agencies on a comparatively larger scale.

The use of commercial manning agencies may bring many advantages to ship managers, which will be reflected in the quality of the service offered. This is because manning agencies are used as a medium towards rationalisation of operation and reduction of costs. By operating through a network of agencies, which in terms of seafarer supply may be located in many advantageous parts of the world, these companies have access to a wide pool of human resources available all the time. In this way, they are able to provide the manning service more efficiently. Efficiency enables companies to serve more clients and manage larger fleets, which may go some way towards explaining the higher annual turnover of companies in the 'rigid' cluster. Based on the above, it can also be inferred that companies in the 'rigid' cluster are more commercially oriented, as they make use of practices to improve efficiency and reduce costs.

The number of employees ashore also reflects the size of companies found in the different clusters. Companies in the 'rigid' and 'reactive' clusters have many more employees than those in the 'friendship' cluster, which are much smaller.

Length of Time in Ship Management

Companies in the 'friendship', 'rigid' and 'reactive' clusters have been in business for a relatively equal number of years. The means calculated are 14, 15.4 and 15.8 years respectively. Companies in the 'investors' cluster have been involved in the ship management business for a longer period (a mean of 21 years). Examination of the exact number of years in business for every company in the clusters revealed that the majority of companies in the 'reactive' cluster have been in business for 1-14 years. The majority of companies in the 'friendship' cluster have been in business for 15-19 years and in the 'investors' cluster between 20-30 years.

Annual Turnover

The annual turnover is only slightly different for companies in the 'investors', 'rigid' and 'reactive' clusters. The highest turnover was reported by companies in the 'rigid' cluster with a mean of £14.8 million. As indicated earlier, companies in this cluster tend to own and operate more ships than companies in any other cluster. This may explain why the annual turnover is higher, as the financial benefits accruing from the operation of a company's own ships are significantly higher than those obtained through management for third parties. This also explains the comparatively lower turnover for companies in the 'friendship' cluster (a mean of £7.35 million). These companies not only manage smaller fleets but are also less likely to be engaged in the operation of owned ships. The number of ships that is owned by companies in this cluster is also small compared to those owned by companies in the other three clusters. Annual turnover may also be regarded as a measure of the size of an organisation, as well as commercial orientation. Hence, this confirms that companies in the 'rigid' cluster are large, whereas companies in the 'friendship' cluster are small. It also supports the earlier assertion that companies in the 'rigid' cluster are more commercially-oriented.

In summary, the following typology can be extracted from the preliminary analysis regarding the organisational characteristics for companies appearing in each cluster. The description of the 'company' in each cluster is construed in accordance with the concept of polythetic typologies, where each member of the group may be close to possessing the properties described, but no member possesses all of the properties (McKelvey, 1978; Sokal and Sneath, 1963).

A Typical Company in the 'Investors' Group

An independent or subsidiary UK-based company engaged in offering ship management services only or operating owned vessels in conjunction with ship management. The company has been established in ship management for more than 20 years and has a fleet of 50-60 vessels under management. The vessels are managed under full management contracts, although crewing only and some commercial management may be undertaken. The company has about 50-60 shorebased employees and more than 1000 seafarers, a small percentage of whom are employed through manning agencies. The company may own a small number of ships and has an annual turnover of about £13 million.

A Typical Company in the 'Friendship' Group

An independent UK-based company offering ship management services only. It has been established for about 14 years and has a fleet of 35-40 vessels mainly under crewing management contracts. It also undertakes technical management. It employs 30-35 shorebased staff and less than 1,000 seafarers. Seafarers are not employed through manning agencies and ship ownership is very limited. The company has an annual turnover of less than £8 million.

A Typical Company in the 'Rigid' Group

An independent company, probably based in a tax advantageous location (Cyprus or the Isle of Man) and engaged in offering ship management services, although it may have expanded into ownership more recently. It has been established for about 15 years and manages a large fleet of more than 60 vessels, mainly under crewing management contracts but also full management. It employs more than 60 staff ashore. A large fleet indicates that the company employs more than 1,000 seafarers, one quarter of whom are employed through manning agencies. There is a high possibility that the company may be building up an owned fleet (currently of small to medium size), and has a high annual turnover (close to £15 million). The company is commercially-oriented, conscious of achieving efficiency and cost reduction, and seeks to invest in profitable maritime business opportunities.

A Typical Company in the 'Reactive' Group

May be based in either the UK or Cyprus, an independent company offering third party management services only. The company has been established for about 15 years and has a very large fleet under management (more than 60 vessels). The company mainly undertakes management under crewing only contracts, although technical and commercial-only may be welcome. About one tenth of the 1,500 seafarers are employed through manning agencies and are supported by more than 60 shorebased staff. The company may be looking to expand into ownership and has an annual turnover of about £12 million. It is associated with the expected form of today's ship management organisations, where management for third parties is a priority and building up a managed rather than owned fleet is the main business activity. Commercially-oriented with regard to management, it may be less reluctant to engage in business outside this area than companies in the 'rigid' cluster.

Profiles with Client Company Characteristics

The characteristics of ship manager-client relationships may be greatly influenced by the organisational characteristics of the major client companies. This is because the client company characteristics partly reflect the resources that the ship manager is able to draw from the major client, and hence the dependence on the major client. Additionally, other characteristics such as the location of the client's company may influence relationship characteristics such as communication or personal contact.

Hence, a profile of the characteristics of client companies found in each ship management cluster is essential for determining whether the relationship characteristics are influenced by the characteristics of the major client company.

Location of Client Companies

Companies in the 'friendship' and 'reactive' groups are more likely to be managing vessels for clients located in the UK. Hence, it seems that all companies managing vessels for UK clients in the 'friendship' cluster, and the majority of those companies in the 'reactive' cluster, are also located in the UK. The geographical location of UK-based companies in the 'friendship' cluster and the high possibility for client companies to be located in the UK may go some way towards explaining the friendship type relationship found in this group of companies. Close personal relationships are more likely to be formed when the parties are in close geographical proximity or have similar cultural backgrounds. In the 'reactive' cluster, most of the companies based in Cyprus have clients based in Germany. These ship management companies are prepared to change certain operational procedures in order to meet the needs of specific clients. There are indications to suggest that these companies may not be prepared, however, to make any investments specific to a client relationship, such as introducing computerised systems to deal with the operations of the major client only.

Companies in the 'rigid' cluster deal with clients based in European countries, including the UK and Germany, but most significantly Eastern Europe and Norway. The relationship between these companies and their client is characterised by rigidity in terms of adaptations and general investments. As explained earlier, the rigidity of these companies may be associated with the fact that they are cost-conscious. This is not the case for Cyprus-based companies and their German clients, where some degree of flexibility is present. It can be inferred that cultural background may have a bearing on the nature of ship management relationships. It must also be noted that the Cyprus-based companies found in the 'investors' cluster also have German clients (hence, these companies may also make major investments for their major German clients). The degree of dependency on the major client, however, is much greater for the 'investors' cluster.

Client's Main Business Activity

Companies in the 'investors' group have clients engaged in a variety of activities. This indicates that major investments may be made for clients in a variety of businesses. However, clients of companies in this cluster are the only ones engaged in shipping pools. This may be important, as shipping pools have always been associated with high quality tonnage and management. It seems that clients requiring high standards of safety and quality management may entrust their vessels to companies found in the 'investors' cluster, since these companies may be prepared to make higher investments into such systems.

The majority of client companies for ship management organisations found in the 'friendship' cluster are engaged in tramp shipping. The same is true for companies in the third cluster, although companies in the 'rigid' and 'reactive' clusters are the only ones that have clients engaged in container liner shipping. The inference that can be made is that ships engaged in container liner shipping may not require flexibility or major adaptations on the part of the manager. Because liner shipping involves fixed schedules, with containerships making voyages between scheduled ports, once a system to cater for the needs of these vessels is in place, it is less likely that major changes will be needed. This is supported in the literature: 'containerships do not require the same high level of technical support as do, for instance, product tankers and gas carriers' (Anon, 1995r, p. 7). Many clients of companies in the 'rigid' cluster, however, are engaged in tramp shipping as well. Therefore, the evidence on whether the client's main business activity accounts for certain relationship characteristics is not conclusive.

Revenue from Major Client

This particular characteristic is extremely important because it may directly account for the level of dependence the ship manager has on the particular client. For instance, if a great percentage of the ship manager's revenue comes from the major client, obviously the manager will be more dependent on the particular client.

In the 'friendship' cluster, the percentage of revenue attributed to the major client is low (13 per cent). This may be accounted for by the fact that only a mean number of four ships are under full management with a mean number of six ships under crewing management. Dependence on the client is low in financial terms, because a ship management company can yield greater profits from full management contracts. This group exemplifies, however, the social/psychological side of a business relationship. Adaptations and investments are made because of the social bonds with the client. Hence, the companies are prepared to change their business processes to accommodate the needs of major clients.

One method of dependency reduction is the cultivation of alternative sources of desired resources (Pfeffer and Leong, 1977). If the required resource is profit maximisation, then expansion into shipowning is the cultivation of an alternative source. About 60 per cent of the companies in the 'rigid' cluster have invested in the purchase of ships. The companies in this cluster also own more vessels than the companies in any other of the three clusters. Because of the alternative source of profit, the dependence on clients is considerably less. This is supported by the fact that companies in this cluster attribute 15 per cent of their revenue to the relationship with the major client. Dependence on the client is low and therefore adaptations are not made. Companies are more reluctant to change their operational procedures to accommodate the needs of the client. The fact that these companies manage a substantial number of vessels for their major clients does not seem to have a great impact on dependency because of the alternative sources of revenue (unlike companies in the 'investors' cluster).

Hallen, Johanson and Seyed-Mohamed (1991) found that adaptation is related to the degree of dependence on the client. The percentage of revenue earned from the major client may be used as a measure of the ship manager's dependence. Up to 80 per cent of the companies appearing in the 'rigid' cluster earn less than 25 per cent of their revenue from their major client. In fact, 60 per cent earn between 1 and 10 per cent, and 40 per cent between 1 and 5 per cent. For the 'reactive' cluster, 28 per cent of the companies earn between 1 and 5 per cent of their revenue from the major client, 55 per cent earn less than 25 per cent of their revenue from the major client and 28 per cent of the companies earn between 46 and 60 per cent of their revenue from the major client. This suggests that adaptations are related to dependence in a ship management context.

This is also supported by looking at the 'investors', where companies make major adaptations. In this cluster we find the only two companies in the sample who earn more than 60 per cent of their annual revenue from a particular major client. On average, the companies in this cluster derive 37 per cent of their revenue from the major client. Hence, the dependence on the client is higher and investments into the relationship are naturally substantial.

Duration of Relationships

Examination of the duration of relationships between the ship management companies in the sample and their major clients indicates that relationships have been long-term. All companies indicate a mean range between 10-12 years. This long-term nature of the relationship is consistent with the high level of trust exhibited by ship managers, and confirms the association found in other studies on exchange relationships. Trust between the parties has been characterised as very high to fairly high by the majority of the companies. The relationship marketing literature indicates that the longer the relationship with exchange partners, the greater the degree of trust among the parties. With increased experience, companies are more likely to have successfully overcome critical periods (Dwyer, Schurr and Oh, 1987; Scanzoni, 1979), and gained a greater understanding of each other's idiosyncracies (Williamson, 1985). Therefore, longer relationships facilitate the prediction of future behaviour and increased confidence and willingness to rely on the other party. Empirically, Anderson and Weitz (1989) found that a channel member's trust in a manufacturer increases with the age of the relationship.

Summarising the above preliminary results, typical companies in the four clusters will have clients exhibiting the characteristics indicated in Table 4.7.

Table 4.7 Typical client characteristics per ship management cluster

Investors	Friendship
Client based all over the world	Client is based in the UK
Client engaged in shipping pools	Few ships under full management are managed for the client
A high percentage of the company's revenue comes from the client	Low percentage of the revenue is attributed to the client
	Longer term relationships
	Client engaged in tramp shipping

Rigid	Reactive
Client based all over Europe	Client based in the UK or Germany
Client engaged in tramp shipping	Client engaged in container liner shipping
Low percentage of revenue comes from the client	The longest relationship with the client
Fairly long relationship with client	

Frequency of Communication

In the relationship marketing literature, communication appears to be one of the most important variables utilised in the understanding of business relationships. Mohr, Fisher and Nevin (1996) argue that the most important element to successful inter-firm exchange is communication. Bleeke and Ernst (1993, p. xvi) state that 'the most carefully designed relationship will crumble without good, frequent communication'.

Higher frequency of communication is likely in conditions of supportive climates, or symmetrical power. This has been referred to as a 'collaborative communication strategy' (Mohr and Nevin, 1990). Communication of lower frequency is likely to appear in non-supportive structures or asymmetrical power. This is called 'autonomous communication strategy' (Mohr and Nevin, 1990). When there is a feeling of shared identity, supportive atmosphere and relationship closeness, exchange parties may seek information from one-on-one verbal modes (Huber and Daft, 1987). It was supported throughout the analysis of results that companies in the 'investors' and 'friendship' clusters interact in a more friendly and supportive manner than those in the 'rigid' and 'reactive' clusters. It can be seen that as far as face-to-face communication is concerned (at operational and senior management level), there is a higher frequency for both the 'investors' cluster and the 'friendship' cluster than for the 'rigid' and 'reactive' clusters.

Face-to-face communication at operational level is much less frequent for the majority of the companies found in the 'rigid' cluster. Some 60 per cent of these companies communicate with their client twice a year or less, compared to only 9 per cent of companies in the 'investors' cluster, 25 per cent of companies in the 'friendship' cluster and 28 per cent in the 'reactive' cluster.

In an analysis of over 100 supplier-customer relationships in international markets, Cunningham and Turnbull (1982) found that, among other roles, personal contact patterns served the roles of information exchange, adaptations and social bonding. Hakansson, Johanson and Wootz (1977) posit that personal contacts provide a significant means of transmitting and responding to the various influencing processes at work. One of these influencing processes is the adaptation and adjustment to the needs of the exchange parties. The companies making no adaptations (found in the 'rigid' cluster) are also those that have the least frequent personal contact with their clients at both operational and senior management level. On the other hand, most frequent personal contact is found in the 'investors' cluster. The companies in this cluster also make major adaptations in the relationship with their major client.

In inter-firm relationships characterised by a high degree of dependency, information exchange interactions tend to occur frequently (Frazier and Summers, 1984). This is also true in this study, where 91 per cent of the highly client-dependent companies in the 'investors' cluster communicate daily with the client at operational level. Only 40 per cent of the companies found in the 'rigid' cluster communicate daily with the client at this level. This cluster has been found to be the least dependent on the client. At senior management level, 73 per cent of the companies in the 'investors' cluster communicate at least once a week with the client, compared to 75 per cent of companies in the 'friendship' cluster, 20 per cent of companies in the 'rigid' cluster and 57 per cent of companies in the 'reactive' cluster. In financial terms, companies in the 'friendship' cluster were found to be least dependent on the client. Despite this, communication was found to be frequent. This may be explained by the fact that these companies are more likely to depend on ship management for their business, rather than ship ownership (companies in this cluster own the least number of ships). Furthermore, the companies in this cluster were found to have a personal/friendship relationship with the client, and, as indicated above, a friendly and supportive atmosphere influences frequent communication. Mummalaneni (1987) found that a personal friendship relationship is associated with greater investments in terms of time. Hence, managers in the 'friendship' cluster seem to invest more time in seeking to communicate with the major client.

Cunningham and Homse (1986) surveyed 59 industrial supplier-customer relationships and found that personal contact patterns varied from approximately 20 times per annum in domestic relationships to six times per annum in international relationships – an overall average of about ten times per annum. The results obtained by Cunningham and Homse (1986) are comparable to those obtained in this study of the ship management industry. It was stated earlier that companies in the 'friendship' cluster are more likely to be located in the UK and manage vessels for UK clients. Hence the higher patterns of personal contact (domestic market). On the other hand, the contact patterns for the 'rigid' cluster are considerably less frequent, as companies will manage vessels for clients located in Europe (mainly Germany, Norway and other European countries).

Summarising the findings, it can be deduced that companies in the 'investors' and 'friendship' clusters communicate with their major client organisations much more frequently than companies in the other two clusters. In particular, companies in the 'rigid' cluster have the lowest frequency of communication and personal meetings at all levels.

Implications for Ship Manager-Client Relationships

The results of the research have widespread implications for the ship management industry in general and ship management companies in particular. Implications for practitioners can be readily drawn with respect to client relationships. Bearing in mind, however, the limited research in the area, and the wealth of information obtained during the study, the results can be used to make reasoned speculations about the ship management industry. Hence, the contribution of the study is not limited to client relationships, but extends to the direction in which ship management is currently moving. In general, the development of relationships can have major benefits for ship management companies and their stakeholders, and on the basis of the study, such relationships are not actively pursued. The implications of the study may provide insights into ship management and client relationships that can facilitate informed decision-making and a possible basis for change in the marketing orientation of the ship management sector at large.

The study revealed that different ship management companies can serve the needs of different types of clients. It is on this basis that ship management companies have been operating, but without due consideration for developing client relationships and serving the needs of the clients better.

It was identified in chapter 3 that ship management companies concentrate on the variables of the marketing mix as part of their marketing effort. The results of the study indicated certain differences in the delivery of the ship management service to the client. In addition, many ship management companies concentrate on the extension of the service offer, and marketing their adherence to quality standards rather than concentrating on the relationship with their clients.

The Delivery of the Ship Management Service

The typology of ship management companies developed from the results indicates some major differences in service delivery among ship management organisations. In broad terms, certain companies seem to concentrate their efforts on the provision of services, and regard this as the major business focus that will assist them in attaining their corporate objectives. Such companies are found in the 'investors', 'friendship' and 'reactive' clusters, although there are distinct differences in terms of providing the actual ship management service. For instance, companies in the 'investors' category seem to regard the provision of services to the client as their major objective. These companies concentrate on the client, and take extra care in satisfying the requirements of the client by making major investments and avoiding conflicts with the client.

On the other hand, companies in the 'friendship' category offer services at a level of personalisation that cannot be attained by companies in any other category. This is because of the nature of the relationship between the executives in the interacting organisations.

Companies in the 'reactive' category seem to be offering ship management services at the expected level. These companies carry out their functions in a manner that would be expected from a client entrusting his vessels to a professional. This includes a certain degree of flexibility and investments and a personalised touch in some instances.

Companies in the 'rigid' category and, to a lesser degree, companies in the 'reactive' category seem to be able to achieve their corporate objectives by pursuing strategies not traditionally associated with offering professional ship management services. These companies seem to be keen on expanding their service offering, operating their own ships and making additional investments in ship purchase. Companies operating their own vessels in conjunction with ship management (mostly found in the 'rigid' cluster) have the highest annual revenue. These companies have either invested in ships, or undertake management as a secondary activity. Those companies that are prepared to invest in the relationship with the client ('investors' cluster) have considerably lower turnovers. This is expected, as the revenue from ship operation is considerably higher than the fee earned by ship management companies providing services. The results suggest that companies in the 'rigid' category are downplaying the delivery of ship management services. In the 'rigid' cluster, relationships with clients are more fragmented and conflict is relatively high.

It is possible that the profitability and growth objectives of these companies are better met by owning ships and operating ships for third parties. This does not mitigate, however, the impact on the ship management organisation, which exists to provide a service. Ship management companies take pride in themselves for delivering the service in accordance with the client's specifications. To do so, flexibility and personalised service are essential. If the ship management companies operating owned tonnage (in cluster 3) continue to be rigid and inflexible in their client relationships, then this may have an impact on the company, since it may be viewed as opportunistic rather than service-oriented and trusting. Companies achieving the right balance in maintaining client relationships whilst investing in business opportunities beyond the 'service-only' scope may be the ones to achieve the highest growth rates and profitability.

It is not suggested here that companies appearing in any particular cluster are inherently applying inadequate business practices. What is suggested is that the problems identified in ship management (and many of these problems were reported to be present in companies participating in the research) may be due to the type of relationship with the client. Hence, companies that have either adjusted their objectives and concentrate on areas other than provision of services in accordance with client specifications, or have diversified from offering ship management services into ship ownership, should not be surprised to find that their client relationships are becoming short-term. Such short-term relationships are found in the 'rigid' cluster. Companies in all other clusters seem to be doing reasonably well with their clients, although they differ in the way they produce and deliver the ship management service. It is important to note that companies in the 'reactive' cluster may in some respect jeopardise client relationships if attention is turned away from the client. At the moment, however, these companies seem to be the most successful, because they have the longer-term client relationships and a high annual turnover, while their costs are kept relatively low by making general investments and minor adaptations in their client relationships. The success of certain companies seems to be luring other traditional ship management companies to diversify into ship ownership (Anon, 1997f). This shows the trend in ship management away from personalised provision of services towards further expansion, diversification and commercialisation, with the ultimate aim of increasing wealth.

Market Segments and Extension of the Service Offer

The four relationship clusters found in this research, and the association with certain organisational characteristics, suggest that many ship management companies exist to serve the needs of different market segments. Success in serving the needs of segments of customers seems to lure companies into extension of their service offer in order to attract more clients having different product (service) needs.

It seems that the expansion of the service offering pursued by many companies can only be justified if it can satisfy the needs of large market segments. Market segments should be large enough to sustain the viability of additional services. However, this does not mean that the production of the service should not be accompanied by a flexible approach to the needs of the client. Service extension must not deprive the core service of essential elements. Expansion of the service offering should not make the service offering impersonal and thus compromise the ability to create a relationship with clients. Diversification and servicing the needs of market niches should only be pursued if the expected returns are not only higher than the original investment, but also higher than the return that would have been achieved, had the same investments been made into resources for satisfying current clients. Otherwise, current clients may turn into in-house management or switch to competitors as identified in chapter 3.

Quality versus Flexibility

Reference to the concept of quality and its importance in ship management was made in chapter 2. Quality management is important in shipping for the improvement of safety and the reduction of accidents and environmental pollution. Ship management companies, however, have seized on the concept of quality as a means of marketing their service offer. Hence, marketing efforts have been directed on the basis of quality rather than flexibility. The result is a lack of differentiability as all major companies have obtained accreditation.

This study provides evidence that suggests a lack of flexibility and major adaptations among many ship management companies. It has been recognised that ship management relationships should be based on a willingness on the part of the manager to respond, change and adapt to the needs of the client (Spruyt, 1994). During the research, some managers indicated that their reluctance to make major changes is attributed to the quality management system, which indicates certain procedures that should be followed and allows little room for flexibility. A review of press advertisements of ship management companies indicates a change from publicising 'personal service', 'flexibility', 'dedication' and 'trustworthiness' in the late 1980s to 'quality assurance', 'safety' and 'training' in the 1990s. The results of the research capture a lack of flexibility, which may account to a great extent for the problems faced by ship management companies and reviewed in chapter 3. It seems that many companies have relied too much on the buzzword of 'quality' and have neglected to a certain extent the primary needs of their clients. There is no indication that clients would prefer 'quality assured management' on the basis of being accredited with quality management certificates, at the expense of a personalised, flexible and trustworthy service. In fact, a quality service with no accidents is the least that a client would expect from a professional. In addition, quality is defined as conformance to specifications and client requirements, hence, companies not having a personal and flexible approach are not in fact offering a quality service, despite being accredited with a quality management certificate. With only a small segment of ship management companies able to offer personalised services, it might not be surprising that switching to competitors or to in-house management have been the problems in ship management.

Marketing Smaller Ship Management Companies

This study has identified the existence of different ship management companies in terms of size and in terms of the amount of resources they command. Large companies are able to pursue further expansion and bid for acquisitions. However, smaller ship management companies will not be able either to participate or to compete with the larger organisations. This view was also expressed by one of the key informants in this study, in a trade magazine (Anon, 1997f, p. 55): 'smaller operators might find themselves going to the wall'. Their owners must adopt a proactive stance in order to maintain their companies' existence. On the basis of this study, the options for smaller companies are twofold:

- develop a close social relationship with current and new clients, which will prevent them from defecting to bigger organisations;
- position and market the company as a small organisation, offering personalised services to only a few clients.

It is clear that the above options require the development of strong relationships with current and new clients. Therefore, relationship marketing is of significant importance to all types of ship management organisations, large and small. The study indicates that managers in the smaller companies found in cluster 2 do have close social relationships with key personnel from the client's organisation. The first option indicated above is thus attained by many of the smaller companies. These companies will need to concentrate on the second option and publicise this particular strength of the company. The results of the study, which indicate the achievement of a greater level of personalisation by smaller companies, are supported by events published in the maritime press. For instance, one of the biggest ship management companies lost a significant part of its management fleet to a newly-formed smaller company. Executives from a client organisation said that the smaller company won the contract because it could 'offer a more personal service because of its size' (Anon, 1995m). The options open to smaller companies are hence justified.

Choice of Ship Manager

Probably the most important issue is that the production and delivery of ship management services vary. Hence, shipowners have a choice and are able to assign management to the third party that can best satisfy their needs. So, for instance, an owner that requires assignment of full management responsibilities and other incidental services (e.g. supervision of major conversions) may opt for those companies that have expanded their service offering. This will give the owner the opportunity to assign all functions to a single management company. The large ship management companies found in the 'reactive' cluster, however, are not able to provide personalised services at a level that can be attained by other smaller companies. Such companies are particularly suited for taking on full management responsibilities for clients engaged in the containership market. Clients should expect a medium to high frequency level of communication. This may be particularly suited to the management of containerships, which are less technically demanding and mostly sail on fixed schedules (Anon, 1995r).

Shipowners that have personal relations with a ship manager and decide to entrust their vessels to him should expect personalised treatment and individual commitment. This is especially true if the ship manager is a small UK-based company and the client is also based in the UK. Such relationships are found in the 'friendship' cluster. Companies in this category are independent, provide mainly third party services and are especially suited for providing crew management to clients engaged in tramp shipping. Clients could expect a very high frequency of communication at operational and senior management level.

It seems that German clients are better off entrusting vessels to German companies based in Cyprus. Evidence from this study suggests that cultural background may prove to be one of the decisive factors in ship management relationships. This is because German companies are entrusting vessels to German ship managers and UK companies to UK ship managers. Spruyt (1994, p. 223) states that 'there is a better working relationship...between German owners and German managers'. It is not clear what the author means by 'better working relationship', however, and this study provides evidence to indicate the preferences of owners with respect to cultural identity and background; the evidence shows that German owners do prefer German managers, while UK owners prefer UK managers. Relationships among German entities have been found in the 'reactive' cluster. Ship management companies in this cluster make general investments and incorporate minor adaptations into the relationship, which is, however, characterised by friendship and a high level of trust. An investment of a general nature that did benefit a particular client was made by one of the companies (with an office in London) that participated in the research and can be found in the 'reactive' cluster. The company acquired a new client in the Far East and, spurred on by an identified increase in demand for ship management services in the area, management decided to set up a subsidiary in Singapore (Osler, 1998). In addition, the company was also involved in opening an office in San Francisco, strongly influenced by the presence of PML – one of its clients. The appointed head of this operation stated: 'a main motivation for the San Francisco location was proximity to PML. However, we feel that there will be significant commercial opportunities and a good customer base which can be serviced from this location' (Osler, 1998, p. 12). This shows commercial orientation, expansion and differentiation as well as investments for the benefit of the client, with a view to attracting more clients. The issue of culture as an important variable in ship management relationships is supported by the move of a London-based Greek ship management company to Athens. The company's director stressed the importance of common language, communication and 'traditional Greek quality of good housekeeping of vessels' as the company's strengths in its attempt to tap the Greek market (Lowry, 1997).

Shipowners wishing to entrust many vessels under full management contracts may also opt for companies in the 'investors' cluster. Ship management companies in this cluster value the customer and make investments in the relationship. Such investments may be extremely important where specialised vessels are involved. The management of such vessels requires flexibility and idiosyncratic investments (investments that are specific to the operation of the vessels). These companies are mainly subsidiaries, which indicates a greater degree of specialisation to particular requirements. Additionally, the complexity of operating specialised vessels requires an attitude of conflict minimisation so far as possible, something which is associated with this cluster of companies. These companies can also provide a similar level of service irrespective of where the client is based. The fact that these companies manage vessels for clients engaged in shipping pools provides evidence to support the contention that they are engaged in the operation of specialised vessels. This is because specialised vessels are more likely to be pooled in order to secure a higher level of continuous employment. These companies exhibit the same relationship characteristics towards the client no matter where the client is based. A high frequency of communication at operational and senior management level should be expected.

Finally, for clients wishing to be assured of the competency of the ship manager in managing his own vessels before deciding to entrust their own ships to him, companies in the 'rigid' cluster may be a viable proposition.

These independent companies are engaged in owned ship operation, and therefore their competency in ship management is undisputed. They are large companies (many employees) and manage vessels under full or crew management contracts, but with very little commercial management on its own. They manage vessels for European clients mainly engaged in tramp shipping. Clients must however, accept a compromise between added assurance in competent ship operation, and lack of adaptability coupled with medium to low communication frequency.

Communication with the Ship Manager

Communication has been identified as a very important factor in ship manager–client relationships. Based on the results of the study, it can be inferred that most of the companies communicate frequently with the client and make investments in the introduction of new technologies to facilitate communication. In fact, only the 'rigid' category of companies was found to have medium to low frequency of communication, probably because the companies are not prepared to make large investments in client relationships.

Spruyt (1994) states that geographical distance between the headquarters of the companies, and cultural differences, may account for an escalation of conflict. The evidence from this study suggests the opposite. It was found that ship management companies in the 'investors' cluster serve the needs of Turkish, American and Japanese owners, and that there has been no conflict between them. Spruyt (1994) assumes that conflict arises because of communication problems due to a combination of geographical distance, time difference, differences in nationality and race, and the fact that the manager serves many different owners. Although the frequency of communication may be related to conflict, the assumptions that geographical distance and time difference contribute to conflict escalation do not seem to be supported by this study. It is also important to note that the general attitude towards conflict was that of resolution by whatever means possible and through close co-operation with the client. Bearing in mind that ship management is becoming a 24-hour business, and with the availability of advance communication systems, communication problems can be minimised. In fact, it was found that companies in the 'investors' cluster communicate with their clients more frequently than companies in the other three clusters at all levels. The results of this study suggest that clients prefer managers of similar cultural background, and that face-to-face contact may be influenced by geographical proximity. However, no relationship between limited communication, geographical time difference and conflict escalation can be supported.

It is also important to note that companies in the UK and mainly Cyprus principally serve the needs of European clients. Hence, it seems that companies in these ship management centres can satisfy the needs of European clients better. It has been suggested that shipowners may be reluctant to move their ship operation too far out of their local time zone (Anon, 1995n), and companies in Cyprus are ideally placed to satisfy this particular need. Despite this, there is no evidence to suggest that companies in Cyprus communicate more frequently with their clients in Europe than with those in Japan and the USA.

The results of the empirical examination suggest the existence of segments of ship management service suppliers. Companies seem to pursue particular courses of action that they perceive will yield the most additional benefits that would fulfil their organisational objectives. Critical aspects in the achievement of organisational objectives for ship management companies include, as this chapter has revealed, the attraction and retention of clients by identifying, anticipating and satisfying the criteria for ship manager selection and evaluation, as dictated by prospects and clients. It is on this premise that the following chapter sets out to reveal the criteria used by shipowners in selecting and evaluating their ship managers, both from the shipowners' and the ship managers' point of view.

5 Ship Manager Selection and Evaluation

Introduction

Client attraction and retention are fundamental aspects in marketing strategy for any ship management company. It follows that knowing the factors or criteria that are most important to clients in selecting a ship manager and evaluating the ship manager's performance is fundamental. This chapter deals with the fundamental aspect of determining the criteria for selecting and evaluating professional ship managers. Dimensions discussed in the services and shipping related literature are highlighted and an empirical investigation is carried out to determine, compare and contrast the views of both ship managers and shipowners.

The Importance of Selection Criteria

As mentioned in chapter 3, one of the main aspects of services marketing is the concept of intangibility. Clients of ship management companies may have difficulty in assessing the quality of the ship management service and the approach offered by the firm. The intangibility and technical complexity of the ship management service may lead certain types of clients to identify and base their assessments on such surrogate indicators of quality as corporate image and advertising (cf. Brown and Swartz, 1989). In addition, most writers agree that customers' expectations are rarely concerned with a single aspect of the service package but rather with many aspects (Berry, Zeithaml and Parasuraman, 1985; Johnston and Lyth, 1991; Sasser, Olsen and Wyckoff, 1978).

Identification of the criteria by which shipowners select ship managers and the criteria used by shipowners to evaluate the performance of the ship manager after the service has been delivered has numerous important implications. One particular issue is identification of what constitutes good service of high quality as defined by the customer. This will facilitate better management of service delivery on a consistent basis, thus reducing the possibility of a service performance gap. The service performance gap is

111

defined as the discrepancy between the specifications for the service and the actual delivery of the service (Parasuraman, Zeithaml and Berry, 1985).

Performing excellent and consistent service and avoiding a service performance gap is of utmost importance for various reasons. It will improve service quality, which is defined as the degree to which perceived service meets customers' expectations (Gronroos, 1984; Parasuraman, Berry and Zeithaml, 1990). The company will be able to demonstrate reliability in service delivery. Reliability has been shown to have an effect on company performance (Buzzell and Gale, 1987). It is also of utmost importance in customer retention (Reichheld and Sasser, 1990) and to develop long-term relationships with customers (Berry, Zeithaml and Parasuraman, 1991; Gronroos, 1984; 1988). In addition, the service performance gap is also important in terms of resource utilisation, because its occurrence generates the costs of correcting and eliminating service failures, costs that, in turn, affect the financial results of the firm (Schlesinger and Heskett, 1991).

The importance of choice selection criteria is also reflected in the need to identify what constitutes 'value' in the context of receiving the service. It is important to identify what customers may perceive as 'value', so as to emphasise the delivery of such aspects in the service package that will increase the customer's perception of the value that he receives.

The organisational procedures and criteria by which shipowners select and evaluate the performance of ship managers have not been the theme of valid scientific analysis before. This is despite the importance attached to choice criteria both in the general shipping industry context and in the marketing literature in particular.

Writers in different fields have suggested different types of dimensions for different industry areas (e.g. Hamilton and Crompton, 1991; Hedvall and Paltschik, 1991; Scott and Shieff, 1993). Different dimensions have been suggested for shipping services in the maritime and logistics related literature, and other services (including professional services) in the services marketing related literature. This idiosyncratic aspect of service selection and evaluation criteria renders the performance of an empirical study imperative in order to obtain valid dimensions for service selection and evaluation in professional ship management. However, prior to such an attempt, it is important to consider the dimensions discussed in other areas.

Selection Criteria in Services

In the marketing literature, the choice selection criteria are often equated with the service quality dimensions, because one would logically expect customers to refer service providers whose service they perceive to be of high quality. As stated by Scott and van der Walt (1995, p. 28):

> The dimensions for service selection should be the same or similar to those of service quality and hence the literature relating to service quality dimensions is of relevance when one is examining the dimensions for service selection.

Parasuraman, Zeithaml and Berry (1985) provided a list of ten determinants of service quality following a series of focus group studies with service providers and customers. They determined that the dimensions of access, communication, competence, courtesy, credibility, reliability, responsiveness, security, understanding and tangibles were critical in the provision of services. They later refined the determinants to five dimensions of tangibles, reliability, responsiveness, assurance and empathy (Parasuraman, Zeithaml and Berry, 1988), also referred to in chapter 3. These dimensions have been used to test the determinants of service quality in various service contexts.

Saporta (1989) found that the qualities considered most important by organisational customers are competitiveness, reliability and adaptability. The supplier must demonstrate an ability to resolve the customer's problem (Hakansson, Johanson and Wootz, 1977; Hakansson and Wootz, 1978). Business-to-business marketing and ship management in particular are also characterised by the importance of the technological dimension, which may represent a source of competitive advantage (Saporta, 1989; Wikstrom and Norman, 1994). In the services area, Stephens et al. (1987) found that four elements are critical and include overall quality, needs, expectations and price. With regard to the latter, studies dealing with competency-based, technical professional services found that low price in such industrial markets may not be an important factor in determining customer value (Lapierre, 1997).

Walker (1990) suggested that the key determinants are product (service) reliability, a quality environment and delivery systems that work, together with good personal service – staff attitude, knowledge and skills. Gronroos (1990a) put forward six criteria of perceived good service quality: professionalism and skills, attitudes and behaviour, accessibility and flexibility, reliability and trustworthiness, recovery, and reputation and credibility. Albrecht and Zemke (1985) postulated care and concern, spontaneity, problem-solving and recovery. Armistead (1990) split the dimensions into 'firm' and 'soft'. The so-called 'firm' dimensions were made up of time, fault-freeness and flexibility. Time included availability, waiting time and responsiveness. Similarly, fault-freeness is further sub-dived into physical items, information and advice, while flexibility includes the ability to recover from mistakes, to customise the service or add additional services. The 'soft' dimensions are style (attitude and accessibility of staff and ambience), steering (the degree to which customers feel in control of their own destiny) and safety (trust, security and confidentiality). Scott and van der Walt (1995) found five underlying factors of choice selection criteria in the context of international accounting firms. These include competitive advantage (fees, reputation, efficiency), personal service, external recommendations, image and product range. The issue of personal recommendations and referral sources may be of particular importance in the ship management business, where business relations play a significant role in acquiring new clients. Zeithaml (1981) stated that consumers seek and rely more on information from personal sources than from non-personal sources when evaluating services prior to purchasing.

Selection Criteria in Shipping and Transport

A number of studies have been carried out in the effort to identify the critical dimensions for selection of providers of shipping, logistics and freight transport services. Many of the dimensions identified are specific to the service provided and would not apply to the context of professional ship management. However, it may be beneficial to make reference to these studies at this stage from two perspectives. Firstly, these dimensions deal with selection of service providers and hence may share a number of factors with ship management. Second, ship managers may benefit from knowledge of what constitutes critical dimensions in the context of shipping services because this aspect may be proximately related with the business of some of their clients. And for service providers, knowledge of the clients' business is of utmost importance in the quest for delivery of client satisfaction.

The importance of the freight transport modal choice is reflected in the number and quality of studies that have been performed in this context since the late 1960s. It was then that Cook (1967) identified transport costs as important, although not necessarily decisive in the choice of freight transport services among manufacturing firms. Early analyses of shipper priorities regarding transportation choice have generally conceded that service variables such as speed, reliability and dependability are more important than rates reflected in dimensions such as shipping charges, cost, direct cost and freight rates (Bardi, 1973; Evans and Southard, 1974; Gilmour, 1976; Saleh and Lalonde, 1972). McGinnis (1980) found that speed and reliability, freight rates, and loss and damage are highly important factors in the transportation choice by shippers, whereas external market influences, market competitiveness and inventories were of moderate importance. In their study, Jerman, Anderson and Constantin (1978) compared the perceptions of carriers and shippers. They found that the most important variables from the carrier's viewpoint were co-operation of personnel, knowledge of the shipper's needs, dependability, quality of service and ability to quickly trace shipments. On the other hand, shippers perceived co-operation among personnel, the ability to quickly trace shipments, total transit time, knowledge of shipper's needs, and carrier assistance in obtaining rate/classification changes as the most important variables.

Burg and Daley (1985) compared carrier and shipper perceptions of the important elements of the service choice decision. According to their study, the most important factors described by shippers include 'satisfies customer requirements', 'dependable transit time', 'low freight rates' and 'allows for large shipments'. On the other hand, carriers perceive the most important factors to be 'low freight rates', 'availability of loading/unloading facilities', 'satisfies customer requirements' and 'provides a low frequency of cargo loss or damage'.

Matear and Gray (1993) performed a study of modal choice criteria in a short-sea and air transport context. The study provided a comparison of the perceptions between shippers and freight service suppliers (freight forwarders). It was found that shippers and freight suppliers employ different criteria in the purchase of sea and air transport services. For shippers, the most important criteria were the carrier's characteristics (relationship with carrier, responsiveness, ability to handle special requirements), timing characteristics (service frequency, transit time, punctuality) and pricing characteristics (low price, value, discounts). For freight suppliers purchasing sea transport services, the most important criterion is the service performance, followed by schedule and price characteristics. Shippers and freight suppliers purchasing sea services have a similar pricing component, whereas schedule, space and price, and frequency components are more important for freight suppliers purchasing air transport services.

Gibson, Sink and Mundy (1993), in a survey of carrier selection, criteria found that the most important considerations from the shipper's point of view were the on-time performance history, the quality of service and the availability of equipment. Whyte (1993) found through an empirical examination that the most important determinants of haulier selection include 'ability to provide good service', 'reputation for integrity', 'price', 'flexibility to future requirements' and 'likelihood of establishing a long-term relationship'. With respect to service evaluation, the most important attributes were 'ability to meet requirements at short notice', 'freedom from loss/damage', 'provision of suitable vehicles', 'ability to understand problems and willingness to help', 'transit time delivery' and 'speed of delivery' (Whyte, 1993).

Brooks (1985) quotes a study by Pearson (1980) reporting a qualitative assessment of shippers' attitudes and policies in a container shipping context. In his survey, Pearson (1980) found that British shippers are more service-oriented than cost-oriented and their selection criteria are comprised of: 'loading/discharge port', 'port accessibility', 'port costs', 'sailing/arrival times', 'transit times', 'regularity', 'reliability' and 'port itinerary'. The most important criteria were identified as: 'flexibility', 'first on the quay', 'speed of transit', and 'reliability' and 'regularity'. In her own study, Brooks (1985) found that both service and cost criteria were perceived by all shippers as important factors in the purchase of marine carriage services for containerised cargo. Brooks (1985) made an important distinction between the perceived importance of choice criteria and the actual determinants of selection. She concluded that service issues are determinants if the shipper does engage in choice set evaluation, and that price is not a key choice determinant although it is a key trigger to re-evaluation of carrier options. In a follow-up study conducted in 1989, it was found that there had been little evolution in the criteria that shippers view to be important in the selection decision, but that the deterministic criteria have changed and transit time had become the sole selection criterion (Brooks, 1990). On the subject of ocean carriers' selection criteria, anecdotal evidence presented in Containerisation International (1999) reports the criteria employed by a large logistics organisation. The criteria include 'general operational efficiency', 'administrative performance', 'people relationships', 'communications', 'route profiles' and 'rates'. Durvasula, Lysonski and Mehta (2000) found that in evaluating the performance of shipping lines, factors related to service recovery, such as claims handling, complaint handling and problem handling (i.e. post performance service activities), are also critical.

In a Ro/Ro ferry trade context, D'Este and Meyrick (1992), found that shippers have a conservative decision-making approach and place emphasis, within price bounds, on quality of service, particularly speed and reliability.

Cullinane and Toy (2000) performed a content analysis of the freight/mode choice decision criteria to identify the most often considered dimensions in the literature. Their sample consisted of seventy-five articles, and the findings from two approaches to content analysis applied suggested five dominant factor categories. These categories include 'cost/price/rate', 'speed', 'transit time reliability', 'characteristics of the goods' and 'service (unspecified)'. The latter factor category, 'service (unspecified)' was used to represent the rather abstract nature of the term 'service', which may encompass different service characteristics.

The conclusions that can be extracted from this review of choice criteria in shipping and transport include the undisputed importance of service quality characteristics which, as determined by the research studies, assume a higher ranking in choice criteria than the price variable alone. The implications of this finding of the review is that it raises an important proposition in the ship management context, viz. to investigate the importance of service quality, service attributes and value vis-à-vis management fee costs and other sacrifices incurred by the client.

Ship Manager Selection and Performance Evaluation

In the context of the dearth of previous studies on such an important concept for professional ship managers, it was deemed of significant importance to undertake a research study in order to identify the dimensions for service selection and evaluation from the ship manager's and the client's point of view.

To accomplish these objectives, a series of telephone interviews with practising ship managers and companies entrusting their vessels to third parties were carried out. In addition, a mail questionnaire was utilised to retrieve the importance of the choice and evaluation criteria and also some key organisational characteristics of the entities. It must be pointed out that the criteria examined relates to the decision of choice among alternative ship management firms, and not the decision of whether to outsource.

Choice Criteria: The Ship Managers' View

The first part of the empirical research involved the conduct of interviews with senior management of a number of ship management companies based in Hong Kong, Cyprus and the UK. The interviews were carried out by telephone and the following issues were reported.

The first Hong Kong-based ship manager thought that the most important factor when a shipowner decides upon his choice of professional ship manager is the reputation of the ship manager, which is determined by the period of time the ship manager has been in business. Price is also a key criterion (price in this context refers to the management fees paid by the shipowner). In addition, the experience and qualifications of key staff such as superintendents is another important aspect according to the ship manager. The quality of management offered may also be a function of whether the ship management company itself owns vessels. If the ship manager is also a shipowner, that may be a criterion that shipowners are looking for.

The second interviewee, also of a Hong Kong-based ship management company, revealed that the most important factors for choosing a ship manager include cost, experience (which is a consequence of the period of time in the ship management business) and the experience and qualifications of personnel. In terms of service evaluation, similar issues have been raised with importance attached to issues of service quality, professionalism and fees.

The vice president and CEO of another major Hong Kong-based ship management company indicated four underlying factors of choice selection criteria. The first factor is reputation, which is a consequence of service quality. Secondly, experience is also an important factor. Unlike previous interviewees, the CEO did not think that history and time in the business are necessarily critical dimensions. He suggests that ship managers who manage a greater number of vessels would be preferable due to the resources that they would have accumulated. Geographical location is another important consideration, and also cost. Lower cost, however, is not always better, but should be viewed in the context of the aforementioned factors. The key criteria that a ship manager should fulfil include a good-quality service at a reasonable price. The price may be largely influenced by the ship manager's network of suppliers. If ship managers can obtain supplies at cheaper prices then they can charge lower fees. The qualifications and experience of personnel are also important factors. According to the views of this ship manager, clients pay particular attention to operating costs, safe operation of vessels, and how well the ship manager maintains the good operating condition of the vessel(s).

A UK-based interviewee of a multinational company offered similar views to the ones expressed by previous interviewees, thus suggesting that ship managers' perception of choice criteria may not vary in accordance with geographical location. According to this ship manager, the most important choice criteria include safe operation at economical price, cost-effectiveness in vessel operation, and the experience and practical ability of personnel. A ship manager should be able to manage cost-effective purchasing. Larger organisations are more able to do that as they can reap the benefits of economies of scale. This raises the issue of size as an important criterion for ship management effectiveness. A trained, qualified and competent staff is of utmost importance. For the evaluation of services the perception of this ship manager is that clients look at price and the reliability of the ship manager in operating the vessel at reasonable cost.

A managing director of another major player in the ship management business noted that trust between ship manager and shipowner is an important factor. The choice of ship manager is largely based on the shipowner's confidence that the manager chosen will deliver the services sought. Communication on paper and other media is also very important. Managers should provide cost-effective vessel operation and highly qualified, experienced and professional officers, and should maintain high technical ability. The quality and competency of shore-based personnel is also a decisive factor according to the interviewee.

Another ship manager offered a slightly different perspective. He considered that one of the most important criteria is the ship manager's degree of specialisation in managing certain types of vessels. He thought that those ship managers who are specialised in managing the type of vessels owned by the shipowner would be preferable. For instance, shipowners who own bulk carriers would choose managers that are specialised in managing bulk carriers. Reputation is also an important factor as famous ship managers are more preferable. Price is an important factor but that has to be evaluated together with the quality of services offered. The lowest price is not necessarily the best choice. An important criterion that ship managers should fulfil during the management process is to offer services and information in accordance to the needs of the clients. Other issues raised include qualification of manpower, technical support, and provision of monthly statements.

The managing director of a company based in Cyprus regarded cost, quality and reliability in the provision of services as the most important factors upon which a shipowner may base his choice of professional ship manager. The key criteria that a ship manager should fulfil include efficient operation and maintenance of vessels, provision of updated information to shipowners, and flexibility in providing such information and services to different situations. In evaluating the services, the managing director contends that shipowners look at such aspects like ability to buy cheap consumables, flexibility and problem-solving ability.

Another ship manager contended that price, safe operation of the vessels, and the range and quality of services offered are the most important criteria upon which a shipowner bases his choice decision. In terms of the key criteria that a ship manager should fulfil, these include low record of accidents, high technical ability and provision of professional and highly qualified crew. In their assessment of the services they receive, shipowners pay attention to the standard of the crew and personnel on-board, and the type and level of complexity in the portfolio of vessels of the ship manager. With respect to the process of selection and evaluation, a ship manager contended that the initial interest that a prospective client may have in third party management would be initiated by the ship management needs of the owner. The owner will rely on information from personal sources and reputation prior to making enquiries with specific ship managers. The ship managers will then be invited to make their bids and proposals, and the owner may require inspections on vessels currently managed by the manager. The manager needs to demonstrate the ability to satisfy the requirements and add value to the shipowner. A potential pitfall in the selection process might include the pricing strategies of competitors that might be pursuing the acquisition of business on price. Post-purchase evaluation may also prove to be a problem for ship managers, particularly if the owner does not have a formal procedure for evaluation and instead relies on the varying views and perceptions of the managers of the different departments that interact with the ship manager. It is thus important for the manager to be proactive in his approach and devise a formal system by which to supply the owner with tangible evidence of the value that the ship manager is adding to the owner's business.

Following the interviews with the ship managers and their clients, and after retrieving a number of key dimensions from the practitioners themselves, a mail survey was utilised to retrieve more specific measures of the choice criteria dimensions. The dimensions that were retrieved from the interviews were edited and used in the survey together with dimensions existing in the choice criteria literature. The mail questionnaire was sent to a sample of ship managers and shipowners. Respondents were asked to rate the choice and evaluation criteria dimensions on a scale of one to five, with one being not important and five being absolutely imperative. Table 5.1 below shows the distribution of the importance of the key dimensions in the selection of professional ship managers as perceived by the ship managers themselves. The table depicts in percentage terms the importance attached to the dimensions by the 48 ship managers who responded to the questionnaire.

Table 5.1 The importance of selection criteria: ship managers' view

Key: 1: Not important; 2: Less important; 3: Important; 4: Very important; 5: Absolutely imperative.

% of respondents with particular response

Dimension	1	2	3	4	5
Price	-	7.0	2.0	57.0	34.0
Size	2.0	11.0	21.0	66.0	-
Advertising	26.0	53.0	17.0	4.0	-
Reputation	-	-	2.0	26.0	72.0
Recommendation	-	-	4.0	64.0	32.0
Technical ability	-	-	4.0	26.0	70.0
Experience	-	-	-	45.0	55.0
Qualifications	-	8.0	8.0	41.0	43.0
Time	-	24.0	17.0	49.0	10.0
Service range	2.0	26.0	26.0	44.0	2.0
Location	2.0	30.0	24.0	40.0	4.0
Specialisation	-	2.0	6.0	57.0	35.0
Large managed fleet	4.0	17.0	26.0	49.0	4.0
Owns vessels	21.0	30.0	28.0	15.0	6.0

The table reveals some important inferences regarding the factors affecting the choice of ship manager as perceived by ship managers themselves. First it must be noted that the most significant dimensions, classified by most respondents as 'absolutely imperative', include the 'reputation' of the company and the 'technical ability' of personnel. These dimensions were rated 'absolutely imperative' by 72 per cent and 70 per cent of the respondents respectively. An obvious distinction can be seen with the 'price' variable, which was classified as 'absolutely imperative' by 34 per cent of the respondents. This is another indication validating the previous findings from the telephone interviews and the literature reviews on choice criteria in services and shipping and transport – that is, price is not the most important criterion in the selection of professional ship managers. Instead, quality of service, evidenced by the reputation the company has managed to build up over the years, and the technical ability of the personnel are ranked higher according to the ship managers' perceptions. The other dimensions that achieve a high 'absolutely imperative' classification include the 'qualifications' and 'experience' of personnel, indicative of the importance attached to the human factor for delivering a high quality service. 'Price', 'size', 'specialisation' and 'recommendations from personal sources' are perceived by ship managers to be very important dimensions that influence considerably the selection process. For the dimensions of 'time in the ship management business', 'range of services on offer', 'location' and 'number of vessels managed' the responses range from very important to less important, and 51 per cent of the respondents view ship ownership as less important or unimportant in the selection process. The least important criterion according to the ship managers is advertising.

On similar lines, the research retrieved the importance of post-performance evaluation criteria from both ship managers and their clients. Table 5.2 shows the distribution of the responses with respect to the evaluation criteria dimensions as perceived by the ship managers themselves. It must be noted that once again the numbers depict the percentage of ship managers classifying a particular dimension in accordance with the scale of importance from 1 to 5.

Although the vast majority of the respondents classifies all dimensions as either 'very important' or 'absolutely imperative', some inferences can be made with regard to the percentage response attached to each dimension. The dimensions of 'responsiveness' and 'trustworthiness' are classified as absolutely imperative by 81 per cent of the ship managers. The fact that ship managers are entrusted with high value assets renders a quick response to problems, complaints and enquiries of the clients imperative. Problem-solving ability, which is inextricably linked with responsiveness, also commands a high percentage in the 'absolutely imperative' scale. The importance of responsiveness and problem-solving ability in post-purchase evaluation in the shipping industry context was also examined and validated by Durvasula, Lysonski and Mehta (2000). The findings also reinforce the results of previous studies that identified the significant value of trust in the ship manager-shipowner relationship (see for example

Panayides and Gray, 1999a; 1999b). As with selection criteria, the dimension of 'technical ability' ranks high on the agenda of ship manager evaluation. Proven technical ability may go a long way towards reinforcing the perception of the client about the quality of the service that he receives. It is also interesting to note that dimensions representing social and psychological attributes, such as trust, integrity and reliability, are perceived to be absolutely imperative by a great majority of the ship managers. It follows that ship managers believe that their performance will not only be judged in terms of their technical competence but also in terms of the social and psychological attributes that they have conveyed and developed, and which are so important in long-term business relationships.

Table 5.2 The importance of evaluation criteria: ship managers' view

Key. 1: Not important; 2: Less important; 3: Important; 4: Very important; 5: Absolutely imperative.

% of respondents with particular response

Dimension	1	2	3	4	5
Problem-solving	-	-	2.0	38.0	60.0
Communication	-	2.0	8.0	66.0	24.0
Staff attitudes	-	-	2.0	49.0	49.0
Flexibility	-	6.0	6.0	43.0	45.0
Technical ability	-	-	2.0	24.0	74.0
Responsiveness	-	-	-	19.0	81.0
Integrity	-	-	6.0	26.0	68.0
Cost-effectiveness	-	-	4.0	43.0	53.0
Reliability	-	-	-	26.0	74.0
Value added	-	2.0	6.0	51.0	41.0
Commitment	-	-	-	47.0	53.0
Trustworthiness	-	-	2.0	17.0	81.0
Accessibility	-	-	2.0	38.0	60.0

Choice Criteria: The Client's View

With respect to clients, qualitative data was obtained from the responses to mail questionnaires and the responses of a chief executive of a major liner shipping company during a relevant conference. The views of the chief executive of the Japanese liner shipping company were particularly incisive. The CEO revealed that the company had used 15 ship managers in the last 12 years, and that at the moment the research was carried out the company was using nine different ship managers. In fact 70, vessels or about 35 per cent of the company's controlled tonnage was under third party ship management. According to the CEO, the critical dimensions as far as his company was concerned included:

- cost competitiveness;
- better asset management;
- good communication;
- flexibility;
- efficiency;
- good understanding of the company's needs.

For the future, the CEO indicated that the manager seeking a competitive advantage should be able to provide 'something of value added' [as he put it].

In addition to the above, a particularly detailed assessment of a number of ship management companies was derived by the author from a client organisation that was considering changing the management of its vessels and was, hence, evaluating its current managers vis-à-vis alternative options. For obvious reasons, the name of the companies will be kept confidential. However, a great deal can be inferred from the criteria that the shipowners themselves practically use in evaluating the performance of their manager and the criteria they employ in choosing another manager.

In choosing a manager, the particular company sent a letter to various candidates identified in advance as potentially able to deliver under the company's remit. The letter invited managers to contribute their ideas about their capabilities in fulfilling the client's requirements. At this stage, the focus was not directed at the budgets of the vessels, but at the methodologies of the individual manager and the systems in place to ensure that eventual budgets did not suffer from cost 'spikes'. This was to ensure that each manager was incident- and risk-averse, illustrating the importance placed on safety in ship manager selection. In addition, the responses of the ship managers were also evaluated in terms of quality and response time. The next stage involved inviting all the ship managers to present their cases in more detail. The short-listed ship managers were then invited to inspect the vessels and refine their prepared budgets. The clients visited the managers' premises for further inspection and evaluation before making an assessment. The above process assisted the clients in 'scoring' each manager under evaluation on a 'management matrix'. This matrix consisted of a table of 15 dimensions/criteria each given a different weighting depending on the significance attached to it by the company. The budgets were then taken into consideration. The budgeting on behalf of the managers needed to be clear and easily understood. The company made it clear that the decision would not be based on the budgets alone and that they were not interested in a manager who cut costs to the bone in order to win the business, only for the ships to suffer rising costs over the ensuing period. The budgets needed to be realistic, and special effort was made to ensure that the managers appreciated this. The criteria indicating the manager's basic qualities that would enable selection by the particular client included:

- organisation and management;
- quality of personnel;
- technical expertise;
- Ro/Ro experience;
- container experience;
- medium speed experience;
- management of the changeover;
- location/convenience;
- flexibility (with the varying size of the fleet);
- IT systems and reporting structure;
- crew management;
- discounts and rebates;
- management fee;
- purchasing;
- claims handling.

Organisation and management refers to the superintendency and the adequacy of the support that is provided to the superintendents. The company recognised that there might be cases where the focus of individual superintendents was placed on a particular ship due to the occurrence of an incident, with the consequence that other ships in the fleet suffered as a result. Focusing on the management structure also highlights any internal politics occurring within the ship management organisation and which could be detrimental to the management of the ships. This is particularly pertinent if it affects the relationships between the superintendent and the purchasing/accounts departments, as a great deal can then be lost in the reporting of incident costs and quarterly running cost variances.

An aspect deemed to be of paramount importance by both ship managers and clients has been the quality of personnel provided by the ship manager. It is imperative that the personnel to be recruited for managing the structure and systems of the ship management organisation are of the highest quality. Special focus is again placed on the quality of superintendent personnel. The manager has to have the ability, presence and appeal to attract high quality individuals. Technical quality is principally related to the quality of the individual superintendents that would be in charge of the vessels. Technical expertise also relates to shore-based individuals who would be able to provide back-up support if so required. For instance, if there is a major incident the manager needs to have the in-house expertise to be able to cope with any given situation.

The specific choice selection criteria of the particular company placed emphasis on the expertise of the ship manager in managing a particular type of specialised vessel. For specialised vessels like Ro/Ro that demand a high level of detailed management, it is recognised that the ship manager should be able to obtain a very high significance rating. This includes the ability to maintain medium speed for these specialised vessels, which requires specific technical in-depth knowledge and experience. Management of the changeover refers to the case when the management of the vessels changes. For a specialised vessel, a greater risk may be associated with such changeover. The process of changing from one manager to another requires great care and detailed planning. In this particular case, each manager evaluated was requested to explain in detail how the process would evolve, the time scale envisaged and how exactly the introduction of the new crews would take place.

Of particular importance seemed to be the location of the manager in relation to the location of the owners of the vessels and the owners' operating departments. Specifically, it was considered of great importance for the manager to be within the owner's time zone in order to ensure direct communication and direct personal interaction. This was considered necessary not least because of the specialised nature of Ro/Ro vessels and the need for direct involvement in the management process from owner and manager. In addition, due to the ownership involvement in the management of the ships and their specialised nature, the location of the manager was considered important. Close proximity between the respective offices of owner and manager was also considered important as it would facilitate regular meetings on various issues such as budgets and owner audits. It must be noted that, in this case, the owner wanted to have direct involvement in the management and close co-operation with the manager, particularly because of the specialised type of vessels to be managed.

The decision to outsource in the first place was the recognition that a professional ship manager would facilitate flexibility in crewing matters that would arise from an increase or decrease in fleet size. Professional ship managers are capable of successfully accomplishing tasks such as crew mobilisation, flag changes and quick arrangement/delivery of certificates. A key criterion for ship manager selection in this particular case was the demonstrable ability of the manager to engage in such tasks swiftly so as to enable the company to engage in asset play without restrictions by incidental ship management concerns. Managers that have the relevant resources and capabilities, such as a pool of human resources and solutions to flagging in and out, are therefore more likely to be approached by clients engaged in asset play. Another requirement with respect to crewing was that the crew should be rotated around the fleet so as to avoid complacency.

The shipowners also stress the importance of information technology (IT) and IT systems in their selection criteria. Information needs should be relayed to the owners accurately and quickly without having to take too much of the superintendents' management time. Ship managers should not just have the management and technological systems for information processing, but need to demonstrate their capability and willingness to update their systems as the systems of their clients develop. Incompatibility between the systems may cause delays and the ship managers should illustrate their ability to cope with the technological and informational demands of their clients.

The ideas put forward by the clients with respect to the management fees, discounts and rebates were particularly insightful. The clients thought that small variations in management fees (up to US$20,000) should have little effect on the overall running cost of the vessels. However, it was believed that management fees represent good value and should be reflected in the ability of the manager to deliver customer satisfaction. In addition, it was generally believed that managers make little profit from the management fee and that they actually make their margins by charging a lump sum and then take advantage of bulk purchasing discounts. Owners may be concerned that discounts and rebates are not fully reflected in the running costs as presented by the managers. Although it is accepted that managers may be able to make a profit from purchasing, the owners may be concerned with the extent to which net prices are shown on the budgets.

The above qualitative assessment exposes the process that clients may employ in evaluating and selecting their professional ship manager. A mail survey that was carried out among clients of professional ship management companies revealed the importance attached to various criteria in selection and evaluation by the clients themselves. The results of this survey are shown in Tables 5.3 and 5.4 below.

Table 5.3 The importance of selection criteria: clients' view

Key. 1: Not important; 2: Less important; 3: Important; 4: Very important; 5: Absolutely imperative

% of respondents with particular response

Dimension	1	2	3	4	5
Price	3.0	14.0	19.0	45.0	19.0
Size	3.0	30.0	39.0	28.0	-
Advertising	25.0	50.0	14.0	8.0	3.0
Reputation	-	-	6.0	55.0	39.0
Recommendation	3.0	11.0	11.0	50.0	25.0
Technical ability	-	3.0	-	25.0	72.0
Experience	-	-	-	45.0	55.0
Qualifications	-	-	3.0	50.0	47.0
Time	-	17.0	25.0	50.0	8.0
Service range	6.0	36.0	22.0	30.0	6.0
Location	6.0	33.0	22.0	36.0	3.0
Specialisation	-	-	14.0	58.0	28.0
Large managed fleet	-	28.0	33.0	36.0	3.0
Owns vessels	22.0	39.0	14.0	22.0	3.0

A number of significant inferences can be made from the results depicted in Table 5.3 and particularly with a comparison of these values and those illustrating the ship managers' views shown in Table 5.1. The highest ranked dimension from the shipowners' perspective is that of the 'technical ability' of the personnel of the ship management company. This dimension, together with the 'experience' and 'qualifications' of personnel, which are also regarded as 'absolutely imperative' by most of the clients, indicates the importance attached to the human factor and clearly illustrates the requirement for a service of high quality.

Table 5.4 The importance of evaluation criteria: clients' view

Key. 1: Not important; 2: Less important; 3: Important; 4: Very important; 5: Absolutely imperative

% of respondents with particular response

Dimension	1	2	3	4	5
Problem-solving	-	-	3.0	44.0	53.0
Communication frequency	-	3.0	28.0	47.0	22.0
Staff attitudes	-	3.0	11.0	47.0	39.0
Flexibility	-	-	-	58.0	42.0
Technical ability	-	-	3.0	42.0	55.0
Responsiveness	-	-	8.0	25.0	67.0
Integrity	-	-	6.0	42.0	52.0
Cost-effectiveness	-	3.0	3.0	44.0	50.0
Reliability	-	-	3.0	39.0	58.0
Value added	-	6.0	22.0	55.0	17.0
Commitment	-	-	11.0	53.0	36.0
Trustworthiness	-	-	-	33.0	67.0
Accessibility	-	3.0	14.0	50.0	33.0

As opposed to the ship managers' view, 39 per cent of the clients think that 'reputation' is 'absolutely imperative' (compared to 72 per cent of ship managers) and 19 per cent think that about 'price' (compared to 34 per cent of the ship managers). Although reputation is classified as 'very important' by the clients, a significant number (36 per cent) classify 'price' as 'important', 'less important' or 'not important'. This is a noteworthy finding that once again supports/underlines the view that ship managers should not regard the 'price' variable as a critical component in their quest for client attraction and retention. Another difference in the views of ship managers and their clients is that clients do not seem to regard the 'size' of the ship management company as such an important criterion for selection as ship managers do. From there on, the views are comparable, with the clients agreeing with the ship managers that 'advertising' plays the least important role in the selection process.

Although clients may not view some dimensions as 'absolutely imperative' in evaluation to the extent ship managers themselves do, the specific dimensions commanding a high rank on the evaluation scale are the same for both ship managers and owners. Hence, as with the ship managers, the dimensions of 'responsiveness' and 'trustworthiness' are perceived to be 'absolutely imperative' by a great majority of clients. In line with the previous findings, 'technical ability' 'reliability', 'integrity' and 'problem-solving' ability are also ranked higher in terms of importance than the rest of the dimensions.

A Process Model for Decision, Selection and Evaluation

The purchase of professional ship management services is a process, commencing with the decision to outsource ship management, the selection and pre-purchase evaluation of the ship manager and post-purchase performance evaluation. It is important to have an understanding of the whole decision process in order to better evaluate the needs and wants of clients and to pursue their fulfilment.

Problem Recognition

The decision of whether to outsource ship management to third parties or choose a different form of organisational arrangement for the management of ships has been discussed in chapter 2 and need not be reiterated. In basic terms, a company will decide to outsource if it perceives that the benefits of such a move on a number of different dimensions will exceed the costs and the benefits to be derived from an alternative arrangement. Typically, companies will employ ship managers on the recognition of specific problems among the following dimensions:

- cost-effectiveness;
- human resource sourcing and management;
- flagging out options and solutions;
- the nature of the problem/need for special skills;
- the lack of special resources;

- legal/regulatory pressures.

Search Process

The method for identifying a suitable ship management company that will satisfy a client's requirements is the second stage in the process model. The search process seems to rely on the prior experience and knowledge of the different managers, as well as their perceived reputation on specific aspects and recommendations from personal sources. Advertising plays little role in the search process and is merely a medium for establishing name recognition rather than reinforcing perceived images. Perceived images can be strongly reinforced through personal recommendations, which is a source of information upon which shipowners may rely during the search process. This is in line with previous studies showing that decision-makers rely heavily on information sources with high expertise and credibility and with low or no intention to influence (Hansen, 1972). Personal sources of information meet these criteria and therefore should be rated high by the decision-maker involved in the purchase of services (Stock and Zinszer, 1987). A number of studies have found that buyers consider personal sources of information important to the industrial purchaser (Kotler and Conner, 1977; Martilla, 1971; Webster, 1970). This is also the case in ship management, as depicted by the empirical results of the study reported in this chapter. In the case of ship management, the search process will be used to derive a shortlist of potential candidates from the information already at hand, and the perception/experience of the people in the company about the ship manager. The short-listed ship managers will then be contacted and the choice/pre-purchase evaluation process will begin. The search process may be complex because of the diverse information about all the potential candidates. A structured and organised approach for collecting and evaluating data is therefore required. Prudent shipowners will undertake a more specific pre-purchase evaluation process before deciding on the preferred candidate.

Choice/Pre-Purchase Evaluation Process

The pre-purchase evaluation/choice process for professional ship managers will involve the rating of alternative ship managers on a number of dimensions. These dimensions will include both general dimensions about the ship managers' ability, service quality and price, and more specific dimensions that are perceived by shipowners to be important for their individual requirements.

The empirical study undertaken in the context of identifying and rating the importance of ship manager selection and evaluation provided some important insights into the perceptions of both shipowners and ship managers with respect to these dimensions. The dimensions retrieved have been discussed in the previous section of this chapter and can also be seen in Table 5.5 below. The table illustrates the mean of the responses, indicating the importance of the dimensions as perceived by both ship managers and shipowners. Means closer to one are not as important, whereas those closer to five are perceived to be absolutely imperative for choosing a particular ship manager.

A readily distinguishable outcome of the responses is that the dimension of price does not seem to be absolutely imperative in the selection of a professional ship manager. This is true for both ship managers and shipowners, and it was also revealed through the telephone interviews. It is interesting to note that the price dimension is perceived to be of less importance by the clients when compared to the ship managers' perception. Although price is a very important dimension, it has not been rated as high as other dimensions in the choice criteria for ship managers, both by ship managers and their clients. In fact, it seems that good service in terms of technical and managerial capabilities is more important than low price alone in choosing ship management services. This finding supports to a great extent the findings of previous studies in various professional service industries. For instance, Banville and Dornoff (1973) found that good service was rated significantly higher than quality of product, low price, location of supplier and the availability of credit in the purchase of major building products. Dempsey (1978) supported this in a study of purchasing managers in two industries: electronic manufacturing and electric utilities. This study has found that price was consistently rated below (based on mean importance ratings) delivery capability and quality in the purchase of capital equipment and component materials.

Table 5.5 Means of importance of selection criteria

Key. 1: Not important – 5: Absolutely imperative

Dimension	Mean	
	Ship Manager n=48	Client n=36
Price	4.19	3.64
Size	3.51	2.92
Advertising	2.00	2.14
Reputation	4.70	4.33
Recommendation	4.28	3.83
Technical ability	4.66	4.67
Experience	4.55	4.56
Qualifications	4.17	4.42
Time in business	3.47	3.50
Service range	3.19	2.94
Location	3.15	2.97
Specialisation	4.23	4.15
Large managed fleet	3.32	3.14
Owns vessels	2.55	2.44

The superior importance of service characteristics to price have also been supported in the case of transportation services, where Jerman, Anderson and Constantin (1978) found that factors like reliability, product availability and service location were consistently rated higher than cost (price) by the buyers of transportation services.

It has been recognised that in the context of technical professional services, price may not be the most important variable in the customer's assessment of value. Wilson (1972) noted that 'the greater the innovation, the further into the value-sensitive area the decision is moved, and the less is the importance of price (p. 140). Value is defined in the pricing literature as the trade-off between customers' perceptions of benefits received and sacrifices incurred (e.g. Leszinski and Marn, 1997). Monroe (1990) and Gale (1994) cited quality as the customers' primary benefit, whereas price is a crucial component of the sacrifice incurred. To the extent that other benefits or components of 'value' as perceived by the client are increased, then price becomes a less crucial aspect in the ship management selection decision.

Other authors have found that past experience was the single most important criterion in the selection process (Cunningham and White, 1973; Wilson, 1972). For instance, Cunningham and White (1973) found that 'the strongest determinant of a buyer's patronage decision is his past experience which is consistent with the...finding that many buyers do not search the market for available alternatives' (1973, p. 201). This may also be true in the case of ship management, where it was revealed by shipowners that past experience or recommendations from personal sources that may be viewed as a substitute of past experience are important criteria in the selection of a ship manager. The dimension of reputation also seems to play an important role in the selection of ship management firms. This was revealed during the interviews and has been supported through the case examined earlier, where the process by which a shipowning company chose its manager was considered. In the original shortlist prepared, there were 14 ship management companies including the existing ship managers. The key reasons for approaching the particular managers, as stated by the prospective client, included the following:

- large, well recognised manager;
- good experience of Ro/Ro operation;
- very large experience of container ships;
- large manager with excellent record;
- alternative manning options;
- long established, experienced;
- extensive experience of ferry operation;
- high quality crew manager;
- existing managers;
- managers of container ships of the company.

It can easily be deduced that considerable weight is placed on the ship manager's experience, establishment and status, i.e. the reputation that the ship manager has accumulated over the years. Lehmann and O'Shaughnessy (1974) suggest that reputation is very important in the selection and evaluation of vendors due to the desire of the decision-makers to reduce risks to their companies and themselves by selecting suppliers with good reputations and high credibility. In ship management, past experience, particularly with the specific ship types that the client requires, is highly important and can become a decisive factor in the choice process. Experience is coupled with the technical ability of personnel, which is deemed to be of great importance by both ship managers and their clients.

This is also reflected by the fact that 74 per cent of the ship managers and 72 per cent of the clients responding to the questionnaire deem technical ability to be absolutely imperative in the ship management selection process.

Post-Purchase Evaluation Process

The complexity of ship operation and ship management services, coupled with the highly intangible nature of the ship management service offering, makes post-purchase performance evaluation difficult to assess and quantify. The perception of the customer with respect to the value and quality of service received is subjective and multi-dimensional. It would be beneficial for the company to develop a series of measures by which the performance of the company with respect to service delivery to customers can be evaluated before and after the purchase. The measures that can be used to evaluate post-purchase ship management service quality and expectations matching have been revealed by this study and can be seen from Table 5.6. The measures were retrieved through interview brainstorming sessions with ship managers and their clients. Table 5.6 shows the mean importance attached to these measures as perceived by both managers and owners. Means closer to one are not as important, whereas those closer to five are perceived to be absolutely imperative in the evaluation of a particular ship manager.

It can be seen from Table 5.6 that high scores have been attached to most dimensions. A question which arises from the results is the extent to which all the criteria specified by the respondents as very important to absolutely imperative are actually utilised in evaluating ship manager performance. As suggested by Aaker and Day (1980), just because an attribute is judged as important does not necessarily mean that it is determinant of the issue. To overcome this problem of importance rating scales, the scale used ranged from 'not important' to 'absolutely imperative'. It may be logically deduced that those dimensions receiving a high score on the 'absolutely imperative' rank may be considered determinant, whereas the salience of the other dimensions may be less. In addition, the research sought qualitative information of the evaluation process. It must be noted that for most clients there has been no specific mention of a formal procedure for evaluating the ship manager's performance, despite being asked directly about this issue in the mail survey.

Table 5.6 Means of importance of evaluation criteria

Dimension	Mean	
	Ship Manager n=48	Client n=36
Problem-solving	4.57	4.50
Communication	4.11	3.89
Staff attitudes	4.47	4.22
Flexibility	4.26	4.42
Technical ability	4.72	4.50
Responsiveness	4.81	4.58
Integrity	4.62	4.47
Cost-effectiveness	4.49	4.42
Reliability	4.74	4.56
Value added	4.30	3.83
Commitment	4.53	4.25
Trust	4.79	4.67
Accessibility	4.55	4.14

Many decision-makers use some form of evaluation of the ship manager's performance, although the methods can be formal and informal, and different dimensions may be used with varying importance as illustrated in the table above. Half of the 16 clients that answered a relevant question in the mail survey indicated that their company does not have any formal procedures for evaluating their ship manager. The responses of the rest of the clients varied, indicative of the variation in performance evaluation approaches. One client indicated that the ISM guidelines are largely utilised for ship manager evaluation. Others mentioned the conduct of periodical inspections of the condition of their vessels and a review of such aspects as manning, office organisation, quality and ability of superintendents, safety and accident/incident rates. Clients also indicated the requirement for submission of reports at regular intervals, detailing costs and budgets. One client indicated the conduct of detailed benchmarking of similar vessels run by different managers.

The results of the study indicate that selection and evaluation of a particular ship management company may be largely based on an assessment of value. This value is a measure of several dimensions of varying importance. In line with previous research studies (see Holmlund and Kock, 1995; Lapierre, 1997; Ravald and Gronroos, 1996), this research reveals that value in a professional ship management context is made up of two levels. The first level is a measure of technical quality (technical expertise, problem-solving ability, qualifications, experience), functional quality (reliability, responsiveness, integrity), relational quality (trustworthiness, commitment, communication), and operational quality (technology, systems) and image (reputation, recommendation, past experience). The second level consists of financial variables (cost-effectiveness, revenue, profitability), strategic variables (location, managerial ability).

The results of this research suggest that a process model for decision, choice and evaluation may be represented as in Figure 5.1.

Figure 5.1 A process model for decision, choice and evaluation

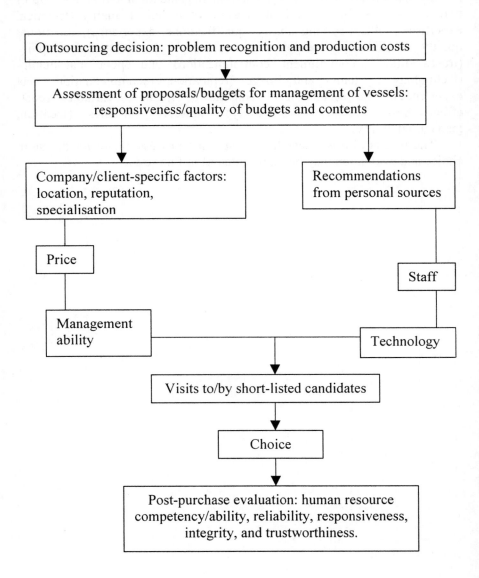

6 Competitive Advantage in Ship Management

Introduction

Ship management companies operate in an environment of intense competition. Competition has actually been viewed by economists as socially desirable because it can lead to greater allocational and operating efficiency. Given the competitive domain of ship management activities, one of the most important challenges for ship management organisations is their ability to achieve a sustainable competitive advantage. This chapter aims to discuss contemporary economic and industrial organisation thought on competition and competitive advantage, and to apply the underlying principles in the context of professional ship management at a conceptual level. The envisaged outcomes include a better understanding of competitive conduct in ship management, and implications for strategy formulation regarding the achievement of a sustainable competitive advantage.

Competition in Ship Management

The concept of competition is of utmost importance in all walks of life, and even more in a business environment such as the one within which ship management companies operate. Competition has a significant impact on the way ship management companies are structured and function. Competition requires companies to make quick responses and adaptations to rival competitive strategies. It requires companies to be proactive in their approach and make innovative moves that will yield an edge over rivals. It also requires companies to improve efficiency and productivity in operations.

Competition is often equated with competition for new business and market share. In fact, competition is a multi-dimensional concept. It can range from price, promotional and product competition to competition in distribution channels, in after-sales service and for greater market share. The latter may be regarded as the most intense form of competition in the ship management context. Ship managers, however, often compete in promotional efforts and in improving service quality.

Competition for business and the securing of contracts is nowadays very intense among ship management companies. Various examples are indicative of the fierce competition that has been intensifying in ship management throughout the 1990s. For instance, in 1995, leading ship management companies were involved in a fierce battle for a lucrative contract to manage six new containerships of American President Lines (Anon, 1995q). Another example is the award of a prestigious crewing contract, after intense competition, to Hanseatic Shipping Co., by the containership operator Sea-Land (Richardson, 1995c). Competition for the acquisition of other companies has also been evidenced in the ship management market (Anon, 1997g).

The intensity of the competition can be assessed by consideration of the determinants of competitive conduct proposed by Phillips (1962), who discussed a number of factors that determine competition among firms. These factors can be applied to ship management companies.

First, competition varies in intensity with the number of rival organisations. Panayides and Gray (1997a) indicate that the number of ship management companies increased from 226 in 1990 to 614 in 1997. As indicated in chapter 2, this number is much higher today and according to some sources may be nearer the 1,000 mark. This remarkable growth is a clear indication of the intensity of rivalry in the ship management sector. Osler (1996) reports that the closure of a UK-based ship management company can be attributed to the crowded nature of the ship management market.

Second, competition varies with the degree of equality in the size of rivals. Ship management is an open market and is not characterised by the dominance of one or a few firms, but rather by the co-existence of many large, medium and small enterprises. Roughly equal market shares would tend to induce greater rivalry than a situation where one or a few organisations dominate a market (Khandwalla, 1981). In the case of ship management, there seems to exist competition among different layers of companies and also between those layers. For instance, companies with roughly equal share (small, medium and large) will compete fiercely for limited resources. In addition, there exists evidence to indicate that smaller companies may poach clients from larger organisations, especially where clients may recognise potential advantages in selecting a smaller organisation.

Barriers to entry are another factor affecting competition. The ship management market is extremely open, due to the relatively low risk involved in setting up a ship management company and the relatively low initial capital investment required. Hence, the low level of barriers to entry indicates a greater degree of rivalry. The formation of new ship management companies and the undertaking of contracts by them is frequently reported in the trade press (e.g. Richardson, 1995d). A key task for the management of established ship management firms is to raise the level at which firms compete, thus erecting entry barriers as a means of coping with the increasingly intensifying rivalry.

Rivalry also varies with the degree of formality of interfirm organisation in the industry. Formality can range from legal cartels (e.g. some shipping conferences) to legally unenforceable gentlemen's agreements. Research carried out indicates that gentlemen's agreements do exist in certain sectors of the ship management fraternity. However, it has been revealed that collusion and poaching clients from competitors is also present. The loss by Wallem Ship Management of a major contract involving the management of four ULCC/VLCC tankers to Ugland/Interocean may illustrate such an example (Richardson, 1995e). Another example could be the award of a major contract to Acomarit (UK) by the National Shipping Company of Saudi Arabia, who transferred vessels that used to be managed by Northern Marine Management, Storli and Denholm Ship Management (Bray, 1996; Thorpe, 1996). Willingale (1992) stated that in many cases any new business coming on to the third party ship management market is competed for fiercely, and efforts to win existing customers away from competitors have intensified. Although made in 1992, this statement was justified throughout the 1990s and also holds today.

Khandwalla (1981) also suggests that rivalry varies directly with the sophistication of an industry's clientele. If an industry's clients are sophisticated and able to evaluate the claims of the rival sellers, as is the case in ship management, the sellers will have to compete harder. In the ship management business it has been getting increasingly difficult to get business, and more often than not there is a fight over new tonnage.

The Competitive Structure of the Ship Management Market

The quest to understand how firms can be successful and achieve a competitive advantage can be traced back to the early theory of strategy, where it was advocated that firms should enter industries that are 'attractive'. The measures of 'attractiveness' suggested were based on growth and past profitability. These initial considerations of strategy and competitive advantage gave rise to increased emphasis on 'industry forces' and their impact on competitiveness (Porter, 1980).

In his analysis of the competitive forces within a given industry, Porter (1985) suggested that five such forces are key determinants of the ability of firms to earn, on average, rates of return on investment in excess of the cost of capital. The five competitive forces include:

- the entry of new competitors;
- the threat of substitutes;
- the bargaining power of buyers;
- the bargaining power of suppliers;
- the rivalry among the existing competitors.

This framework seems to place increased emphasis on the structure of an industry as a determinant of firm profitability. It is also suggested that, although the five forces may not be equally important for different industries, their overall and relative strength can positively or negatively influence profitability. In addition, it is thought that firms, through strategy formulation, can influence the five forces and can therefore fundamentally change an industry's attractiveness positively or negatively.

The conceptual application of the proposed model in a ship management context can be beneficial for understanding the competitive structure of the market. In ship management, the threat of new entrants can be said to be quite high. As discussed above, barriers to entry are relatively low. Smaller companies are more likely to suffer from this as larger companies are already established, have wide client bases and good reputations and can already achieve economies of scale. Nevertheless, there have been instances in the past where large ship management companies lost business in the form of current clients to smaller new entrants.

Apart from barriers to entry, the other force that seems to be of significant importance in ship management is the bargaining power of the clients (buyers). The major determinants of buyer power that would apply to ship management include buyer volume, buyer switching costs, buyer information, ability of the buyer to integrate backwards, and price sensitivity. Buyer volume can have an influence on the bargaining power of clients over their ship manager. Large clients that have a greater number of ships under a particular ship manager can exert considerable influence. The well-established theoretical underpinnings of power-dependence relations, as succinctly depicted by Yuchtman and Seashore (1967) and Pfeffer and Salancik (1978), justify this assertion. This may be exacerbated by the fact that switching costs for the clients are relatively low. It is not unknown for a single large shipping corporation to be using more than one ship manager at the same time, sometimes maybe up to five ship managers or more. If demands are not satisfied it will not cost the client a great deal to transfer new contracts to another of the existing ship managers. The fact that information about other ship managers in the market is freely available and easily accessible and companies may co-operate with ship managers and have first-hand information about their performance contributes to such a development.

In addition, clients also have an ability to integrate backwards when circumstances are right. Hence, it has not been uncommon in recent years for oil major companies in particular to withdraw from third party ship management or limit their involvement by setting up their own in-house ship management department. This propensity of certain types of clients to move back to in-house management may have been aided by advances in technology that facilitate ship operation and the wider availability and accessibility of specialised supplier companies that companies can deal with directly. There is also the availability of experienced staff in the market to undertake such in-house tasks. The question which a company needs to ask in deciding between in-house, third party or even a combination of the two, is how ship management for the company can be co-ordinated more efficiently. This means co-ordination of the resources for the sustenance of the ship as a revenue-earning entity at a lower cost but without compromising safety and quality. It is also true to assert that, all other things being equal, the clients of ship management companies are price-sensitive. Price sensitivity combined with information availability and readily available substitutes such as competitors or the possibility of moving in-house are strong determinants of the bargaining power of clients and represent a significant element of the competitive structure of the ship management industry.

Suppliers of ship management companies cannot be viewed as a competitive threat the same way buyers can. They may, however, have a significant impact on other issues that may determine the competitiveness of ship management firms. Suppliers of manpower, for instance, need to be efficient and effective in serving the needs of ship management companies. As on-board manpower mainly comes from developing countries, suppliers in these countries may not be able to fully satisfy the demands of ship management companies. As a result ship management companies may co-operate in joint ventures with suppliers and invest in effective training and efficient selection of manpower. Hence, although a different power-dependence relationship in this case, it is still critical for professional ship managers to have good relationships with suppliers in their efforts to deliver a high quality ship management service.

Strategies for Competitive Advantage

There have been a number of approaches developed in the literature and applied in practice for the achievement of competitive advantage. It may be beneficial to review the various approaches that have been applied in the strategy formulation of companies in many industries as a means for assessing their potential applicability in a ship management context. In addition, such a conceptual application may go some way towards highlighting issues that may be of importance to practising strategists in ship management companies and provide a firm foundation for further research. The various approaches advocated include budgetary planning and control (Steiner, 1969), diversification and portfolio planning (Boston Consulting Group, 1970), competitor analysis and relative competitive advantage (Ohmae, 1982; Porter, 1980), the resource-based view of the firm (Barney, 1991; Wernerflet, 1984), core competencies (Prahalad and Hamel, 1990) and the quest to understand industry-specific competitive characteristics (D'Aveni, 1994).

Portfolio Planning

The portfolio planning approach reflected in BCG's Growth Share Matrix distinguishes product lines on two dimensions: the growth of the market in which the product is situated, and the product's market share relative to the share of its next largest competitors. The matrix's primary focus is on the current status of a company's product portfolio relative to its main competitors (Hedley, 1977). Depending on their position in the matrix, products warrant different strategies. Hence, products in the high growth-high market share segment require further investment. Products with high growth potential in low market share segments should be divested or supported for increasing market share. Products with low growth potential but high in terms of market share should be harvested, and strategies for maintaining the market share should be pursued. Finally, products in low growth-low market share segments should be divested or liquidated. The international scope of professional ship management, coupled with the wide range of services on offer, provides ample opportunity for service portfolio classification and the formulation of strategy based on the outcomes.

Ohmae's Four Basic Routes

Ohmae's Four Basic Routes to Strategic Advantage (Ohmae, 1982) capture competitor analysis and competitive advantage approaches. This model emphasises a firm's market position relative to its competitors by arguing that a good business strategy should enable a company to gain significant ground on its competitors at an acceptable cost to itself. The model offers four basic routes to competitive advantage, viz.:

- strategic degrees of freedom;
- key success factors;
- aggressive initiatives;
- relative superiority.

The first route advocates identification of the critical axes or degrees on which a strategy can be worked out. For instance, taking into account the objective pursued by the firm (e.g. profit maximisation), the task is to develop strategies to achieve the objective through the deployment of innovations in new markets or in new products while avoiding direct competition. For instance, in ship management at least two degrees can be identified: improvements to the service delivery system and improvements to the perceived quality of the product. To the extent that such improvements can be effected in new services and/or in new markets, then this strategy will lead to competitive advantage. The second strategy involves thoroughly dissecting the industry to identify key factors of success or studying winners and losers to determine distinguishing characteristics. Once again, identification and emphasis on such factors in a ship management context can lead to competitive advantage. Aggressive initiatives are implemented when the company can no longer expect improvement based solely on cost and operations efficiencies. In ship management, this implies anticipation of changes with regard to how the industry operates, and re-conceptualisation of company structure and the processes of service delivery. Innovation of this kind may lead to differentiation and achievement of advantage. Relative superiority strategies require a systematic comparative analysis of a firm's products with those offered by competitors. Relative advantages should not be easy to imitate by competitors and can lead to competitive advantage. This may be particularly applicable to smaller ship management companies that may not be able to compete with their larger counterparts in terms of price but can have relative superiority on the delivery of a personalised service offering.

Hamel and Prahalad's Core Competency Agenda Matrix

Hamel and Prahalad's (1989) model captures the internal resources and core competencies approach. The development and acquisition of core competencies is seen as critical to a company's long-term survival. The nature and characteristics of competencies that are critical for competitive advantage are discussed later in this chapter. The focus of the Core Competency Agenda Matrix is on obtaining new resources and combining or reconfiguring them with resources the organisation already possesses (McGrath, MacMillan and Venkataraman, 1995). The model offers four alternative strategies for developing and allocating core competencies, viz.:

- mega opportunities;
- white spaces;
- premier plus ten;
- fill in the blanks.

Mega opportunities involve the development of new core competencies for new markets. This can be achieved through joint ventures and strategic partnerships or the acquisition of companies already possessing the desired competencies. This is a strategy particularly applicable to ship management. It has been employed in the past through strategic partnerships with manning agencies for instance, but it has wider appeal in terms of acquiring competencies in information technology. The information technology sector may offer desirable opportunities for ship management companies, but it also entails undertaking significantly high risks. Through a strategic partnership, the opportunities may be tapped whilst risk is minimised owing to the competencies possessed by the partner. White spaces refer to the deployment of existing core competencies in new markets. With the range of competencies and skills developed by ship management companies in the process of managing ships, opportunities might arise for deploying such skills to other situations (e.g. the establishment of a shipowning company). For example, the competency in the management of containerships developed by the Schoeller Group and one of its companies, Columbia Shipmanagement, in particular, may have contributed to the establishment of Columbia Container Shipping Ltd. The company's business has been specified as the ownership and operation of feeder container vessels. The company would have not recognised the opportunities presented in the feeder container market and would have not gone ahead with the initial purchase and operation of ten vessels, had it not possessed core competencies in most aspects related to the operation and trading of such ships within the group. Premier plus ten strategies involve the development of new core competencies to be deployed in existing markets. For instance, expansion of the original service offering to current clients involves the development of such competencies. The last strategy involves using existing core competencies to support current markets. This may be essential when aiming to strengthen the position in particular markets the company is operating in and importing competencies residing elsewhere in the company or group.

D'Aveni's Hypercompetition Model

D'Aveni (1995) developed the hypercompetition model in response to the increasingly turbulent competitive environment in which firms find themselves today. This environment is characterised by the rapid erosion of competitive advantages (Williams, 1992), established rules of competition (D'Aveni, 1995), industry barriers to entry and customer loyalty (D'Aveni, 1994). It is argued that such an environment requires greater comprehension of four competitive arenas of specific industries, viz.:

- cost and quality;
- timing and know-how;
- strongholds;
- deep pockets.

In the first arena, firms differentiate themselves on the basis of price and quality. Hence, differences in quality are reflected by differences in the price of the service. If quality is not differentiated then price wars will result as this will become the major point of competition. Escalating hypercompetition tends to drive costs down and quality up. Ship management companies are able to differentiate themselves on the basis of quality, although this is increasingly becoming more difficult owing to the imitation among competitors. However, both client relationships and client evaluation criteria discussed in the previous chapters can be critical in achieving differentiation and being able to maintain a stable price level. This leads to the second strategy, which involves moving to another new level of quality that cannot be easily imitated or improved upon by competitors. Many innovations currently taking place in the ship management market can be imitated by competitors. Even companies that try to achieve first mover advantages and make substantial investments may not be assured of sustainability in their leapfrog innovations. The third arena involves the creation of strategic strongholds that are insulated from competitive attacks. This may involve strongholds in geographic markets or service segments, although it is extremely doubtful that such a strategy can be practised in a ship management context and provide sustainable competitive advantage. Lastly, deep pockets strategies involve larger, financially strong companies that can engage in sustained attacks on smaller competitors. Financial resources do play a role in the ability of a company to maintain competitiveness, and a lack of them may lead companies to termination of their existence. However, despite the expectations of smaller ship managers going to the wall throughout the 1990s, such an event has not occurred to date, particularly on the scale evidenced in other industries.

Michael Porter's Generic Strategies

One of the traditional approaches for the achievement of a sustainable competitive advantage is Michael Porter's classification of the three generic strategies for strategic positioning (Porter, 1980; 1985). The three generic strategies for achieving above-average performance in an industry that can lead to a sustained competitive advantage as advocated by Porter include cost leadership, differentiation and focus. Sletmo and Holste (1993) also suggest the use of such strategies for achieving a competitive advantage in the shipping industry context.

Porter (1980; 1985) explained differential performance among competitors as a function of the ability of each firm to harness the so-called 'drivers of competitive advantage' in a specific industry. Harnessing these drivers would place the firm in a more advantageous position relative to 'industry forces' compared with rivals. For example, if responsiveness and reliability in service provision are critical drivers of differentiation advantage in ship management, those firms who can offer such services will be positioned to make higher profits than competitors who offer lower reliability/responsiveness in their service delivery. Porter has classified the drivers of competitive advantage into asset stocks, cost drivers and uniqueness drivers. Asset stocks that may be perceived to be of importance in a ship management context include:

- firm's reputation;
- R&D capability;
- technological know-how;
- relationships with suppliers;
- customer loyalty;
- market knowledge;
- human capital (managerial skill and employee competence);
- information technology systems;
- relationships with government/regulators.

Similarly, cost drivers relevant to the ship management industry include:

- economies of scale;
- vertical linkages and value chain linkages;
- level of vertical integration;
- interrelationships with other business units;
- first mover versus follower advantages;
- service performance;
- mix and variety of services offered;
- level of service provided;
- spending on marketing and R&D;
- human resource policies.

Uniqueness drivers are similar to cost drivers, with emphasis on achieving high service quality where applicable.

The first generic strategy of cost leadership entails the achievement of a cost advantage relative to competitors. The firm sets out to become the low-cost producer in the industry. This means that the company should be able to achieve lower costs if it is going to set prices at levels below those offered by the competition or near the industry average. A ship management company must be able to achieve a reduction in its own costs in producing the ship management service, if it is to pursue such a strategy. Relocation of headquarters, consolidation and a drive for greater efficiency by adopting new technologies have been the principal means by which companies try to manage costs. If a firm can achieve and sustain overall cost leadership, then it will be an above-average performer in its industry provided it can command prices at or near the industry average. A problem arises with the fact that ship management fees are relatively low. It follows that the price variable alone cannot ultimately be used for the achievement of a sustainable competitive advantage in ship management. In addition, as empirically determined in chapter 5, a low price is not widely regarded as absolutely imperative in selecting a professional ship manager, particularly when other credentials such as service quality, technical ability and reputation lag behind. Two important points should also be noted. A cost leader must achieve parity or proximity to the differentiation bases of the competitors. In addition, a firm must be the cost leader and not just one of several firms trying to achieve this status. Only in this way can a company achieve a competitive advantage in accordance with what is suggested by this strategy.

Differentiation entails the offering of the service, which is perceived to be unique by buyers in some dimensions when compared to that of competitors. This uniqueness should enable the firm to offer the service at a premium price. It is questionable to what extent such a strategy may be successful in a ship management context. Firstly, being a professional service, it is difficult for professional ship managers to differentiate their service and provide hard evidence of that differentiation or uniqueness. In addition, the unique dimensions should be extremely important and critical to the ship management service offer, otherwise buyers will not be prepared to pay a premium price for it. Strategies of differentiation are also quickly copied by competitors in the ship management market. Of course, companies may be able to achieve a first mover advantage if they manage to differentiate themselves by being first to introduce a new service, use a new process or enter a new market. Order of entry into a market and market share are believed to be causally related (Urban and Star, 1991). An important aspect of the differentiation strategy is that it can be achieved not only by concentrating on the core elements that make up the service, but also through the delivery system, the marketing approach adopted, relationships and communication with clients and a broad range of other factors.

The third generic strategy is focus or specialisation. The underlying principle in this case is that the firm chooses a target group, segment, or group of segments within an industry, upon which it tailors its strategy in satisfying their needs alone. The firm aims to achieve a competitive advantage in the target segments without necessarily having a competitive advantage overall. The firm can achieve above average performance through either cost leadership (cost focus) or differentiation (differentiation focus). Although cost focus may not be a viable strategy as far as ship management is concerned, there seems to be scope for achieving focus on the basis of differentiation. Smaller companies in particular may be better off specialising in serving the needs of particular segments of clients. The basis for segmentation may vary, with the most obvious one being specialisation in the operation of particular ship types, particularly specialised vessels. The fact that companies may be smaller provides a measure of differentiation in itself, as the smaller company may be able to offer a more personalised service, something that may be more difficult for the largest companies. In reality, few ship management companies actually pursue the generic strategy of concentrating on special niches. The requirement of making substantial investments into specialised facilities may render specialisation a high-risk strategy, which may result in limited returns and may also not be available to a great number of ship management companies.

Until now, the ship management industry has been continually expanding in terms of a greater number of companies the introduction of new services, the diversification of companies into other services (related and unrelated to shipping), and investments in ship ownership. Expansion has been assisted by the continuous supply of new clients (although different types of clients, i.e. oil majors, investors, banks, traditional shipowners). Ship management has been extremely successful on the basis of cost reduction and the achievement of economies of scale. Cost reduction was the driving force for shipping companies in the late 1970s and 80s. Ship management thrived because managers could reduce costs for shipowners by offering advice on flagging-out strategies, recruiting seafarers from less developed countries, and re-location. Additionally, by providing similar services and systems for a large number of vessels, ship management firms were able to create markets large enough to obtain greatly reduced average costs (Sletmo, 1986). These cost savings were passed on to the clients.

Nowadays, however, the increasing regulation in shipping puts more pressure on ship managers to maintain higher standards. Hence, flagging-out and crews from less developed countries become less effective options unless investments are made into training competent crews. In addition, the recent successful policies of traditional maritime nations in their quest to retain, regain and expand ship registration under their flag may set a trend that might have an impact on flagging-out, if other countries follow their example. For instance, the Dutch model as expounded in The Dutch Maritime Network's inventory/cluster approach and the recent policies of the UK government obtained favourable responses from shipowners. The advancement of technology indicates that the future trend is towards the requirement for greater efficiency and productivity rather than the short-term measure of cost reduction (without wishing to suggest the abandonment of strategies to achieve the latter). Client involvement and specialisation may achieve greater efficiency.

It has been evident in recent years that clients themselves have become choosier and more demanding. Client satisfaction rests on building expertise and specialisation rather than contributing towards cost reduction alone. Specialisation will enable ship management companies to acquire expertise on the management of certain vessel types and easier adaptation to the clients' requirements. Specialisation can be achieved in a variety of ways. It was suggested earlier that smaller companies may concentrate on offering a limited number of services or services for certain ship types, hence satisfying the requirements of specific market segments. This will assist in the development of client relationships by building on service personalisation and service competence. For larger companies, specialisation can be achieved through the development of specialised departments that will deal with important clients, i.e. clients placing a large number of vessels with the company. Only one of the largest ship management companies is currently adopting such an approach (Anon, 1996i). In this company, the actual ship management work is done by so-called 'management cells' responsible for about 12 ships each and consisting of three superintendent engineers, two ship operators and one group assistant. The management cells receive support from the accounting, personnel and general administration departments.

The Sustainability of Competitive Advantage

To achieve a competitive advantage in the shipping/ship management context, Sletmo and Holste (1993) suggest pursuance of the three generic strategies of absolute cost advantage, differentiation and specific adaptation to customer needs. Such strategies may be necessary but not necessarily sufficient for achieving a sustainable competitive advantage in professional ship management.

The application of stand-alone generic strategies and concentration on tangible resources seem to have limited potential for achieving competitive advantage in professional ship management. Grant (1991, p. 114) states:

> Although the competitive strategy literature has tended to emphasise issues of strategic positioning in terms of the choice between cost and differentiation advantage, and between broad and narrow market scope, fundamental to these choices is the resource position of the firm.

The resource position of the firm referred to above is definitely among the most important concepts of contemporary strategic management thought in the quest for understanding the basis for achieving a sustainable competitive advantage. The concept is well explained in the literature and referred to as the resource-based view. The resource-based view originates from renewed interest in the works of Ricardo (1891), Coase (1937) and Penrose (1959), and has been given increasing emphasis during the 1990s by various thinkers in strategic management and industrial economics. It is imperative to consider this body of theory and its empirical assessment in various industries prior to applying the concepts to professional ship management.

The Resource-Based View of the Firm

The resource-based view has received impressive attention in recent years, to the extent that it has been regarded by some as having momentous paradigmatic potential in the field of strategic management (Peteraf, 1993). As mentioned above, the work of Penrose (1959) has been an influential force, followed by other notable contributions from leading scholars including, among others, Lippman and Rumelt (1982), Wernerfelt (1984), Barney (1991), Dierckx and Cool (1989), Conner (1991) and Mahoney and Pandian (1992). In the resource-based view, the firm is viewed as a bundle of resources, the services of which may have multiple uses (Penrose, 1959). Resources may be divided into three categories:

- tangible resources: plant and capital;
- intangible resources: patents and trade marks;
- knowledge about products, services and processes, which may be embedded in individuals.

In advocating the usefulness of analysing economic units in terms of their resource endowments, Wernerfelt (1984) argued the following:

- the resource view leads to different immediate insights than the product perspective;
- resources that can lead to high profits can be identified;
- resource position barriers, analogous to entry barriers, can be identified and developed;
- strategy for bigger firms involves striking a balance between exploiting existing resources and developing new ones;
- an acquisition can be seen as a purchase of resources, and acquiring rare resources can be highly beneficial in an imperfect market.

According to Grant (1991) the resource view provides a basis upon which a firm can establish its identity and frame its strategy – the primary sources of a firm's profitability. Further, he states that the key to a resource-based approach to strategy formulation is understanding the relationship between resources, capabilities, competitive advantage and profitability, and in particular understanding how competitive advantage can be sustained over time. A more in-depth perspective of capabilities and sustainable competitive advantage is provided in the following paragraphs.

Core Competencies and Organisational Capabilities

Integral in the resource-based view have been the concepts of core competencies and organisational capabilities and their significance in achieving a sustainable competitive advantage. Core competence has been defined by Prahalad and Hamel (1990, p. 82) as:

> The collective learning in the organisation, especially how to co-ordinate diverse production skills and integrate multiple streams of technologies.

Stalk, Evans and Schulman (1992) note that the examples provided by Prahalad and Hamel (1990) place emphasis on underlying production skills and technological know-how. In this way, there might be no difference between resources and competencies. Eriksen and Mikkelsen (1996) view competencies as more than just a function of prior resource deployment. They further note:

Competence is not just another resource, which may be applied to the production of intermediate or end products. The important words in Prahalad and Hamel's definition are *learning, co-ordinate, and integrate.* It is the accumulated organisational and social capital, which makes co-ordination and integration possible (Eriksen and Mikkelsen, 1996, p. 61).

Organisational capital refers to the aspects that facilitate the efficient communication and co-operation of people and may be embodied in the organisational structure. Social capital reflects the corporate culture that has been identified to be a significant factor in achieving organisational efficiency (Barney, 1986). Without proper communication of an informal nature through social networks in the organisation, it will be more difficult to achieve efficiency.

In order for core competencies to contribute to the sustainability of competitive advantage, certain key criteria should be fulfilled. Core competencies should be valuable, they should be heterogeneous in nature, they should be imperfectly imitable and difficult to substitute.

Valuable competencies are those that are helpful in delivering some combination of value and cost that is superior to that of competitors. Since, in a ship management context, the services that can be offered by one company may also be offered by another at a similar price, what is important is the way that a service is offered. By offering the same service differently, companies can create additional value for the clients. Competencies in learning, co-ordinating and integrating resources for delivering additional value are thus critical in the ship management context. It may also be true to assert that companies have not viewed such aspects as critical in service delivery in the past. Competencies and social and organisational capital can be developed in an organisation, and it is up to senior management to proactively initiate its development and instil a corporate culture that can contribute to efficiency.

Core competencies should also be heterogeneous. This means that the resources deployed in order to create value should be different than those deployed by competitors. In the general industry, there have been instances where research and development (R&D) was done differently because of ties a particular company fostered with university departments. The knowledge of organising R&D in the university was both valuable and unique to the particular company, and culminated in its achieving a competitive advantage.

Core competencies should be imperfectly imitable. This means that companies should install some form of isolating mechanism to prevent imitation from competitors. Trademarks and legal restrictions represent such isolating mechanisms, protecting tangible and intangible assets. In the case of services, core competencies may be more difficult to imitate, as intangible aspects and the organisation of the service-offer may be unique to a firm. Despite this, the threat of substitution always exists. The more difficult it is for core competencies to be substituted, the better it is for the firm.

There are some additional issues with respect to core competencies that are notable and extremely important in the ship management context. First, the core competencies of a firm, and a ship management firm in particular, are quite complex and not easy to identify. A company may be able to identify what it does better than competitors, but may fail to identify *why* the firm is better and *how* such activities may be imitated by competitors. Hence, the point is not to identify that you are better in technical management, but why you are better and how to safeguard current and future superiority.

Core competencies can assist in the achievement of a sustained competitive advantage due to their inherent uniqueness. The firm's core competencies are created during the complex interactions between entities and individuals. Such interactions are not possible to replicate, hence competencies are idiosyncratic and unique to a firm. The process and interactions that form the firm's core competencies take place over time and throughout the firm's lifetime. This historical perspective may have an influence over the firm's future decisions. In many instances, historical dependence, or what has been referred to as 'administrative heritage', has influenced firms to compete in structurally unattractive segments (Collis, 1991). The administrative heritage creates path dependence.

In the current competitive age, aspects of cost reduction and tangible assets cannot guarantee competitive advantage. Intangible resources and capabilities such as accumulated knowledge, corporate culture and attitudes are significant. The pace of advancement, be it in terms of technology or knowledge, is so fast that one cannot afford to rest on pillars of traditionalism and experience. The latter are important in so far as they can highlight the importance of advancement and change.

The Relational Resource Advantage

The resource position for professional ship management companies is largely related to the ability of the companies to form strong and stable client relationships.

As explained in previous chapters, one of the problems faced by ship management companies is competition of an opportunistic nature, directed towards attracting clients from competitors. The results of the research on client relationships described in chapter 4 indicate that companies are not systematically implementing strategies for strengthening relationships with existing clients. For instance, when respondents were asked to describe aspects of the relationship with their major client during a telephone interview survey, none of them made any specific reference to actions taken for strengthening the relationship. Stronger client relationships, however, can contribute to a unique competitive advantage for ship management companies. According to the resource-advantage theory (Hunt, 1995; 1997a; 1997b), competitive advantage can be attained through acquiring and creating organisational, informational and relational resources. Relational resources can be reaped in ship management through the development and maintenance of client relationships, as advocated in chapter 4.

On this basis, it is clear that two groups of ship management companies with particular client relationships (the 'rigid' and 'reactive' groups as identified in chapter 4) make few or no adaptations or specific investments in the relationship with the client. On this premise, it is evident that many of the ship management companies cannot attain a relational resource advantage.

It is quite clear from the results depicted in chapter 4 that ship management companies do not actively pursue the achievement of a relational competitive advantage. It seems that practitioners have not yet fully recognised the presence of intangible resources which may contribute towards achieving a competitive advantage. Although ship manager–client relationships are characterised by the variables discussed in the relationship marketing literature, the pursuance of client relationships is neither structured nor coherent.

A relational competitive advantage is unattainable by many companies on the grounds of adaptability and flexibility. It has been suggested that adaptation to the needs of the client may have important consequences for the long-term competitiveness of the firms (Hallen, Johanson and Seyed-Mohamed, 1991). For example, when a client forces a ship management company to introduce a new system, this may enable the company to become competitive in other client relationships. For instance, a client envisaging a stable long-term relationship with a ship management company may request the introduction of a computerised information system that will enable direct communication via satellite linking the offices of the interacting organisations and the ship(s). A company willing to change its communication procedures and adapt to such needs would almost certainly make such an investment. However, such an investment may be used in other client relationships, thus contributing to their stability. The development of mutual trust in the relationship can also be a source of competitive advantage (Barney, 1991). Barney and Hansen (1994) discuss three types of trust present in economic exchanges, viz. weak, semi-strong and strong. In the case of ship management relationships, most of the respondents indicated a strong level of trust existing in their client relationships, or that 'trust is fairly high'. However, others also indicated that 'we would not trust this client'. Three levels of trust were hence identified in ship management relationships. Although a minority, those managers indicating the presence of weak trust must actively pursue the build-up of mutual trust with clients. This can be achieved by showing individual dedication towards the clients and responsiveness to their changing needs. Frequent communication of an informal nature is essential for developing a climate of trustworthiness.

A corporate culture of trust and flexibility, and the development of a client knowledge base, are intangible organisational assets that accumulate over time and are acquired through a process of learning and investing in these areas. Competitive duplication of these assets is only possible through the similar time-consuming processes of irreversible investments or learning that the firm itself underwent (Barney, 1989; Dierickx and Cool, 1989). The greater the irreversible investments made by the firm, the more difficult the duplication of the product market position of the firm. Hence, ship management companies making specific investments and learning about their clients will be able to secure their distinctive value and achieve competitiveness. Acquiring data and building a client knowledge base will require frequent and systematic communication at all levels of the organisational structure. The data from the various sources should be processed and integrated in order to produce information of value to the decision-makers. With communication in many ship management companies being infrequent and on an *ad hoc* basis, it is more difficult to retrieve the data required for building a client knowledge base and achieving competitive advantage.

Client relationships can contribute to ship management companies producing and delivering their service more effectively and/or efficiently. Competitive advantage theory (e.g. Porter, 1985) indicates that competitive advantages determine superior/inferior financial performance. Competitive advantages of efficiency and effectiveness can be achieved by knowing and understanding the customers' needs and delivering the service to satisfy those exact needs. Stable long-term client relationships will ensure that the service is produced and delivered more effectively and efficiently. Such relationships are based on the investment of tangible and intangible resources, frequent communication of a formal and informal nature, and flexibility. The lack of these attributes among certain segments of the ship management fraternity indicates that the pro-competitive nature of a relational advantage is more difficult to attain. Companies that seem to be able to achieve this form of competitive advantage are found in the 'investors' cluster.

A key to sustainable growth and profitability for ship management is the achievement of a sustained competitive advantage. This chapter exposed the major conventional and contemporary theoretical underpinnings for achieving competitive advantage as applied in the ship management context. Apart from these concepts, ship management companies may pursue a number of other strategies in their effort to achieve competitiveness, growth and profitability. Such fundamental strategies are the subject of the chapter that follows.

7 Strategy in Ship Management

Introduction

Leading strategic management gurus Rumelt, Schendel and Teece (1994, p. 9) stated that 'the strategic direction of business organisations is at the heart of wealth creation in modern industrial society'. This statement underpins the importance of strategy in the ship management market, where ship management firms strive to achieve growth and create wealth. The aim of this chapter is to present the fundamental concepts of strategy that are thought to be imperative for the future viability and success of professional ship management firms. Although empirical investigations of the concepts are pending in the professional ship management context, current trends in the industry strenuously suggest that such concepts are of immense practical value.

In broad terms, this chapter aims to address the issues of why ship management firms aim at producing particular mixes of services, and how they go about organising their activities in terms of internal organisation as well as through relationships with other business organisations. Issues of scope and diversification, inter-organisational relationships and organisational structures, as well as the choice of markets in which to compete, are critical and will be addressed in the ship management context.

The chapter is classified into six sections to be addressed: establishment of strategic direction, diversification, mergers and acquisitions, coalitions and joint ventures, and entering international markets. Finally, after a course of action or strategy has been adopted, it is essential to determine the effectiveness of the strategy in accomplishing the envisaged outcomes. It is for this reason that performance measurement for ship management firms will be discussed in this chapter.

Establishing a Strategic Direction

Prior to discussing the establishment of a strategic direction, it would be beneficial to consider a definition of strategy, since scholars in the past had diverse opinions on the issue. Strategy is developed over time and predominantly arises from the moulding of corporate culture, structured plans to achieve objectives, and human perceptions of the best course of action. These are the major outcomes emanating from the definition provided by Lorsch (1986), which seems to capture the essence of strategy. Lorsch (1986, p. 95) defines strategy as:

> The decisions taken over time by top managers, which, when understood as a whole, reveal the goals they are seeking and the means used to reach these goals. Such a definition of strategy is different from common business use of the term in that it does not refer to an explicit plan. In fact, by my definition strategy may be implicit as well as explicit.

In addition to the above, authors have stressed the importance of strategy formulation on the basis of systematic and concrete research and establishment of specific objectives. Lorenzoni and Baden-Fuller (1995) make explicit reference to the value of formal strategic centres, which had a significant impact on the success of alliance partners in particular. Hence, a systematic approach to strategy formulation is essential and this chapter will aim to highlight those aspects that are thought to be at the forefront of a systematic strategic approach in a ship management context.

An integral part of strategy formulation and the establishment of a strategic direction is the drawing up of a formal plan. Its purpose is to define the business in which the company operates, indicate financial objectives which have to be accomplished, specify how revenues are to be generated through various marketing programmes, and assess the various costs which will be incurred in achieving these objectives. In essence, such a plan should identify the current business position of the company, establish realistic objectives and expectations to attain, and indicate how resources should be organised to achieve the objectives.

Of significant importance in establishing a strategic direction is the identification of internal and external influences that may have an impact on strategy direction and formulation. Various techniques are available to an organisation wishing to determine the possible impact of environmental forces, market trends, economic trends, competitive trends and socio-cultural and technological trends. Such techniques include cross impact analysis, gap analysis, and associated techniques for investigating the potential of specific projects on the basis of forecasts and quantitative measures. In addition, SWOT analysis and the TOWS matrix provide useful starting points for the identification of suitable business strategies for an organisation to follow.

Strategic direction entails the implementation of various strategies for achieving stated objectives. According to Proctor (1997) such strategies may include diversification, vertical integration, cost reduction, joint ventures and strategic alliance formation, as well as placing emphasis on the development of core competencies. This chapter will provide a detailed discussion of these issues in the professional ship management context.

Diversification in Ship Management

Different perspectives have been used in past attempts to define diversification. In essence, diversification is a means of spreading the base of a business to achieve improved growth and/or reduce overall risk, which:

- includes all investments apart from those directed at supporting the competitiveness of existing businesses;
- may take the form of investments that address new products, services, customer segments, or geographic markets;
- may be accomplished by different methods, including internal development, mergers, acquisitions and joint ventures;
- entails changes in organisational structures, systems and management processes.

Using this perspective, Ramanujam and Varadarajan (1989, p. 525) defined diversification as 'the entry of a firm or business unit into new lines of activity, either by processes of internal business development or acquisition, which entail changes in its administrative structure, systems, and other management processes'. Strategies of diversification have been part of corporate practice for most firms in industrial economies, and over the last few decades an increasing propensity towards greater product-market diversity has been significantly evident. As far back as the 1960s, it was suggested that successful firms first expand their operations geographically, then integrate vertically, and finally diversify their product offerings (Chandler, 1962).

An examination of corporate practice in ship management suggests that various types of corporate diversification have been taking place over the recent history of the ship management sector. Various reasons may culminate in the decision to pursue corporate diversification in ship management. It is possible that the restructuring taking place in other sectors of shipping and the oil industry in particular may be forcing third-party ship management companies to diversify in order to be able to serve their customers better. Hence ship management companies may be looking at vertical and horizontal moves of diversification as a means of serving the interests of their clients on a global scale. The general literature offers a comprehensive theoretical framework upon which rationales for corporate diversification in ship management can be explained. In addition, other key issues that need to be addressed in the ship management context include identification of the degree, type and mode of diversification that contribute to improved performance for the companies.

Rationales for Corporate Diversification in Ship Management

Reed and Luffman (1986) suggested that firms diversify for both proactive and defensive reasons. Various specific reasons may account for a firm's decision to diversify. Miles (1982) highlights the influences of the general environment (i.e. the legal, political, economic, technological, social and ecological milieu where the firm operates), the industry's competitive environment, characteristics specific to the firms themselves, and the firms' performance. Obviously, such factors have an influence on the decision of ship management firms to diversify. However, their impact is not easy to assess. Montgomery (1994) has suggested three firm-specific and comprehensive perspectives that are made up by a number of reasons underpinning the rationales for corporate diversification. These perspectives include the market-power view, the agency view and the resource view.

The market-power point of view entails that firms diversify in order to achieve market power. Market power can be achieved in ways which have been deemed anti-competitive, such as cross-subsidisation. Hence, a firm may possess power in a market not by virtue of its position in that market but because it possesses market power in other markets and uses that to support predatory activities in the particular market. This view argues that diversified firms will 'thrive at the expense of non-diversified firms not because they are more efficient, but because they have access to what is termed conglomerate power' (Hill, 1985, p. 828). Market power can also be achieved by taking advantage of scale and scope economies, and attainment of financial synergies as a result of diversification. It is also widely accepted that pursuing a strategy of acquisitions will lead directly to an increase in the size of the firm and consequently the market power that it commands. Brush (1996), for instance, established through an empirical investigation that merger activity was positively related to an increase in market share and an improvement in the performance of the merged entity mainly arising from the attainment of operational synergies. The potential for achieving financial synergies is another argument for pursuing a diversification strategy. Portfolio strategy requires a firm to develop a portfolio of businesses that will ensure a stable and adequate cash flow with which to finance its activities.

Agency theory has been utilised to explain the motives for diversification and excessive diversification. The theory proposes that managers may pursue strategies of diversification in order to promote their own self-actualisation objectives through empire-building (Mueller, 1969), job-entrenchment (Shleifer and Vishny, 1991) or reduction of their own employment risk (Ahimud and Lev, 1991). There is no evidence in a ship management context that managers may pursue such objectives to accomplish individual interests at the expense of corporate interests. Whilst it may be the case that individual interests are promoted when actively engaging in growth strategies, agency theory does not seem to be widely applicable to the ship management context.

The resource-based view expounded in the previous chapter can also be utilised in a diversification context. In fact, the resource-based view can be used to explain how diversification may contribute to a firm's competitive advantage. It basically argues that firms possess resources that have accumulated through time and which, if underused, the firm can use outside its normal line of activity in order to achieve growth. Penrose (1959) argues that economies of scale can be achieved from spreading the firm's under-utilised managerial and organisational resources to new areas. This view of the underlying rationale for diversification has been expanded with the concepts of the firm's core competencies (Prahalad and Hamel, 1990) and organisational capabilities (Stalk, Evans and Shulman, 1992). Teece (1980; 1982) contended that the Penrosian perspective on firm diversification is true unless a firm can efficiently sell its unused resources in the market place. A strategy of firm diversification will assist both in the utilisation of existing resources and capabilities that are unused, and at the same time in the development and acquisition of new ones (Mahoney and Pandian, 1992). Chatterjee and Wernerfelt (1991) found through an empirical examination that firms diversify in part to utilise productive resources which are surplus to current operations. In particular, they suggest that internal financial resources are associated with unrelated diversification, whereas other resources such as physical, knowledge-based and external financial resources are associated with unrelated diversification. Peteraf (1993) also asserted that the direction of a firm's diversification is associated with the nature of the resources available and the market opportunities in its external environment.

The resource-based view seems to have wide applicability in the ship management context. Due to the demanding nature of ship management and operation, companies are bound to accumulate a multitude of diverse resources and, in particular, intangible resources such as technical knowledge, marketing know-how and reputation. In addition, the companies are able to develop skills in co-ordinating resources to satisfy the requirements of many different clients. The resources, together with the capabilities present in the firm's routines in making decisions and management of internal processes, can be used outside the offering of core services when the opportunities arise. Hence, companies can diversify by targeting new market segments but still using the core competencies and organisational capabilities already possessed. It would seem that diversification into related lines of activity would be a logical course of action.

An application of the resource-based view in the ship management context is evident in the case of Barber International. An additional aim was the achievement of greater market power. This may be reflected in the strategy of Barber International to establish a new company called International Tanker Management Holding in June 1998. The company was set up to specifically target the tanker market. The company aimed at offering a comprehensive range of services to tanker owners, including ship management, manning, commercial operations and post-fixture services, and technical and newbuilding consultancy. Crewing has been sub-contracted to Barber International. It is quite clear that the company took advantage of the resources of the group and employed its core competencies to address a specific market segment. In less than a year since its establishment, the company has taken over the activities of Barber Ship Management (Hong Kong) and Barber Ship Management Singapore Pte through acquisition. The aim was clearly to combine the managed assets into a larger pool of vessels and command a greater market-power. Hence, with what may be viewed as internal business development, Barber has specifically focused on a target market, set up a new company, and made acquisitions and internal consolidation to increase its market share. Barber aimed at increasing market power by addressing a new market segment, through specialisation, internal development and acquisition, with the restructuring of businesses within the Barber empire.

Direction of Diversification

An integral decision to the diversification choice is the direction of diversification, i.e. whether the diversification move will be related or unrelated. Related diversification involves moving into a new line of business activity that is linked to the company's existing line of activity by commonality between one or more components of each activity's value chain. Unrelated diversification refers to expansion into a new business area that has no obvious connection to a company's existing areas. Many factors will have a bearing upon the particular direction of diversification for specific firms. In general, however, it has been empirically supported that firms pursuing related diversification strategies tend to be more successful than unrelated diversifiers with regard to economic performance (Rumelt, 1974). This is because related diversification allows the transferability of core skills (Rumelt, 1982) and results in associated synergistic benefits like economies of scale and scope (Teece, 1980). On the other hand, Leontiades (1986) posits that unrelated diversification is a desirable strategy when ageing markets result in the firm's profit erosion or to modulate risk in a highly cyclical industry. Williamson (1975) also suggests that, given the right structure, unrelated diversified firms are often in a better position to allocate capital than the external capital market. Ship management companies nowadays appreciate the importance of diversification, and many of them with the requisite financial muscle have diversified into shipowning. This is the case with Interorient Navigation, for example, which invested into containerships at first and then diversified further from its long-standing containership involvement to invest in bulk carriers. As stated by its chairman, 'it is wise not to have all your eggs in one basket, especially because of the rate of container newbuildings recently'. Of particular interest, in terms of the direction of diversification, is the German-owned international shipping company, Schoeller Holdings Ltd. The company owns one of the five largest independent ship management companies, Columbia Shipmanagement, which manages a fleet of about 287 vessels (93 containerships) and is based in Cyprus. Apart from the ship management company, Schoeller also has equity interest in 25 vessels (six containerships), owns and operates liner feeder and multi-purpose liner shipping service companies, and has interests in and operates two hotels in Germany. In Cyprus, Columbia also has had interests in a tropical plant-growing company and hotels. Recognising the opportunities presented in the feeder container business, Schoeller diversified further by making substantial investments in ten feeder container vessels in 1999, to be operated by the newly formed Columbia Container Shipping Ltd (Lustrin, 1999). The vessels were to be managed by Columbia Shipmanagement. It is clear that the strategy of the group was feasible due to the resources and capabilities it possessed, which enabled it to recognise the opportunities presented and to manage and operate the vessels profitably. The transferability of core skills within the Schoeller group is evident from the related diversification strategies pursued.

Mode of Diversification

Ramanujam and Varadarajan (1989) classify the available modes of diversification as being on a continuum of two polar extremes, viz. internal growth and acquisition-based growth. The two polar extremes have been widely discussed in the literature (Pitts, 1980; Salter and Weinhold, 1978; Yip, 1982). Lamont and Anderson (1985) suggest that the two modes can be mixed, whereas a number of other modes, like joint ventures and strategic alliances, which would fall somewhere along the continuum, have also been discussed in a number of studies (Roberts and Berry, 1985). Internal growth involves the exploitation of internal resources in order to establish a business new to the firm and also related to innovation. Mergers and acquisitions on the other hand involve assessments of the strengths and weaknesses of target firms and their value to the acquiring firm. In general, Datta, Rajagopalan and Rasheed (1991) contend that both approaches have advantages and disadvantages, and the preferred approach will depend on a variety of industry and organisational factors.

Diversification and Performance

A key issue in pursuing strategies of diversification is due consideration of the effects on performance. The absence of studies dealing with this aspect in the ship management context dictates the need to review the major seminal studies performed in other industries in order to provide an assessment of the potential effects in the ship management context.

Firms diversify in order to achieve certain objectives, which should, in principle, contribute to improvement in firm performance. In order to have a realistic expectation of achieving a particular diversification objective, firms should diversify to some optimal point. On many instances, firm performance has actually deteriorated due to over-investment in diversification. Markides (1995) presents four reasons for excessive investment in pursuing diversification objectives. These include agency theory, the hubris hypothesis, wrong signals and incentives provided by the capital market, and a gradual decrease in the optimal firm diversification level over the past few decades.

It has generally been accepted that the evidence on the relationship between diversification and performance emanating from a number of studies is inconclusive (Datta, Rajagopalan and Rasheed, 1991). This seems to be confirmed by the view that, even in cases where a positive relationship between diversification and performance was found, it was also suggested that diversification itself may have been caused by the profits available to the company from its primary industry (Grant, Jammine and Thomas, 1988; Luffman, and Reed, 1982).

Rumelt (1974) in his seminal work put forward the 'relatedness' hypothesis, where it was suggested that related diversifiers outperform unrelated diversifiers. This was later supported in a number of works including Bettis (1981), LeCraw (1984), Palepu (1985) and Varadarajan and Ramanujam (1987). Other studies, however, including those of Michel and Shaked (1984), Luffman and Reed (1984), and Grant and Jammine (1988), did not support this hypothesis. Moreover, studies in a related v. unrelated context failed to support the hypothesis (Chatterjee, 1986; Lutbakin, 1987; Singh and Montgomery, 1987).

A number of studies utilising a purely financial perspective on evaluating firm performance, particularly at the post-merger stage, have also been carried out. Healy, Palepu and Ruback (1992) studied the post-acquisition performance of the 50 largest US mergers that took place between 1979 and 1984. Their findings do not show significant change in cash flow margin on sales, but do indicate significant improvement of asset turnover and the return on the market value of assets, which suggests better asset management.

Corporate finance theory has taken a negative view of acquisitions in which diversification is the main motive, primarily due to the disservice to stockholders, who could diversify their stock portfolios if they wished, without the acquisition of another entity by the company whose stocks they already hold (Levy and Sarnat, 1970). To test the implications of corporate finance theory, Ravenscraft and Scherer (1988) compared the performance of the stocks of the 13 leading conglomerates in the 1960s with that of the market as a whole. They concluded that diversified firms do not provide investors a benefit when they diversify, and that the fact that a firm is a conglomerate does not improve its probability of yielding higher than normal returns. This rather pessimistic view was contradicted, however, by a number of other studies which showed that returns to stockholders in conglomerate acquisitions are greater than in non-conglomerate acquisitions (Elgers and Clark, 1980). Substantial gains were said to be made by stockholders of seller firms and moderate gains by those of buying firms. This finding was confirmed by Wansley, Lane and Yang (1983) who found that returns to stockholders were larger in horizontal and vertical acquisitions than in conglomerate acquisitions.

Berger and Ofek (1995) examined a large sample of firms over the period of 1986-1991 and found that diversification resulted in a loss of firm value to the order of 13-15 per cent. Although there was no positive relationship between loss of firm value and firm size, the loss was found to be less when diversification occurred within related industries. The reasons for this loss in value were associated with lower operating profitability and over-investment in diversified segments. In support of this finding, Comment and Jarrell (1995) found that increased specialisation or corporate focus was positively related to shareholder wealth maximisation.

In the ship management context, companies seem to be keen on pursuing strategies of related diversification, particularly through expansion into ship ownership or through involvement in high tech information technology projects. There is no evidence to suggest, however, that diversification in the ship management context contributes directly to an improvement in economic performance. Nevertheless, there are clear strategic benefits to be derived, not least from the reduction of risk and the exploitation of arising opportunities by investing in technological advances. In addition, ship ownership has conventionally been more profitable than third party ship management. Hence, such a diversification strategy, particularly bearing in mind its related nature and the potential for transferability of core skills and resources, can achieve the sought-after objectives. It will be extremely interesting, however, to empirically determine the effects of diversification on the financial performance of, let's say, a ship management group, as it will provide concrete evidence upon which strategy formulation may be based.

Coalitions and Competitor Alliances

Many firms cannot afford to own or internally dominate all needed service activities. They may, however, require the offering of a particular service that will complement current activities and further utilise currently under-utilised resources. When there are two or more companies sharing the same concerns and opportunities, it might be feasible for them to co-operate in the particular activity. The two companies may even be competing for the same business in other areas. However, if the situation arises where both companies can be winners through co-operation (what has been termed as a 'win-win situation'), then the companies should co-operate. Through co-operation, the two organisations are not fighting for a share of the pie, they are actually creating a bigger pie and sharing it. This concept has been termed *co-opetition* (combining co-operation and competition) and is lucidly described by Nalebuff and Brandenburger (1997).

The revolutionary concept of co-opetition directs managers towards lateral thinking in their strategic thought process. For instance, the traditional approach defines competitors as the other companies in the particular industry, i.e. other ship managers in the case of professional ship management. This would seem logical, as ship management companies offer more or less a similar service. However, one must try to determine competitors by virtue of the offering for satisfying certain customer needs. For instance, ship management companies nowadays employ software for assisting and facilitating efficiency in ship operation. However, companies that design and develop such software, although not traditional ship managers, may be able to satisfy the clients of ship managers by selling software to the clients. Hence, the clients may find it more effective to have their own in-house department as advances in technology make it more economical to do so, as opposed to hiring a third party ship manager. Nalebuff and Brandenburger (1997, p. 17) state:

> The right way to identify your competitors is to put yourself in the customers' shoes. This will lead you to ask: What else might my customers buy that would make my product less valuable to them? How else might customers get their needs satisfied? These questions will lead to a much longer and more insightful list of competitors.

By identifying a longer and more insightful list of competitors and potential competitors, ship management companies can then develop strategies for potential collaboration. Collaboration with companies that have complementary skills and resources may be particularly beneficial, as it may allow for continued prosperity in the shared business without invading the partner's market. This would be the case if a ship management company was to collaborate with a shipping-related software manufacturer or an information technology company that seeks to enter the shipping market.

The concept of co-operation between competitors to attain a win-win situation has received increasing attention from a practical perspective in a number of industries in recent years. The result has been an increase in the incidence of strategic alliance formation (Glaister and Buckley, 1994; Hergert and Morris, 1988). The formation of strategic alliances has also been accelerating throughout the 1990s in other sectors of the shipping industry like liner shipping (e.g. Midoro and Pitto, 2000; Ryoo and Thanopoulou, 1999). The concept of co-operation has also found applications in the port sector. Hence, previously competing ports have discovered that co-operation can lead to mutual benefits, unlike competition, which may be damaging for all the entities concerned.

Although the concept of strategic alliance or collaboration with competitors has not been considered widely in the ship management context, it is important to identify the potential advantages and disadvantages of such an approach. It is also important to consider the potential instances where the formation of strategic alliances might be feasible in the ship management context.

Hood and Young (1979) note that strategic alliances were the traditional vehicle with which multinational enterprises sought to enter the markets of developing countries that enforced restrictive conditions on foreign investment. An alliance has been defined as an 'inter-firm collaboration over a given economic space and time for the attainment of mutually defined goals' (Buckley, 1992, p. 91). The definition, according to Buckley (1992) entails the following important characteristics:

- it covers only agreements between firms;
- the venture must be collaborative in that it should entail input of resources from all the partners;
- the alliance can range from local to global and can be defined in real time or until certain goals are reached;
- while the alliance aims for the achievement of certain goals, the partners may not necessarily have the same view of the objectives.

The underlying motives and rationales for the formation of collaborative arrangements such as joint ventures and strategic alliances mainly originate from the potential influences of such strategic behaviour on the competitive positioning of the firm (Kogut, 1988). Mariti and Smiley (1983) identified a number of core strategic motives for alliance formation, whereas Harrigan (1985) groups the various motives into three divisions consisting of internal benefits, competitive benefits and strategic benefits. Contractor and Lorange (1988) enumerate the following benefits as possible outcomes of co-operative ventures:

- risk reduction;
- economies of scale and/or rationalisation;
- technology exchanges;
- co-opting or blocking competition;
- overcoming government mandated trade or investment barriers;
- facilitating initial international expansion of inexperienced firms;
- vertical quasi-integration advantages of linking the complementary contributions of the partners in a 'value-chain'.

Strategic alliances are seen as an attractive organisational adjustment for hedging risk, because neither of the partners will bear the full risk and cost of the activities of the alliance. More specifically, Contractor and Lorange (1988) identified the following ways in which an alliance can reduce a partner's risk:

- product portfolio diversification, thus reducing the market risk of being associated with only one or a limited number of products/services;
- spreading the risk of a large project over two or more firms;
- faster market entry and quicker establishment in the market, which culminates into faster payback on the investment;
- cost of subaddivity, (i.e. the cost of the partnership is less than the cost of investment undertaken by each firm alone);
- political risk reduction because of a local partner's contacts or government endorsement of ventures seen as beneficial to its economic policy agenda.

Added potential for economies of scale and rationalisation in the production of the service exist in the context of professional ship management. Economies of scale may be achieved in various ways. First, a joint venture may facilitate establishment in a particular country to serve both partners, as opposed to having two establishments in different countries. In addition, it might be feasible to relocate particular aspects of the ship management supply chain (e.g. the crewing service) through the joint venture. In this way, the sourcing cost may be lower due to the highest comparative advantage attributed to the new location. Moreover, serving the needs of two parent companies, instead of one, may render the accomplishment of further reduction in average unit cost due to larger economies of scale.

The formation of strategic alliances or joint ventures can also have important implications in influencing competition. Porter and Fuller (1986) note that strategic alliances can influence who a firm competes with and the basis of competition. For instance, joint ventures could blunt the abilities of competing firms to retaliate by binding potential enemies to the firm as allies. Joint ventures can defend current strategic positions against forces that may be too strong for a single firm to withstand on its own. A joint venture entity may develop the ability to compete more effectively due to the combined internal resources of the parent companies (Harrigan, 1985). Strategic alliances may, therefore, be used defensively to reduce competition by co-opting potential or existing competition into an alliance. On the other hand, an alliance may be used as an offensive strategy, for example by linking with a rival in order to put pressure on the profits and market share of a common competitor (Contractor and Lorange, 1988). Although such moves have not occurred in ship management to the same extent as in other sectors of the shipping industry, there have been instances where companies have joined forces for competitive reasons.

Strategic alliances and joint ventures may also play a key role in accessing markets that are otherwise inaccessible. The latter may be due to the legal exclusion of foreign companies, which may be overcome by forming a joint venture entity with a local partner. Such protectionist policies are predominantly in place when it comes to developing countries and former planned economies, but can also occur in advanced market economies like Japan. Certain ship management companies have recorded considerable successes in obtaining new business by co-operating with national or private companies from developing countries.

The advantages postulated from a theoretical perspective have accrued to professional ship management companies that have been pursuing strategies of collaboration. For instance, in late 1996 it was announced that the UK-based ship management company Acomarit was to form a joint venture ship management company with the National Shipping Corporation of Saudi Arabia to manage a fleet of 30 vessels. The joint venture company was named Mideast Ship Management, is based in the United Arab Emirates and acts as technical in-house manager for the National Shipping Corporation. This joint venture company was formed after a tender process and competition among ship management companies. The advantages for Acomarit include increased influence in a particular geographical market (the Middle East) and the pressure exerted on competition, which occurred with the transfer of vessels from Denholm Ship Management to the new venture company.

The applicability of joint ventures as a means of entering new markets and diversification strategy in ship management is illustrated by the case of Interorient Navigation. The company has steadily branched out over the 1990s with a number of novel alliances, and at the same time has shown an increasing interest in involving itself with a more diverse range of tonnage. The company formed Latinter Maritime SA in 1992, in a joint venture with the Riga-based Latvian Shipping Company. In 1993, Interorient was awarded one of its most significant management contracts by the Baltic Shipping Company, clear indication that the opening made in Eastern Europe was already bearing fruit. Following this, the company again joined forces with Baltic Shipping, this time to set up Baltinter, a company which mainly deals with recruiting seamen for its parent operators and for third parties.

Another notable example of a joint venture in ship management is that between Thome Ship Management of Singapore and Samudra Petrindo Asia, a leading Indonesia-based shipping company. The companies joined forces to establish SPA-TSM Ship Management. The co-operation aimed at combining the expertise of Thome in ship management and the local knowledge and crewing expertise of SPA.

International Market Strategy

The term entering international markets is construed in this case to refer to entry in foreign markets with the aim of offering professional ship management services. This may happen for a variety of reasons, the most important being:

- there is demand or potential demand for ship management services in the identified market;
- to serve existing clients that have expanded in the region;
- saturation of the current marketing region resulting in diminishing returns from the application of additional marketing expenditures.

According to Terpstra and Yu (1988) a large number of service firms enter foreign markets primarily to serve the foreign subsidiaries of their domestic clients. This phenomenon of client following, while not unheard of in the manufacturing sector, is nevertheless a unique characteristic of service firms in terms of its occurrence and importance. It is also a quite common phenomenon in the case of professional ship management, where companies have in the past demonstrated willingness to follow key clients by establishment in foreign markets. The other type of entry is described as the market-seeking entry (Erramilli and Rao, 1990). This second entry situation refers to the case where a service firm enters foreign markets primarily to serve foreign customers, i.e. customers in that particular overseas market. Weinstein (1977) found significant variations in entry mode between client followers and market seekers. It was found that client followers were 'early entrants' in particular markets, whereas market seekers were 'later entrants'. According to Weinstein (1977), client followers tend to be associated with more aggressive entry behaviour than market seekers.

It is a fact that physical presence, in some form or another, closer to the client and/or the supplier brings many advantages to ship management companies. If properly structured and managed this presence need not cost much, whereas the benefits to be accrued would be considerable. This strategy may at first seem to conflict with the moves of consolidation evident across the ship management spectrum over recent years. Consolidation has been occurring at industry and also firm level, so it may seem unrealistic to embark on an international expansion strategy by forming new subsidiaries and establishing in new locations. It is definitely a fine balancing act, but ship management companies nevertheless need to weigh the economic advantages of consolidation with the necessity of maintaining a local presence close to clients and suppliers. There have been instances where, despite the additional burdens of local requirements, ship management companies have adopted particular approaches that ensured reaping the benefits of international presence. The case of American V. Ships Marine is illustrative of the importance of proper planning and structuring for success in international market strategy. Companies based in the US and managing US-flagged vessels are faced with an array of challenges. These include the strict enforcement of maritime and financial rules and laws, the danger of facing litigation, and special demands placed on owners involved with the US military or the domestic oil trade (Anon, 2000a). To cope with these challenges and maintain local presence and market share, American V. Ships Marine formed a joint venture with GE Capital to handle the operational and technical side of the ship management business. On the other hand, the company transferred back office activities to the headquarters of the V. Ships Group in Monaco. According to the president of American V. Ships Marine:

> In ship management it makes sense to centralise some services. But then you have to take a more hands-on approach on the operational and technical side and that is where regionalisation comes in. It's about being close to where the ship and owners are (Anon, 2000b, p. 30).

Once a decision to enter a foreign market has been made, the critical point is to decide upon the mode of entry. A foreign market entry mode is 'an institutional arrangement that makes possible the entry of a company's products, technology, human skills, management or other resources into a foreign country' (Root, 1987, p. 5). Firms can enter foreign markets via exporting (direct or indirect), contractual methods and foreign direct investment (joint ventures and wholly-owned subsidiaries). The mode of foreign market entry decision is one of strategic importance and has crucial implications for the achievement of a competitive advantage (Erramilli and Rao, 1993; Hill, Hwang and Kim, 1990; Wind and Perlmutter, 1977). According to Madhok (1998), the dominant perspective in addressing the choice of foreign market entry mode has been internalisation theory (Rugman, 1986). This perspective raises the question of the most optimum form of foreign market entry, between internalisation of a firm within its own boundaries (forming a subsidiary) or through some form of collaboration with a partner. The decision is once again a measure of the transaction costs associated with the alternative governance structures. The transaction cost approach favours internalisation, i.e. formation of subsidiaries, as it is associated with minimisation of transaction costs and hence a more efficient governance structure for foreign market entry. So under this theoretical principle, ship management companies that possess some rent-yielding firm-specific advantage should be better off establishing a subsidiary as a means of entering a foreign market. This means that companies having specific capabilities that can be exploited in a foreign market may be better off with the 'go it alone' option. This seems to be the case with certain ship management groups such as V. Ships, which has been establishing subsidiary offices on a global scale in its effort to develop commercial opportunities. When V. Ships established its Singapore subsidiary a few years ago, its aim was clearly to gain business from the fast-growing cruise and leisure market in South East Asia. Its rent-yielding advantage was the established expertise and capabilities from its operations in Europe where it had already been managing around ten cruise ships. On the other hand, where it was identified that collaboration with a competitor possessing a specific capability would be beneficial, V. Ships was also swift to embark on the challenge – hence the V. Ships and Celtic Marine venture.

Despite the above argument, it must be stressed that under different conditions, entering a foreign market through a collaborative venture may be more beneficial to the firm even if transaction costs are high. This is the case when the company can gain from the knowledge and capabilities of a partner firm. The perspective of organisational capabilities that was discussed in the previous chapter is also applicable to foreign market entry and ownership-related decisions. In fact, according to Kogut and Zander (1993) and Tallman (1991), this perspective is becoming increasingly prominent and holds strong potential as an explanation of ownership-related decisions. In a dynamic and intensely competitive environment on a global scale, firms are increasingly inadequately equipped to remain competitive through reliance solely on their own capabilities. Therefore, collaborations occur in order to complement and reinforce a firm's knowledge and capability base (Kogut, 1988; Mody, 1993). Accordingly, collaborative governance modes should not be regarded simply as a cost-efficient alternative to markets or wholly-owned subsidiaries, but as an alternative to other modes of knowledge acquisition and deployment (Hamel, 1991). In addition, the careful choice of partner may limit transaction costs, increase the inflow of capabilities and knowledge, and have limited impact on the outflow of capabilities that will inevitably occur in a collaborative venture. For the firms that have international scope, a local partner may not be a direct competitor when compared to other expanding companies on a global scale. Hence, the outflow of capabilities to local, in scope companies becomes less important, whereas the inflow of capabilities from local partners can enhance the competitive advantage of the company vis-à-vis other more global competitors.

The ship management companies that feature prominently in their global approach have arguably been the V. Ships and Acomarit Groups. The V. Ships Group's approach has been to concurrently and continuously enter and develop new markets on a global basis. It has achieved this objective through the establishment in many new locations by setting up offices and recruiting centres, increasing the number and diversifying the range of services on offer and embarking on diversification of its core business activities. Hence, apart from the core ship management services, V. Ships may also supply financing, insurance, agency, bunkering, average adjusting and legal services. In addition, apart from its headquarters in

Monaco, the company has technical management offices in major shipping centres such as New York, Miami, Rio de Janeiro, Southampton, Oslo, Limassol, Dubai and Singapore. It also boasts recruiting offices in Manila, New Delhi, Odessa, Genoa, Hamburg and Gdynia, in addition to further financial and/or support centres in several other locations (Jaques, 1998).

Acomarit has also been extremely successful in its international market entry strategies. The company has tried to enter foreign markets, either through joint ventures, acquisitions or establishment of subsidiaries. In 1994, for instance, the company formed a joint venture with a local company in its effort to enter the apprehensive Greek market. The venture was later on dissolved and Acomarit has taken full responsibility for the operation (Anon, 1998a). In 1999 the company entered into a deal with Brazil's state-owned oil company Petrobas to provide ship management services to 30 vessels controlled by Transpetro, the oil company's transportation unit. The importance of the deal for Acomarit lies not only in the sheer volume of business but also in the fact that the new subsidiary established to oversee the contract will provide a concrete base for broader expansion into the South American market (Gray, 1999). In a similar fashion, Acomarit established an office in Montreal, Canada, after clinching a deal to handle technical management for the entire Canada Steamship Lines domestic fleet. Once again, the management of the company stressed the importance of establishing a foothold in North America to serve as a springboard for further expansion (Osler, 1999b).

Another way of entering a new geographical market or pursuing international market expansion is through horizontal integration. This entails the merger with or acquisition of a similar firm operating in a different geographical area. Mergers and acquisitions, whose importance is becoming increasingly evident in the ship management context, will be dealt with next.

Mergers and Acquisitions

Integral to the issues of corporate diversification and entrance into new markets are the strategies of merger and acquisition. These are becoming increasingly important in the corporate practice of professional ship management firms. Current indications show that merger and acquisition strategies will be fundamental for the future shaping and re-structuring of the ship management industry.

There are different types of mergers that are pursued to achieve the accomplishment of diverse objectives. Mergers may have a major influence in the economic organisation of a particular industry, and are therefore controlled and regulated by governments, mainly in order to avoid the exploitation of monopoly powers. This is true of horizontal mergers in particular. Horizontal mergers involve the coming together of two firms operating and competing in the same kind of business activity. Thus, two ship management companies merging would constitute a horizontal merger. If companies merge horizontally, then the number of firms in the industry decreases and there are, potentially, negative effects on competition. Hence, horizontal mergers may result in the creation of monopoly power and may enable firms to engage in anti-competitive practices.

Horizontal integration may result in an increase in market share (expansion of client base), which can have a significant impact on market power. Gaughan (1996) notes that whether market power actually increases depends on the size of the merging firms and the level of competition in the industry. Market power is sometimes referred to in economic theory as monopoly power that results from the ability of firms to set and maintain price above competitive levels and may be the result of horizontal integration. The monopolist has the ability to select the price-output combination that will maximise profit. In ship management, companies are not in a state of monopoly, nor are they in a market of perfect competition. The latter is the direct opposite of monopoly and regards firms as price takers (no ability to influence market price). In the ship management context, market power is attained through the build-up of a larger client-base, which reduces dependency, and the expansion of the resource base, which reduces risk. The company may not be able to influence market price as such, but it can negotiate a competitive price and terms that would suit particular requirements. Merging horizontally reduces client-dependency and risk for the merged entities and competition in the ship management industry. It may also raise the barriers to entry in the market and the level at which ship management firms compete. It follows that horizontal mergers may have beneficial effects for the firms pursuing them. Outsiders, however, may suffer, as will the ship management industry at large if it is to be dominated by a few larger players.

Vertical mergers on the other hand occur between firms at different stages in the production process. In the case of ship management, the production of the service involves co-ordination of the firm with suppliers as well as clients. Service production (by ship management firms) and consumption (by clients) are inseparable. The merging of adjacent members in this service channel would constitute a vertical merger. The vertical integration of two originally separate entities in the supply chain of the ship management service may result in a series of economic benefits. The underlying economic principles involved in this type of organisational co-ordination can be found in the transaction-cost approach originally suggested by Coase (1937) and further developed mainly by Williamson (1979; 1981) and Teece (1980; 1982). The firm is explained by Coase (1937) in terms of 'natural' market failures due to what he referred to as 'marketing costs', now known as 'transaction costs'. These are the costs of carrying out market exchanges. These costs consist of 'discovering the relevant prices' of the factors of production, and of 'negotiating and concluding a separate contract for each exchange transaction' (Coase, 1937, pp. 90-91). In the case of services in particular, Coase argues that a contract which allows for the co-ordination of the resources by an entrepreneur is desirable because it reduces uncertainty and 'marketing costs'. A firm thus emerges when the co-ordination of resources, within the limits of a contract, becomes dependent on the buyer. The theoretical framework of the transaction-cost approach seems to be adequate in attempting to explain the nature and existence of professional ship management firms. Ship managers are involved in the co-ordination of resources on a contractual basis because they can achieve greater efficiency and lower costs in market exchanges for sustaining ship operation and management.

Professional ship management companies have engaged in the past in what can be referred to as backward integration decisions (as opposed to forward integration). Backward integration entails the acquisition of suppliers. This would mean acquisition of a company specialising in manning and crew supply and located in a country with human resource availability. The greatest motivation for this type of vertical integration is the assurance of a dependable source of crew supply. Dependability would include the reliable availability of manpower, quality maintenance, and timely delivery and co-ordination considerations. Cost savings will ultimately accrue to the ship management company embarking on a vertical acquisition. The cost savings will be from the reduction in transaction costs discussed above, such as the reduction in uncertainty and costs in the re-negotiation of supply agreements, reduction in disruptions when contracts with independent suppliers end, etc. It must be pointed out, however, that the fact the company will not have to pay profits to the supplier will not result in the realisation of cost savings. This is because the supplier subsidiary should be incurring losses if the parent acquirer is to be making a cost saving in that respect.

Various other motives and determinants for mergers can be identified, many of which are closely related to the determinants of corporate diversification discussed earlier in this chapter. Companies often merge in an attempt to diversify into another line of business activity.

For ship management companies, the inclination to merge vertically or horizontally may be equated to the various objectives that may be pursued. One such objective may be the achievement of synergy, which refers to the greater effect that can be produced from both companies working together than from the effect of each one if it was to operate independently. The term 'operating synergy' refers to the efficiency gains or operating economies that are derived in horizontal or vertical mergers. Operating synergy results in cost reduction due to the combination of the two companies that culminates as a result of economies of scale. Through mergers, ship management companies can acquire tangible and intangible resources that will facilitate a greater network by which to serve clients globally at a lower cost per unit. For instance, setting up an office in another country to serve a limited number of clients directly may not be economically feasible. Acquiring a company with local offices not only expands the acquirer's client base, but also provides the opportunity for it to serve its existing clients at a lower overall cost. Another concept of particular importance in ship management is the effect of mergers on the achievement of economies of scope as opposed to economies of scale. Economies of scope result from the ability of a firm to utilise one set of inputs to provide a broader range of services. Therefore, it is possible that the merging of ship management companies will result in the ability to economically sustain additional services that can be offered and that could have not been provided otherwise. Merging can provide the additional resources to facilitate the sustainability of more departments that can offer additional services.

Over the past couple of years, a number of professional ship management companies have been actively and openly pursuing strategies of merger and acquisition. The statement of the Acomarit chief executive is characteristic of the trend in ship management:

> There are two ways for a company like Acomarit to grow internationally: either attract new clients or acquire the competition - and we are looking at both options (Anon, 1998b, p. 7).

Among the most notable acquisitions of Acomarit has been that of the ship management business of Nordic Oriental in Singapore from Frontline and

ICB. The company also bought out 100 per cent of Acomarit-LPL, a previously joint venture entity that it re-named to Acomarit (Hellas). With respect to the acquisition of Nordic Oriental, the chief executive of Acomarit stated:

> We are delighted to be able to acquire a mature ship management business in the strategically important Singapore market which, together with our operation in Hong Kong, will be a further stepping stone in the development of Acomarit's Asia-Pacific business (Anon, 1997h, p. 1).

In the Asian scene, Jardine Ship Management, which is based in Hong Kong, has been among the most active in the pursuance of acquisitions. Its managing director declared in mid-1999 that the company has held discussions with other companies for possible mergers, and that it is looking for a company of similar size, plus or minus five or ten ships. Jardine Ship Management was at the time managing 52 vessels – 21 under technical management and 31 under crewing management – and was employing approximately 700 officers and ratings. The acquisition of a 50 per cent interest in Singapore-based Northsouth Ship Management by Interocean Ugland Management aimed at expanding the acquirer's traditional European focus. Through an international outlook, the company aimed at boosting its third party business.

A significant merger in the ship management market occurred in 1999 with the joining of Monaco-based V. Ships and Celtic Marine. Both companies were deemed to be among the most reputable prior to the merger, hence the benefits of keeping the name of Celtic Marine intact after the merger. Through this merger, V. Ships was aiming to increase its network of offices and expertise on a global basis as a result of Celtic Marine's successful establishment in the Greek and South African markets. The plans of V. Ships to expand into the Far East were also expected to benefit. The president of V. Ships reportedly said that the company had for some time been evaluating possible acquisitions of ship management companies in the Far East as part of its plans to establish a foothold in the area. In addition, he stated:

> In an era of depressed ship management fees the possibility of offering a high quality service – which means high investments in crew training, quality control, safety and information technology – is proportional to the dimension of the business. This is why we believe that the V. Ships–Celtic Marine merger will not be the last one on the market (Anon, 1999a, p. 9).

A significant underlying reason for the merger has been the willingness of V. Ships to acquire resources possessed by Celtic Marine. These include tangible resources as well as intangible competencies and capabilities. Hence, V. Ships was looking to enhance its capabilities and resources in crewing management by acquiring Celtic Marine's expertise in crew manning. The distinct capabilities of the company in manpower supply in particular acted as a catalyst for the merger. The company had some 150 ships under crew management at the time of the merger, and could draw from a pool of up to 5,000 seafarers sourced directly from the Philippines, India, Poland and Croatia. The scope of added value was also further enhanced with the integration of the offices of the two companies in Manila (Philippines), Mumbai (India) and Gdynia (Poland). In addition, the reputation of Celtic Marine for specific expertise in crewing, consultancy, vessel inspection and emergency response were seen as critical factors for the completion of the merger. Other important underlying reasons for the merger included the bargaining power of the combined entity, the power of size in continuing with investments in information technology, training, safety and quality management, and the achievement of cost-effectiveness by virtue of scale economies.

The merger resulted in an increase in the market share of V. Ships. The managed fleet has grown to more than 370 ships after the merger, with about 200 under full management. Office staff also increased to 500 in total, and seafarers to 11,000. In terms of revenue, Celtic Marine was estimated to be making a contribution of 10 per cent.

The bidding for corporate acquisitions among ship management companies is a relatively recent characteristic of the ship management industry. In late 1997, for example, there was a bid for the acquisition of the Australian ship management company ASP by the UK-based ship management company Seahorse (Anon, 1997g). The UK-based ship management company was one of four bidders (three of which were UK-based companies). The company viewed the acquisition as a means of expanding into the South East Asian market. It was believed that the acquisition would provide the basis for resource expansion, as the Australian company managed 23 ships (Anon, 1997g). The number of ships indicates that companies susceptible to acquisitions may be smaller in terms of fleet size. This supports the fact that smaller companies may not be able to compete with the much larger organisations. Acquisitions of other companies do, however, have important implications for client relationships. These include the current clients of the acquirer company, as well as the clients of the acquired company. It is inevitable that acquisitions will result in major changes in the structure and top management of acquired firms (Shanley, 1994), and that such changes will disrupt employees (Hirsch, 1987). Such changes may affect the relationships with the clients of the acquired firms. Acquisitions will also have an effect on the acquirer, its management and employees, and may well disrupt current clients, who will view large-scale structural changes with anxiety. Hence relationship marketing becomes extremely important, as the strength of the bonds with clients will serve as a means for reducing client uncertainty. Additionally, relationship initiation with the current clients of the acquired firm is important, as they themselves will be faced with even greater uncertainty, bearing in mind the restructuring of top management and the introduction of other parties into the management of their vessels.

Performance Measurement

At the heart of success, accomplishment of objectives and future strategy setting is the past, current and most importantly the future performance of the firm. This includes operational performance and strategic performance. Without a benchmark of operational performance it is impossible to determine whether the firm has made progress in productivity and efficiency. In addition, without a strategic performance referent, managers cannot objectively determine or consistently evaluate the quality of their strategic decisions (Chakravarthy, 1986). In recent years, there has been renewed interest in business performance measurement, both from a practical and academic point of view. This is reflected in the number of conferences organised by commercial entities and the number of delegates attracted, as well as by the literature on the subject area. According to Neely (1999) there are certain reasons for this renewed interest – reasons that apply wholly to the nature of professional ship management. The reasons put forward include the changing nature of work, increasing competition, specific improvement initiatives, national and international awards, changing organisational roles, changing external demands and the power of information technology.

It follows that measurement of performance is imperative in ship management. It is also widely accepted nowadays that measures of financial performance, which mainly rely on accounting data, are not sufficient for providing a complete picture of the performance of a firm. For instance, measures of performance derived from financial accounting have been criticised in the past. The main problems with such measures, as stated by Chakravarthy (1986), include:

- scope for accounting manipulation;
- under valuation of assets;
- distortion consequent of depreciation policies, inventory valuation and treatment of certain revenue and expenditure items;
- differences in methods of consolidating accounts;
- differences arising from lack of standardisation in accounting conventions internationally.

Eccles and Pyburn (1992) argue that one of the major limitations of using financial measures of performance is that they are 'lagged indicators' which are 'the result of management action and organisational performance, and not the cause of it' (p. 41). Traditional financial measures have also been criticised on the grounds that they:

- encourage short-termism, such as delay of capital investment (Hayes and Abernathy, 1980);
- lack strategic focus and fail to provide data on quality, responsiveness and flexibility (Skinner, 1974);
- encourage local optimisation (Hall, 1983);
- encourage managers to minimise the variances from standard rather than seek to improve continually (Turney and Anderson, 1989);
- fail to provide information on what customers want and how competitors are performing (Kaplan and Norton, 1992).

It is not suggested, of course, that conventional measures of financial performance should not be considered. In fact, authors suggested that profitability measures such as Return on Investment (ROI) and Return on Sales (ROS), despite their inherent limitations, are essential to the comprehensive representation of performance when properly complemented by other measures (Reece and Cool, 1978). The latter issue is significant, as many authors have contended that a multi-factor model of performance assessment should be used as a means of determining 'excellence' in firms (Bagozzi and Phillips, 1982; Benson, 1974). In the quest to determine 'excellence', Chakravarthy (1986) applies such a multi-factor model and shows that, although financial measures such as profitability Z score, Market/Book ratio and Debt/Equity ratio are important, they are not the sole determinants of excellence. Companies should also apply a stakeholder satisfaction index that will prevent alienation of stakeholders in the quest for satisfying stockholders. Strategic performance measures need to be applied to ensure that the ability to adapt to future environments and hence future performance is not compromised.

The implications for performance measurement of ship management firms are numerous. First, the importance of performance measurement for professional service firms is undisputed (see also Brignall and Ballantine, 1996). It is not enough to apply measures for achieving high quality, attracting/retaining clients and making profit; firms need to assess how well they have managed to achieve such objectives. As in other businesses, performance measurement in ship management firms has traditionally been based on financial/accounting measures. Although at departmental level other measures may have been used, there is a need for applying a systematic and organised performance measurement approach at corporate and strategic level. This approach should first seek to identify the determinants of business performance in ship management. Such determinants may include customer satisfaction, service quality, incident and accident rates, customer attraction, new services and other issues specific to the nature of ship management. The next step will be to determine how best to measure the performance of the company on these issues. For instance, customer satisfaction surveys, reports from the vessels, etc. should be consolidated and used by management in the assessment of performance. Financial measures also play an important role. Once performance measures have been adopted, implemented, and the results interpreted, the task of performance measurement does not end. In fact, managers should seek to improve the measures on the basis of previous results and performance, and also adapt the measures as the business environment changes.

8 Conclusion

Introduction

The aim of this chapter is to present the major implications emanating from the conceptual and empirical applications to ship management carried out earlier. Particular emphasis will be placed on managerial implications and the current direction of the professional ship management industry.

Ship Management Service Solutions

Professional ship management has been defined in chapter 2 as the contractual rendering of services related to the systematic organisation of economic resources and transactions required for the sustenance of a ship as a revenue-earning entity. The historical review carried out explaining the evolution of ship management underpins the importance of professional ship management in the international shipping scene.

Nowadays, the professional ship management service may be preferred by different types of shipowning organisations for various reasons, whereas others may prefer other forms of organisation to manage their ships. Outsourcing ship management is purely a function of the costs and benefits as perceived by the shipowner and as influenced by the prevailing market and economic conditions. Ship managers cite the traditional arguments of expertise, quality, professionalism, and cost competitiveness due to the achievement of scale economies in their effort to make the case for third party management. Nevertheless, it is also important to analyse the external environmental factors prevailing at the time, including the opportunities that can be reaped in ship operation, and devise solutions for particular shipowners in their effort to reinforce the outsourcing rationale. Ship management should move forward towards offering innovative solutions as opposed to operating a fleet of ships by following fixed procedures applicable to everybody. The economics of vertical disintegration suggest that outsourcing ship management may lower the costs of production of ship operation and management for the shipowning entity. Arguing for the efficiency benefits and cost effectiveness of outsourcing is one thing, however and attracting and retaining the business is another. Shipowners who choose other organisational forms for ship management, such as in-house departments or subsidiaries formed to manage the vessels of a parent company, may appreciate the current outsourcing rationale, which may nevertheless be insufficient. It is noted that professional ship management has achieved competitive status by virtue of improved efficiency in organising the economic resources and transactions required for ship operation. This, however, translates into a lower cost of production, but not in identifying and fulfilling client requirements – even if the former leads to a lower price this has been found to be important but not absolutely imperative in the selection of a professional ship manager. Attracting and retaining the business requires identification and anticipation of specific customer needs and development of service solutions to satisfy those needs.

Markets, Location and Entry

One of the most difficult tasks is to establish with a certain degree of validity the number and geographical dispersion of ship management companies. Various statistics that exist are highlighted in the book and an idea of ship management market structure is provided. Choice of location has once again been an outcome of lowering production costs and efficiency. Fewer companies have established in particular locations for marketing and strategic reasons. Marketing reasons would include serving, for instance, existing clients whereas strategic reasons may entail the prospects of a particular location for creating business.

The reduction of production costs and efficiency that account for establishment in particular locations tax reasons, lower operating costs, proximity to supply sources, especially crew, proximity to ships and proximity to clients. The ideal situation – with the company objectives always in mind – would be to have headquarters in a tax advantageous location, but at the same time maintain physical links (through subsidiaries/joint ventures) with important locations of supply sources and key clients. It is evident that ship managers may set up offices in certain locations after having been awarded with a major contract from a new client. This seems to be a reasonable strategy, as companies are not only seen as making a major investment in their effort to provide customer satisfaction, but are also establishing a foothold in a new market where potential opportunities for further expansion may exist. Rarely will companies set up a subsidiary in a new market without a substantial contract. A notable exception has been Acomarit and its efforts to establish a foothold in the Greek market. Initially a joint venture operation with a local partner, Acomarit moved on to maintain a wholly-owned subsidiary in 1994 after the withdrawal of the partner. The first breakthrough seemed to have come some six years later with a landmark contract to manage the LMZ-Transoil fleet. This has been a relatively high-risk strategy in the effort of Acomarit to sway the Greek shipping community to appreciate the advantages of outsourcing. The next breakthrough for professional ship management companies in Greece might come from the smaller owners that are reluctant to invest in new technologies, particularly IT. Information technology represents another input required for efficient ship management, and hence another cost of producing the service. As the resources required for efficient ship operation continue to expand, smaller owners may find it increasingly difficult to organise such resources cost effectively. They will need to outsource either full ship management or aspects of the ship management operation – the efficiency reasons for growth-minded companies are compelling. On the other hand, small local ship management start-ups in Greece are certain to pose serious competition threats for the international companies.

Problems and Panaceas

Fierce competition on a multitude of aspects, client uncertainty and defections, human resource sourcing and training, and the relatively low level of management fees are the major problems facing the ship management industry. Success in coping with such problems is determined, to a large extent, by the ability of management to apply the strategies, policies and tactics that have been the centre of discussion throughout this text. The relatively recent expansion of the industry at large, but also of individual companies in particular, however, is the most concrete justification that the prospects are promising, so long as change is forthcoming.

The behaviour of ship management companies in terms of adopted strategies reviewed in the book signifies a trend with numerous underlying implications. Those companies that have adapted to new states of affairs in international shipping, that applied new strategies and concepts such as diversification, that had growth-oriented objectives and specific plans to achieve them have made significant progress over the last ten years. Only a brief look at the recent history of ship management suggests that companies that have made significant advances were those that have been engaging in continuous transactions and exchanges with the external environment. These included but are not limited to identifying new markets and new suppliers, devising new solutions for efficiency and expanding by co-operation or acquisition.

As mentioned above, adaptation to a new state in the affairs of international shipping is of extreme importance and the ISM Code and IT provide good examples of this. The ISM Code has numerous implications and should not be regarded as a mere marketing tool or a necessary evil, but as a business philosophy that permeates the organisational structure in its entirety. It is also quite clear that ISM implementation has not crystallised the panacea expected by many for third party ship management. The advent of information technology has meant that new opportunities and challenges have been presented to ship management companies, and many of them, have reacted accordingly to the new state of technological advances. Information technology not only presents an operational tool for improving efficiency but may have strategic implications for ship managers. This may be true in particular with respect to owners in various locations that still seem reluctant to embrace new technologies and might be doing themselves a disservice. It also has implications in the identification of potential competitors.

Client Relationships

Ship management may be moving away from the provision of personalised services and individual dedication towards greater commercialisation and expansion. This may have been brought about by the greater need for efficiency and rationalisation that has swept across the whole shipping industry. A parallel can be drawn with liner shipping companies. Liner companies are themselves operating in a service industry, where reliability, trustworthiness and good client relationships are essential features. These maritime organisations have diversified enormously to the extent of becoming involved in the provision of a complete range of services for the carriage of goods by sea and land. Liner shipping companies have invested in logistics systems and are also becoming involved in the operation of port terminals, facilitated by the swing towards privatisation. It is possible that the bigger ship management companies will themselves seek expansion and rationalisation of the service by vertical and horizontal integration. Vertical integration may involve acquisitions of suppliers like manning agencies or ship chandlers. This may be the way for achieving greater efficiency, rationalisation of the service offer and greater profits, and this is the direction in which ship management may currently be moving. Additionally, liner companies have formed strategic alliances in order to reap greater economies of scale, acquire greater market and bargaining power at the expense of shippers, and yield greater profits. It seems logical to deduce that the large ship management companies may themselves seek greater co-operation rather than damaging competition. Strategic alliance formation in ship management may take the form of more than two companies sharing resources that they command internationally. For instance, if one company has expertise in technical management and supply of spare parts and another in crewing, the potential for co-operation in the areas of comparative advantage for the achievement of greater efficiency is quite rational. The trend away from personal services to the achievement of greater profits through increased power and expansion suggests that strategic alliances among ship management companies may be the next major change in the ship management industry. The viability of co-operative arrangements in ship management will, to a large extent, depend on the ability of companies to forge stable long-term relationships. Hence, the importance of relational capability for ship management companies. The forms that such co-operative arrangements may take will depend on various factors, including the power relationship of companies and the objectives sought. The recent merger of V. Ships and Celtic Marine provides a prominent example of such co-operation of two companies each having a comparative advantage in a particular area of ship management. This high profile merger also confirms the findings of previous research (Panayides, 1998) of the trend towards greater co-operation and integration of ship management companies.

Client Needs and Expectations

Ship management companies are concerned with two fundamental marketing issues in particular. On one hand they are interested in attracting new clients, whereas at the same time they are looking to retain their existing client base amidst an environment of intense competition for market share. Central to client attraction and retention is identification of the important and determinant dimensions for ship manager selection and evaluation. As empirically determined and expounded herein, clients are more interested in attributes of service quality, evidenced by such factors as technical ability and experience of personnel and supported by the reputation of the company, in choosing a ship manager. The level of the management fee plays a secondary role in the selection procedure – cutting costs to the bone at the compromise of quality is not a recommended course of action for ship management companies. Reputation is built up over time, and the attitudes and behaviour of personnel and senior management are instrumental not only in delivering high level service but also in achieving respect among clients and competitors.

Client retention rests to a large extent on delivering on promises made and clients' expectations. The determinant characteristics that ship managers must convey and upon which clients are more likely to base their performance evaluation include trust, reliability and integrity, proven technical ability and responsiveness, and problem-solving ability. To the extent that ship managers are able to demonstrate such abilities and foster a relationship based on trust, they would erect strong barriers against defections of clients to competitors.

The process of client attraction and retention may be conceptualised to consist of six phases. Client attraction and retention begins from the foresight of managerial staff in devising solutions that would satisfy target markets, what may be termed the 'discovery' (of solutions) and the 'exploration' (of markets). Phase three is the 'initiation' or 'inquiry' phase and involves the demonstration of an ability to deliver on promises made. Once a contract is agreed, the process moves on to the 'transaction' phase. At this point, there is no assurance of the long-term nature of the relationship – a client may defect at the end of the contract. The ship manager needs to demonstrate an ability to deliver on the promises made and even to exceed contractual obligations. Evidence of service quality, technical ability and responsiveness, coupled with the integrity of the manager, will assist towards the build-up of trust and the gradual shift from the 'transaction' phase to the 'relationship' phase. The latter entails the presence of social/psychological bonds in addition to economic bonds, fostering the ties between ship manager and client. The last phase involves the continuous improvement of the 'relationship' quality and the service offered, and the development of new solutions to meet more and changing client needs and expectations.

The Sustainability of Competitiveness

Various models and dimensions have been proposed for the achievement of a competitive advantage in business industries. In the ship management context, it is not the application of a single model that would seem to achieve such an objective. Rather, it is a combination of certain key drivers that will ensure sustainable competitiveness. The achievement of a competitive advantage is certainly not a function of top management alone, and recent advances advocating the importance of certain asset stocks that require input from everybody in the organisation exacerbate this. Service performance, for instance, or relationships with customers and suppliers are not the function, of management alone, but of all those employees that may come in direct contact with customers or influence the delivery of a high quality service.

The basic tenets of achieving competitive advantage include cost advantage relative to competitors, adaptation to customer needs, and differentiation. How cost advantage will be achieved depends largely on management's ability to improve efficiency in the internal organisation of resources. Staff must be competent and need to be productive. Human resource management is critical, and continuous assessment of improvement and capabilities should be undertaken. A major cause of under-performance in service quality and delivery may be the incompetence of certain staff. The cultivation and development of core competencies and organisational capabilities seems to be the next level upon which ship management companies will compete. The collective organisation of resources for delivering high service quality and continuous integration of available technologies in the company's processes are fundamental aspects for ensuring sustainable competitiveness. Their accumulation is accomplished over time, and needs to be identified and appropriately harnessed and utilised. Ship managers should be looking at the level of core competencies and organisational capabilities to identify the next level of sustainable competitive advantage.

Strategic Directions

Expansion through merger, acquisition and diversification seem to be the prevailing strategies at the forefront of the agenda for the big players in ship management.

The contemporary scene on ship management strategy may be analysed by a simple classification of the companies in accordance with their strategic direction, as evidenced by recent moves and behaviour. Hence, one may identify small companies to be at the core of a model and concentrating on the provision of services for satisfaction of current clients.

This may be followed by companies that, in addition to the above, are also keen and more proactive in attracting more clients, but without embarking on high-profile strategic moves and content to work diligently within their given market. Following this type of company are the companies that are content to embark on a certain number of international expansion strategies and diversification, without diverting too much from their core business activity and markets. Columbia Shipmanagement and Denholm Ship Management may represent such companies. At the outer end of the model are the bigger players emulated by companies such as V. Ships and Acomarit. These companies seek to expand continuously, embarking on diversification, joint ventures and mergers and acquisitions. At this moment in time, there does not seem to be a clear indication that a particular strategic direction is superior or inferior to another. From a pure business perspective, however, size does matter, and the bigger players that have embarked on successful expansion strategies may be better able to satisfy their shareholders.

Professional Ship Management: Marketing and Strategy

The theme of this book, and the ensuing empirical examinations and discussions, culminated into the delimitation of a number of important issues in professional ship management encapsulated as follows.

Efficient Organisation of Resources

This is one of the most important aspects for professional ship management firms, i.e. the achievement of Pareto efficiency to:

- minimise costs of production;
- gain competitiveness in relation to other forms of ship management organisation;
- gain absolute cost advantage in relation to competitors.

Marketing

Adoption of contemporary principles of marketing will assist companies in the achievement of key objectives. Marketing is essential in professional ship management for:

- creating new markets;
- understanding and anticipating changing client needs and developing service solutions to satisfy those needs;
- creating new services to satisfy new and changing client needs;
- attracting new clients;
- identifying homogeneous groups of clients through market segmentation;
- targeting specific market segments;
- retaining existing clients by developing client relationships;
- improving service quality through investment in new technologies and concepts and internal marketing.

Strategy

Strategy is longer term, and can be used in the specification of courses of action to achieve organisational objectives including marketing objectives. Formulation of strategy and strategic planning is essential in professional ship management for:

- growth and profitability – companies that do not aim for growth will eventually stagnate and decline; without proper strategic planning and clear objectives companies like Acomarit and V. Ships would have not achieved the success they are currently enjoying;
- change – without change there is no progress; change should permeate all levels of the organisation and should include operational and organisational aspects;
- recognising and combating potential problem areas;
- identifying and seizing opportunities arising in the external environment;
- achieving sustainable competitiveness through the cultivation of core organisational competencies and capabilities.

Professional ship management is no longer just in the business of managing ships; it is also in the business of business.

Bibliography

Aaker, D. A. and Day, G. S. (1980), *Marketing Research: Private and Public Sector Decisions*, John Wiley & Sons, Toronto.

Achrol, R. S., Reve, T. and Stern, L. W. (1983), 'The Environment of Marketing Channel Dyads: A Framework for Comparative Analysis', *Journal of Marketing*, vol. 47, Fall, pp. 55-67.

Ahimud, Y. and Lev, B. (1991), 'Risk Reduction as a Managerial Motive for Conglomerate Mergers', *Bell Journal of Economics*, vol. 12, pp. 605-617.

Airey, A. J. (1995), 'Ship Management', in G. P. Gunton, *Lloyd's Nautical Yearbook*, Lloyd's of London Press, London, pp. 25-35.

Albrecht, K. and Zemke, R. (1985), *Service America*, Dow-Jones Irwin, Homewood, IL.

Alchian, A. and Demsetz, H. (1972), 'Production, Information Costs, and Economic Organisation', *American Economic Review*, vol. 62, no. 5, pp. 777-795.

Alderson, W. and Martin, M. W. (1965), 'Toward a Formal Theory of Transactions and Transvections, *Journal of Marketing Research*, vol. 2, May, pp. 117-127.

Alles, M., Newman, P. and Noel, J. (1998), 'The Value of Information in Internal Management Communication', *Journal of Economic Behaviour and Organisation*, vol. 36, no. 3, pp. 295-317.

Ambler, T. (1994), 'The Relational Paradigm: A Synthesis', in J. N. Sheth and A. Parvatiyar, (eds), *Relationship Marketing: Theory, Methods and Applications*, 1994 Research Conference Proceedings, Centre for Relationship Marketing, Emory University, Atlanta.

Anderson, E., Lodish, L. M. and Weitz, B. (1987), 'Resource Allocation Behaviour in Conventional Channels', *Journal of Marketing Research*, vol. 24, February, pp. 85-97.

Anderson, J. C. and Narus, J. A. (1990), 'A Model of Distributor Firm and Manufacturer Firm Working Relationships', *Journal of Marketing*, vol. 54, January, pp. 42-58.

Anderson, E. and Weitz, B. (1989), 'Determinants of Continuity in Conventional Industrial Channel Dyads', *Marketing Science*, vol. 8, no. 4, pp. 310-323.

Ang, S. (1998), 'Production and Transaction Economies and IS Outsourcing: A Study of the US Banking Industry', *MIS Quarterly*, vol. 22, no. 4, pp. 535-552.

Anon (1985), 'AMA Board Approves New Marketing Definition', *Marketing News*, vol. 19, no. 5, p. 1.

Anon (1987), 'Keeping Abreast', *Seatrade Business Review*, March/April, pp. 139-141.

Anon (1989a), 'Third Party Ship Management Moving Forward and Adapting to Change', *Lloyd's Ship Manager* supplement, March, pp. 1-2.

Anon (1989b), 'Navigo's Expansion has been Rapid in its Relatively Short History', *Lloyd's Ship Manager* supplement, March, p. 10.

Anon (1991), 'Reservations over Group of Five's Proposed Code for Ship Management Standards', *Lloyd's Ship Manager,* March, pp. 30-35.

Anon (1992), 'ISMA's First Year Membership Target Reached, but Few Audits are in Hand', *Lloyd's Ship Manager,* March, p. 9.

Anon (1994a), 'Review of Ship Management', *International Bulk Journal,* vol. 14, no. 2, pp. 87-91.

Anon (1994b), *A Profile of the International Ship Managers' Association,* ISMA publication.

Anon (1995a), 'Safman Keeps Full-Time Crews', *Lloyd's List,* Wednesday, October 18, p. 7.

Anon (1995b), 'V. Ships has Key Role in Plan for Former Soviet Hull', *Lloyd's List,* Wednesday, June 14, p. 6.

Anon (1995c), 'Ugland Links up with Interocean', *Lloyd's List,* Wednesday, April 26, p. 1.

Anon (1995d), 'Firms Differ on In-House Option', *Lloyd's List,* Wednesday, July 12, p. 7.

Anon (1995e), 'Barber Consolidation Moves Operation to Kuala Lumpur', *Lloyd's List,* Wednesday, August 16, p. 9.

Anon (1995f), 'DML Builds to Put Down Roots', *Lloyd's List,* Wednesday, October 18, p. 7.

Anon (1995g), 'Quality Management: Jury out on QM Benefits', *Lloyd's Shipping Economist,* vol. 17, no. 11, pp. 6-8.

Anon (1995h), 'ISMA: Managing the Future', *Lloyd's Ship Manager Supplement,* October, p. 19.

Anon (1995i), 'ISMA: Managing the Future', *Lloyd's Ship Manager Supplement,* October, p. 13.

Anon (1995j), 'Acomarit Joins Argument on Safety Codes', *Lloyd's List,* Tuesday, January 31, p. 5.

Anon (1995k), 'Dorchester Stays out of ISMA', *Lloyd's List,* Wednesday, June 28, p. 9.

Anon (1995l), 'ISMA Prepares for a New Role by Extending its Influence, *Lloyd's List,* Tuesday, October 10, p. 5.

Anon (1995m), 'Wallem Maintains Numbers', *Lloyd's List,* August 16, p. 10.

Anon (1995n), 'London Steals March on Norway', *Lloyd's List,* Wednesday, June 28, p. 9.

Anon (1995o), 'Glasgow Wins Place as Base for Managers', *Lloyd's List,* March 10, p. 7.

Anon (1995p), 'Providing the Right Environment for Business to Flourish', *Lloyd's List,* October 30, p. 11.

Anon (1995q), 'Midocean Expands into New HQ', *Lloyd's List,* October 18, p. 7.

Anon, (1995r), 'Columbia Wins APL Deal in Fierce Race', *Lloyd's List,* January 17, p. 5.

Anon (1996a), 'Columbia Targets Newbuilding Supervision', *Lloyd's List*, October 29, p. 6.

Anon (1996b), 'Blue-chip Columbia Puts Training at the Forefront', *Lloyd's List*, June 14, p. 7.

Anon (1996c), 'Interorient Blooms with New Ventures', *Lloyd's List*, September 3, p. 8.

Anon (1996d), 'Major Ship Managers Rely on Dedicated Networks', *Lloyd's List*, July 15, p. 6.

Anon (1996e), 'V Ships Takes Growing Cruise Sector Role', *Lloyd's List*, October 29, p. 7.

Anon (1996f), 'Company Case Studies Highlight Differing IT Issues', *Lloyd's List*, November 23, p. 10.

Anon (1996g), 'ISMA Wins Code Benefits', *Lloyd's List*, September 17, p. 10.

Anon (1996h), 'Austrian Lloyd Tips Major Transition with ISM', *Lloyd's Ship Manager*, vol. 16, no. 10, p. 29.

Anon (1996i), 'Acomarit Expands from its Geneva Base', *Lloyd's List*, February 1, p. 9.

Anon (1997a), 'Universal Marine and Techno Marine Join Forces', *Lloyd's List*, December 4, p. 5.

Anon (1997b), 'V. Ships Eyes New Markets', *Lloyd's List*, April 12, p. 3.

Anon (1997c), 'Managing Costs Gives Barber Something to Smile About', *Lloyd's List*, July 4, p. 5.

Anon (1997d), 'Tax Regime Aids Shipmanagers', *Lloyd's List*, Wednesday, February 27, p. 7.

Anon (1997e), 'Eurasia Seeks to Expand Network', *Lloyd's List*, July 31, p. 6.

Anon (1997f), 'Ship Managers Face Good Times', *Lloyd's Ship Manager*, vol. 18, no. 6, pp. 55-56.

Anon (1997g), 'Seahorse Wins Race for ASP: Australian Stakeholder ANL Set to Sell Stake to UK Shipmanager', *Lloyd's List*, October 13, p. 1.

Anon (1997h), 'Acomarit Buys Nordic', *Lloyd's List*, January 17, p. 1.

Anon (1998a), 'Acomarit Loses Greek Partner', *Lloyd's List*, March 5, p. 1.

Anon (1998b), 'Acomarit Looking for two Kinds of Growth', *Lloyd's List*, June 9, p.7.

Anon (1999a), 'Supply Cloud over Glasgow Managers' Future', *Ship Management – Special Issue of the Baltic Magazine*, February, pp. 8-9.

Anon (1999b), 'Hong Kong Battles High Costs to Stay Ahead', *Ship Management – Special Issue of the Baltic Magazine*, February, pp. 15-17.

Anon (2000a), 'Management: Pros and Cons', *World Ship Owner*, March, pp. 37-39.

Anon (2000b), 'Managing the Trade', *Lloyd's Ship Manager*, January, pp. 30-32.

Armistead, C. G. (1990), 'Service Operations Strategy: Framework for Matching the Service Operations Task and the Service Delivery System', *International Journal of Service Industry Management*, vol. 1, no. 2, pp. 6-17.

Arndt, J. (1983), 'The Political Economy Paradigm: Foundation for Theory Building in Marketing', *Journal of Marketing*, vol. 47, Fall, pp. 44-54.

Bagozzi, R. P. (1974), 'Marketing as an Organised Behavioural System of Exchange', *Journal of Marketing*, vol. 38, October, pp. 77-81.

Bagozzi, R. P. (1975), 'Marketing as Exchange', *Journal of Marketing*, vol. 39, October, pp. 32-39.

Bagozzi, R. P. (1978), 'Marketing as Exchange. A Theory of Transactions in the Marketplace', *American Behavioural Scientist*, vol. 21, no. 4, pp. 535-556.

Bagozzi, R. P. (1979), 'Toward a Formal Theory of Marketing Exchanges', in O. C. Ferrell, S. W. Brown and C. W. Lamb, (eds), *Conceptual and Theoretical Developments in Marketing*, American Marketing Association, Chicago, pp. 431-447.

Bagozzi, R. P. and Phillips, L. W. (1982), 'Representing and Testing Organisational Theories: A Holistic Construal', *Administrative Science Quarterly*, vol. 17, pp. 459-489.

Banks, R. L. and Wheelwright, S. C. (1979), 'Operations versus Strategy – Trading Tomorrow for Today', *Harvard Business Review*, May-June, pp. 112-120.

Banville, G. R. and Dornoff, R. J. (1973), 'Industrial Source Selection Behaviour – An Industry Study', *Industrial Marketing Management,* vol. 2, June, pp. 251-260.

Bardi, E. J. (1973), 'Carrier Selection from One Mode', *Transportation Journal*, vol. 13, no. 1, pp. 23-24.

Barnes, J. G. (1994), 'Close to the Customer: But is it Really a Relationship?', *Journal of Marketing Management*, vol. 10, pp. 561-570.

Barney, J. B. (1986), 'Organisational Culture: Can it be a Source of Sustained Competitive Advantage?' *Academy of Management Review*, vol. 11, no. 3, pp. 656-665.

Barney, J. B. (1989), 'Asset Stocks and Sustained Competitive Advantage: A Comment', *Management Science*, vol. 35, pp. 1511-1513.

Barney, J. B. (1991), 'Firm Resources and Sustained Competitive Advantage', *Journal of Management*, vol. 17, pp. 99-120.

Barney, J. B. and Hansen, M. H. (1994), 'Trustworthiness as a Source of Competitive Advantage', *Strategic Management Journal*, vol. 15, pp. 175-190.

Beaton, M. and Beaton, C. (1995), 'Marrying Service Providers and their Clients: A Relationship Approach to Services Management', *Journal of Marketing Management*, vol. 11, pp. 55-70.

Beaumont, P. B. (1992), 'The US Human Resource Management Literature: A Review', in G. Salaman, (ed), *Human Resource Strategies*, Sage, London

Benson, J. K. (1974), 'Comment on Price's 'The Study of Organisational Effectiveness', *Sociological Quarterly*, vol. 14, pp. 273-276.

Benson, J. and Ieronimo, N. (1996), 'Outsourcing Decisions: Evidence from Australia-based Enterprises', *International Labour Review*, vol. 135, pp. 59-73.

Berger, P. G. and Ofek, E. (1995), 'Diversification's Effect on Firm Value', *Journal of Financial Economics*, vol. 37 no. 1, 39-65.

Berry, L. L. (1981), 'Perspectives on the Retailing of Services', in R. W. Stampfl and E. C. Hirschman (eds), *Theory in Retailing: Traditional and Non-traditional Sources*, American Marketing Association, Chicago, pp. 9-20.

Berry, L. L. (1983), 'Relationship Marketing', in L. L. Berry, G. L. Shostack, and G. D. Upah, (eds), *Emerging Perspectives on Services Marketing*, American Marketing Association, Chicago, pp. 25-28.

Berry, L. L. (1995), 'Relationship Marketing of Services – Growing Interest, Emerging Perspectives', *Journal of the Academy of Marketing Science*, vol. 23, no. 4, pp. 236-245.

Berry, L. L. and Parasuraman, A. (1991), *Marketing Services: Competing Through Quality*, The Free Press, New York.

Berry, L. L., Zeithaml, V. and Parasuraman, A. (1985), 'Quality Counts in Business Too', *Business Horizons*, vol. 31, May-June, p. 46.

Berry, L. L., Zeithaml, V. and Parasuraman, A. (1991), 'Refinement and Re-assessment of the Servqual Scale', *Journal of Retailing*, vol. 67, Winter, pp. 420-450.

Berry, L. L., Parasuraman, A. and Zeithaml, V. A. (1994), 'Improving Service Quality in America: Lessons Learned', *Academy of Management Executive*, vol. 8, no. 2, pp. 32-45.

Berry, L. L. and Thompson, T. W. (1982), 'Relationship Banking: The Art of Turning Customers into Clients', *Journal of Retail Banking*, vol. 4, no. 2, pp. 64-73.

Bettis, R. A. (1981), 'Performance Differences in Related and Unrelated Diversifiers', *Strategic Management Journal*, vol. 2, pp. 379-383.

Bitner, M. J. (1993), 'Tracking the Evolution of the Service Marketing Literature', *Journal of Retailing*, vol. 69, Spring, pp. 61-103.

Bleeke, J. and Ernst, D. (1993), *Collaborating to Compete*, John Wiley & Sons, New York.

Blois, K. J. (1996a), 'Relationship Marketing in Organisational Markets: When is it Appropriate?' *Journal of Marketing Management*, vol. 12, pp. 161-173.

Blois, K. J. (1996b), 'Relationship Marketing in Organisational Markets – Assessing its Costs and Benefits', *Journal of Strategic Marketing*, vol. 4, pp. 181-191.

Bolton, R. N. and Drew, J. H. (1991), 'A Multistage Model of Customers' Assessments of Service Quality and Value', *Journal of Consumer Research*, vol. 17, March, pp. 375-384.

Bonoma, T., Bagozzi, R. P. and Zaltman, G. (1978), 'The Dyadic Paradigm with Specific Application Toward Industrial Marketing', in T. V. Bonoma, and G. Zaltman, (eds), *Organisational Buying Behaviour*, American Marketing Association, Chicago, IL., pp. 49-66.

Booms, B. H. and Bitner, M. J. (1981), 'Marketing Strategies and Organisation Structures for Service Firms', in J. Donnelly and W. R. George, (eds), *Marketing of Services*, American Marketing Association, Chicago, IL., pp. 47-51.

Boston Consulting Group (1970), *Perspective on Experience*, BCG, Boston.

Bowen, D. E. and Lawler, E. E. (1992), 'Total Quality-Oriented Human Resources Management', *Organisational Dynamics*, vol. 20, no. 4, pp. 29-41.

Branch, A. E. (1989), *Elements of Shipping*, Chapman and Hall, London.

Bray, J. (1996), 'Saudi Contract for Acomarit', *Lloyd's List*, July 16, p. 1.

Brignall, S. and Ballantine, J. (1996), 'Performance Measurement in Service Business Revisited', *International Journal of Service Industry Management*, vol. 7, no. 1, pp. 6-31.

Brodie, R. J., Coviello, N. E., Brookes, R. W. and Little, V. (1997), 'Towards a Paradigm Shift in Marketing? An Examination of Current Marketing Practices', *Journal of Marketing Management*, vol. 13, no. 5, pp. 383-406.

Brooks, M. R. (1985), 'An Alternative Theoretical Approach to the Evaluation of Liner Shipping. Part II: Choice Criteria', *Maritime Policy and Management*, vol. 12, no. 2, pp. 145-155.

Brooks, M. R. (1990), ' Ocean Carrier Selection Criteria in a New Environment', *Logistics and Transportation Review*, vol. 26, no. 4, pp. 339-356.

Brown, S. W. and Swartz, T. (1989), 'A Gap Analysis of Professional Service Quality', *Journal of Marketing*, vol. 53, April, pp. 92-98.

Brush, T. H. (1996), 'Predicted Change in Operational Synergy and Post-Acquisition Performance of Acquired Businesses', *Strategic Management Journal*, vol. 17, pp. 1-24.

Buckley, P. J. (1992), 'Alliances, Technology and Markets: A Cautionary Tale', in P. J. Buckley, *Studies in International Business*, Macmillan, London.

Bundock, M. (1989), 'Few Firm Pointers to a Manager's Legal Status', *Seatrade Business Review*, September/October, pp. 81-87.

Burg, H. B. and Daley, J. M. (1985), 'Shallow Water Transportation: Marketing Implications of User and Carrier Attribute Perceptions', *Transportation Journal*, vol. 24, no. 3, pp. 55-67.

Buttle, F. (1996), 'Relationship Marketing', in F. Buttle, (ed), *Relationship Marketing: Theory and Practice*, Paul Chapman Publishing Ltd, London, pp. 1-16.

Buzzell, R. D. (1964), *Mathematical Models and Marketing Management*, Harvard University, Boston.

Buzzell, R. D. and Gale, B. T. (1987), *The PIMS principles – Linking Strategy to Performance*, The Free Press, New York.

Camerer, C. and Vepsalainen, A. (1988), 'The Economic Efficiency of Corporate Culture', *Strategic Management Journal*, vol. 9, Special Issue, pp. 115-126.

Chadha, K. K. (1996), 'Univan Creates Joint Venture', *Lloyd's List*, Thursday, April, 25, p. 3.

Chakravarthy, B. S. (1986), 'Measuring Strategic Performance', *Strategic Management Journal*, vol. 7, pp. 437-458.

Chandler, A. D. (1962), *Strategy and Structure: Chapters in the History of the American Industrial Enterprise*, MIT Press, Cambridge, MA.

Chapman, S. (1992), 'Flagging Strategies', in *Leading Developments in Ship Management,* 2nd International Lloyd's Ship Manager Ship Management Conference, Lloyd's of London Press, London, pp. 59-67.

Chapman, S. (1994), 'Ship Management Under Pressure', in *International Ship Management-4,* 4th International Ship Management Conference, Lloyd's of London Press, London, pp. 7-12.

Chatterjee, S. (1986), 'Types of Synergy and Economic Value: The Impact of Acquisitions on Merging and Rival Firms', *Strategic Management Journal,* vol. 7, no. 2, pp. 119-140.

Chatterjee, S. and Wernerfelt, B. (1991), 'The Link Between Resources and Type of Diversification', *Strategic Management Journal,* vol. 12, pp. 33-48.

Christopher, M., Payne, A. and Ballantyne, D. (1993), *Relationship Marketing: Bringing Quality, Customer Service and Marketing Together,* Butterworth-Heinemann, Oxford.

Clark, M., Peck, H., Payne, A. and Christopher, M. (1995), 'Relationship Marketing: Towards a New Paradigm' in A. Payne (ed), *Advances in Relationship Marketing,* Kogan Page, London, pp. 263-280.

Coase, R. H. (1937), 'The Nature of the Firm', *Economica,* vol. 4, pp. 386-405.

Cochran, I. (1995), 'Ship Management: In Search of Quality', *Lloyd's List Maritime Asia,* July, pp. 6-7.

Cole, R. E. (1993), 'Learning from Learning Theory: Implications for Quality Improvement of Turnover, Use of Contingent Workers, and Job Rotation Policies', *Quality Management Journal,* vol. 1, no. 1, pp. 9-25.

Collis, D. (1991), 'A Resource-Based Analysis of Global Competition: The Case of the Bearings Industry', *Strategic Management Journal,* vol. 12, pp. 49-68.

Comaner, W. and Wilson, T. (1974), *Advertising and Market Power,* Harvard University Press, Cambridge, MA.

Comment, R. and Jarrell, G. (1995), 'Corporate Focus and Stock Returns', *Journal of Financial Economics,* vol. 37, no. 1, pp. 67-87.

Congram, C. A. (1991), 'Building Relationships that Last', in C. A. Congram, and M. L. Friedman, (eds), *The AMA Handbook of Marketing in the Service Industries,* AMACOM, New York, pp. 263-279.

Conner, K. (1991), 'A Historical Comparison of Resource-Based Theory and Five Schools of Thought within Industrial Organisation Economics: Do we Have a New Theory of the Firm?', *Journal of Management,* vol. 17, pp. 121-154.

Containerisation International (1999), 'Carrier Selection', October, pp. 45-47.

Contractor, F. J. and Lorange, P. (1988), 'Why Should Firms Co-operate? The Strategy and Economics Basis for Co-operative Ventures', in F. J. Contractor and P. Lorange (eds), *Co-operative Strategies in International Business,* Lexington Books, Lexington, MA., chapter 1, pp. 3-28.

Cook, W. R. (1967), 'Transport Decisions of Certain Firms in the Black Country', *Journal of Transport Economics and Policy,* vol. 1, no. 2, pp. 326-344.

Cooney, P. (1992), 'Ship Management: What Price Quality?', *Seatrade Review,* February, pp. 83-85.

Cowell, D. (1984), *The Marketing of Services*, Heinemann, London.

Cross, J. (1995), 'IT Outsourcing: British Petroleum's Competitive Approach', *Harvard Business Review*, vol. 73, no. 3, pp. 94-103.

Crozier, M. (1964), *The Bureaucratic Phenomenon*, University of Chicago Press, Chicago, IL.

Cullinane, K. and Toy, N. (2000), 'Identifying Influential Attributes in Freight Route/Mode Choice Decisions: A Content Analysis', *Transportation Research Part E*, vol. 36, pp. 41-53.

Cunningham, M. T. and Homse, E. (1986), 'Controlling the Marketing-Purchasing Interface: Resource Development and Organisational Implications', *Industrial Marketing & Purchasing*, vol. 1, no. 2, pp. 3-25.

Cunningham, M. T. and Turnbull, P. W. (1982), 'Inter-organisational Personal Contact Patterns', in H. Hakansson (ed), *International Marketing and Purchasing of Industrial Goods - An Interaction Approach*, John Wiley & Sons, Chichester, pp. 304-316.

Cunningham, M. T. and White, J. G. (1973), 'The Determinants of Choice of Supplier', *European Journal of Marketing*, vol. 7, Winter, pp. 189-202.

D' Aveni, R. (1994), *Hypercompetition*, The Free Press, New York.

D'Aveni, R. (1995), 'Coping with Hypercompetition: Utilising the 7S's Framework', *Academy of Management Executive*, vol. 9, pp. 45-60.

Datta, D. K., Rajagopalan, N. and Rasheed, A. M. A. (1991), 'Diversification and Performance: Critical Review and Future Directions', *Journal of Management Studies*, vol. 28, no. 5, 529-558.

Dean, J. and Bowen, D. (1994), 'Management Theory and Total Quality: Improving Research and Practice Through Theory Development', *Academy of Management Review*, vol. 19, no. 3, pp. 392-418.

D'Este, G. M. and Mayrick, S. (1992), 'Carrier Selection in a RO/RO Ferry Trade. Part I: Decision Factors and Attitudes', *Maritime Policy and Management*, vol. 19, no. 2, pp. 115-126.

Deming, W. E. (1986), *Out of the Crisis*, MIT Press, Cambridge, MA.

Deming, W. E. (1993), *The New Economics*, MIT Press, Cambridge, MA.

Dempsey, W. A. (1978), 'Vendor Selection and the Buying Process', *Industrial Marketing Management*, vol. 7, August, pp. 257-267.

Dickey, A. (1995), 'Sea Malta in Management Project for Med Owners', *Lloyd's List*, Wednesday, October 18, p. 14.

Dierickx, I. and Cool, K. (1989), 'Asset Stock Accumulation and Sustainability of Competitive Advantage', *Management Science*, vol. 35, pp. 1504-1511.

Dixon, D. F. and Wilkinson, I. F. (1989), 'An Alternative Paradigm for Marketing Theory', *European Journal of Marketing*, vol. 23, no. 8, pp. 59-70.

Donthu, N. (1993), 'Comparative Advertising of Professional Services', *Journal of Professional Services Marketing*, vol. 9, no. 1, pp. 95-103.

Dorey, J. (1989), 'Who will be the Ship Managers' Customers in the 1990's and what Services will they Require?', in *International Ship Management: Profit or*

Loss from Shipping's Revival, Lloyd's Ship Manager and Shipping News International Conference, Lloyd's of London Press, London.

Downard, J. M. (1981), *Running Costs*, Fairplay, Surrey.

Downard, J. M. (1987), *Managing Ships*, Fairplay, Surrey.

Drewry (1996), *Shipping Finance: A High Risk–Low Return Business?*, Drewry Shipping Consultants, London.

Duncan, R. (1972), 'Characteristics of Organisational Environments and Perceived Environmental Uncertainty', *Administrative Science Quarterly*, vol. 17, pp. 313-327.

Durvasula, S., Lysonski, S. and Mehta, S. C. (2000), 'Business-to-Business Marketing: Service Recovery and Customer Satisfaction Issues with Ocean Shipping Lines', *European Journal of Marketing*, vol. 34, no. 3/4, pp. 433-452.

Dwyer, F. R., Schur, P. and Oh, S. (1987), 'Developing Buyer-Seller Relationships', *Journal of Marketing*, vol. 51, April, pp. 11-27.

Eccles, R. G. and Pyburn, P. J. (1992), 'Creating a Comprehensive System to Measure Performance', *Management Accounting*, October, pp. 41-44.

Elgers, P. and Clark, J. (1980), 'Merger Types and Shareholder Returns', *Financial Management*, vol. 9, Summer, pp. 66-72.

Eriksen, B. and Mikkelsen, J. (1996), 'Competitive Advantage and the Concept of Core Competence', in N. J. Foss and C. Knudsen (eds), *Towards a Competence Theory of the Firm*, Routledge, London, chapter 4, pp. 54-74.

Erramilli, M. K. and Rao, C. P. (1990), 'Choice of Foreign Market Entry Modes by Service Firms: Role of Market Knowledge', *Management International Review*, vol. 30, no. 2, pp. 135-150.

Erramilli, M. K. and Rao, C. P. (1993), 'Service Firms' International Entry Mode Choice: A Modified Transaction-Cost Analysis Approach', *Journal of Marketing*, vol. 57, pp. 19-38.

Etgar, M. (1979), 'Sources and Types of Intrachannel Conflict', *Journal of Retailing*, vol. 55, no. 1, pp. 61-78.

Euske, N. A. and Roberts, K. H. (1987), 'Evolving Perspectives in Organisation Theory: Communication Implications', in F. M. Jablin, L. L. Putnam, K. H. Roberts and L. W. Porter (eds), *Handbook of Organisational Communication: An Interdisciplinary Perspective*, Sage Publications, Newbury Park, pp. 41-69.

Evans, R. E. and Southard, W. R. (1974), 'Motor Carriers and Shippers Perceptions of the Carrier Choice Decision', *The Logistics and Transportation Review*, vol. 10, no. 2, pp. 145-147.

Ewart, W. D. (1982), *Bunkers: A Guide for the Ship Operator*, Fairplay, Surrey.

Feigenbaum, A. V. (1991), *Total Quality Control*, McGraw-Hill, New York.

Fisk, G. (1994), 'Reality Tests for Relationship Marketing', in J. N. Sheth and A. Parvatiyar (eds), *Relationship Marketing: Theory, Methods and Applications*, 1994 Research Conference Proceedings, Centre for Relationship Marketing: Emory University, Atlanta.

Ford, D. (1982), 'The Development of Buyer-Seller Relationships in Industrial Markets', in H. Hakansson, (ed), *International Marketing and Purchasing of*

Industrial Goods: An Interaction Approach, John Wiley & Sons, Chichester, pp. 288-303.

Ford, D. (ed) (1990), *Understanding Business Markets: Interactions, Relationships and Networks*, The Dryden Press, London.

Franco, T. (1992), 'Political Factors Affecting Flag Choice', in *Leading Developments in Ship Management*, 2nd International Lloyd's Ship Manager Ship Management Conference, Lloyd's of London Press, London, pp. 78-80.

Frazier, G. L., Spekman, R. E. and O'Neal, C. R. (1988), 'Just-in-Time Exchange Relationships in Industrial Markets', *Journal of Marketing*, vol. 52, October, pp. 52-67.

Frazier, G. L. and Summers, J. O. (1984), 'Interfirm Influence Strategies and their Application Within Distribution Channels', *Journal of Marketing*, vol. 48, Summer, pp. 43-55.

Fry, D. (1993), 'Determining the Right Price for the Right Service', in *International Ship Management: The Right Product at the Right Price*, 3rd International Lloyd's Ship Manager Ship Management Conference, Lloyd's of London Press, London, pp. 31-35.

Gale, B. Y. (1994), *Managing Customer Value. Creating Quality and Service that Customers Can See*, The Free Press, New York.

Gaskell, N. J. J., Debattista, C. and Swatton, R. J. (1994), *Chorley & Giles' Shipping Law*, Pitman Publishing, London.

Gaunt, I. and Morgan, J. (1994), 'Finance Options', in *International Ship Management-4*, 4th International Ship Management Conference, Lloyd's of London Press, London, pp. 69-71.

Gaughan, P. A. (1996), *Mergers, Acquisitions, and Corporate Restructurings*, John Wiley & Sons, Inc., New York.

Gentry, J. W., Macintosh, G. and Stoltman, J. J. (1993), 'Reconsideration of the Structure of the Marketing Core Curriculum: Implications of the Trend Toward Relationship Marketing', in J. N. Sheth and A. Parvatiyar (eds), *Relationship Marketing: Theory, Methods and Applications*, 1994 Research Conference Proceedings, Centre for Relationship Marketing: Emory University, Atlanta.

Gibson, B. J., Sink, H. L. and Mundy, R. A. (1993), 'Shipper-Carrier Relationships and Carrier Selection Criteria', *Logistics and Transportation Review*, vol. 29, no. 4, pp. 371-382.

Gilbert, H. (1994), 'Ship Management: The How and Why of the Third Party', in *The Shipmanagers Register*, Ocean Press and Publications, London, pp. 189-193.

Gilmour, P. (1976), 'Some Policy Implications of Subjective Factors in the Modal Choice for Freight Movements', *The Logistics and Transportation Review*, vol. 12, no. 1, pp. 33-57.

Glaister, K. W. and Buckley, P. J. (1994), 'UK International Joint Ventures: An Analysis of Patterns of Activity and Distribution', *British Journal of Management*, vol. 5, no. 1, pp. 33-51.

Gorton, L., Ihre, R., and Sandevarn, A. (1990), *Shipbroking and Chartering Practice*, Lloyd's of London Press, London.

Grant, R. M. (1991), 'The Resource-Based Theory of Competitive Advantage: Implications for Strategy Formulation', *California Management Review*, vol. 18, pp. 114-135.

Grant, R. M. and Jammine, A. P. (1988), 'Performance Differences Between the Wrigley/Rumelt Strategic Categories', *Strategic Management Journal*, vol. 3, pp. 333-346.

Grant, R. M., Jammine, A. P. and Thomas, H. (1988), 'Diversity, Diversification and Profitability Among British Manufacturing Companies, 1972-1984', *Academy of Management Journal*, vol. 31, no. 4, 771-801.

Gray, T. (1997), 'Managing Costs gives Barber Something to Smile About', *Lloyd's List*, Friday, July 4, p. 5.

Gray, R. and Panayides, Ph. M. (1997), 'The Ship Manager–Shipowner Relationship: An Interaction Approach', in *Essays in Honour of Prof. Dr. B. N. Metaxas*, University of Piraeus, Department of Maritime Studies, Piraeus, pp. 407-422.

Gray, T. (1999), 'Acomarit Clinches 30-ship Petrobras Contract', *Lloyd's List*, August 3, p. 1.

Grey, M. (1995), 'Acomarit Aims to Improve Contact', *Lloyd's List*, Tuesday, March 14, p. 5.

Gronroos, C. (1984), 'A Service Quality Model and its Marketing Implications', *European Journal of Marketing*, vol. 18, no. 4, pp. 36-44.

Gronroos, C. (1988), 'New Competition of the Service Economy', *International Journal of Operations and Production Management*, vol. 8, pp. 9-19.

Gronroos, C. (1989), 'Defining Marketing: A Market-Oriented Approach', *European Journal of Marketing*, vol. 23, no. 1, pp. 52-60.

Gronroos, C. (1990a), *Service Management and Marketing*, Lexington, MA, Lexington Books.

Gronroos, C. (1990b), 'Relationship Approach to Marketing in Service Contexts: The Marketing and Organisational Behaviour Interface', *Journal of Business Research*, vol. 20, pp. 3-11.

Gronroos, C. (1991), 'The Marketing Strategy Continuum: Towards a Marketing Concept for the 1990s', *Management Decision*, vol. 29, no. 1, pp. 7-13.

Gronroos, C. (1994), 'From Marketing Mix to Relationship Marketing: Toward A Paradigm Shift in Marketing', *Management Decision*, vol. 32, no. 2, pp. 4-32.

Gronroos, C. (1996), 'Relationship Marketing: Strategic and Tactical Implications', *Management Decision*, vol. 34, no. 3, pp. 5-14.

Gronroos, C. (1997), 'Value-Driven Relational Marketing: From Products to Resources and Competencies', *Journal of Marketing Management*, vol. 13, no. 5, pp. 407-419.

Groth, J. C. and Dye, R. T. (1999), 'Service Quality: Guidelines for Marketers', *Managing Service Quality*, vol. 9, no. 5, pp. 337-351.

Grove, S. J. and Fisk, R. P. (1996), 'The Dramaturgy of Services Exchange: An Analytical Framework for Services Marketing', reprinted in C H. Lovelock, (ed), *Services Marketing*, 3rd ed., Prentice-Hall, Upper Saddle River, NJ, pp. 97-105.

Guest, A. (1994), 'Three Ways towards a Brighter Future', *Lloyd's List*, Tuesday, September 27, p. 5.

Guest, A. (1995a), 'Acomarit in Dubai Venture', *Lloyd's List*, Wednesday, October 11, p. 1.

Guest, A. (1995b), 'Acomarit Posts Slender Profit', *Lloyd's List*, Saturday, June 24, p. 2.

Guest, A. (1995c), 'Costs May Kill Small Players', *Lloyd's List*, Tuesday, July 4, p. 5.

Gummesson, E. (1978), 'Toward a Theory of Professional Service Marketing', *Industrial Marketing Management*, vol. 7, pp. 51-67.

Gummesson, E. (1987), 'The New Marketing - Developing Long-Term Interactive Relationships', *Long Range Planning*, vol. 20, no. 4, pp. 10-20.

Gummesson, E. (1991), 'Marketing-Orientation Revisited: The Crucial Role of The Part-Time Marketer', *European Journal of Marketing*, vol. 25, no. 2, pp. 60-75.

Gummesson, E. (1994), 'Making Relationship Marketing Operational', *International Journal of Service Industry Management*, vol. 5, no. 5, pp. 5-21.

Gunton, G. P. (1993), 'Ship Management', *Lloyd's Nautical Yearbook 1994*, Lloyd's of London Press, London, pp. 25-34.

Gunton, G. P. (1994), 'Ship Management', *Lloyd's Nautical Yearbook 1995*, Lloyd's of London Press, London, pp. 25-34.

Gunton, G. P. (1995), 'Ship Management', *Lloyd's Nautical Yearbook 1996*, Lloyd's of London Press, London, pp. 25-35.

Haas, J. E., Hall, R. H. and Johnson, N. J. (1966), 'Toward an Empirically Derived Taxonomy of Organisations', in R.V. Bowers, (ed), *Studies on Behaviour in Organisations*, University of Georgia Press, Athens, pp. 157-180.

Hackett, B. (1989), 'Who Manages What and for Whom?', in *International Ship Management: Profit or Loss from Shipping's Revival*, Lloyd's Ship Manager and Shipping News International Conference, Lloyd's of London Press, London.

Hakansson, H. (ed) (1982), *International Marketing and Purchasing of Industrial Goods - An Interaction Approach*, John Wiley & Sons, New York.

Hakansson, H., Johanson, J. and Wootz, B. (1977), 'Influence Tactics in Buyer-Seller Processes', *Industrial Marketing Management*, vol. 6, pp. 319-332.

Hakansson, H. and Wootz, B. (1978), 'A Framework of Industrial Buying and Selling', *Industrial Marketing Management*, vol. 8, pp. 28-39.

Hall, R. W. (1983), *Zero Inventories*, Dow-Jones Irwin, Homewood, IL.

Hallen, L., Johanson, J. and Seyed-Mohamed, N. (1987), 'Relationship Strength and Stability in International and Domestic Industrial Marketing', *Industrial Marketing and Purchasing*, vol. 2, no. 3, pp. 22-37.

Hallen, L., Johanson, J. and Seyed-Mohamed, N. (1991), 'Interfirm Adaptation in Business Relationships', *Journal of Marketing*, vol. 55, April, pp. 29-37.

Hallen, L., Seyed-Mohamed, N. and Johanson, J. (1989), 'Relationships and Exchange in International Business', *Advances in International Marketing*, vol. 3, pp. 7-23.

Hamel, G. (1991), 'Competition for Competence and Interpartner Learning within International Strategic Alliances', *Strategic Management Journal*, vol. 12, pp. 83-103.

Hamel, G. and Prahalad, C. K. (1989), 'Strategic Intent', *Harvard Business Review*, May-June, pp. 69-81.

Hamilton, J. A. and Crompton, J. L. (1991), 'Identifying the Dimensions of Service Quality in a Park Context', *Journal of Environmental Management*, vol. 32, pp. 211-220.

Hansen, F. (1972), *Consumer Choice Behaviour*, The Free Press, New York.

Harrigan, K. R. (1985), *Strategies for Joint Ventures*, Lexington Books, Lexington, MA.

Hayes, R. H. and Abernathy, W. J. (1980), 'Managing our Way to Economic Decline', *Harvard Business Review*, July-August, pp. 67-77.

Healy, P. M., Palepu, K. G. and Ruback, R. S. (1992), 'Does Corporate Performance Improve after Mergers?', *Journal of Financial Economics*, vol. 31, pp. 135-175.

Hedley, B. (1977), 'Strategy and the Business Portfolio', *Long Range Planning*, vol. 10, pp. 9-15.

Hedvall, M.-B. and Paltschik, M. (1991), 'Intrinsic Service Quality Determinants for Pharmacy Customers', *International Journal of Service Industry Management*, vol. 2, no. 2, pp. 38-48.

Hergert, M. and Morris, D. (1988), 'Trends in International Collaborative Agreements', in F. J. Contractor and P. Lorange (eds), *Co-operative Strategies in International Business*, Lexington Books, Lexington, MA, chapter 6, pp. 99-109.

Heskett, J. L., Jones, T. O., Loveman, G. W., Sasser, W. E. and Schlesinger, L. A. (1994), 'Putting the Service-Profit Chain to Work', *Harvard Business Review*, March-April, pp. 164-174.

Heyerdahl, T. (1978), *Early Man and the Ocean - The Beginning of Navigation and Seaborne Civilisations*, Allen and Unwin, London.

Hill, C. W. L. (1985), 'Diversified Growth and Competition: The Experience of Twelve Large UK Firms', *Applied Economics*, vol. 17, October, pp. 827-847.

Hill, C. (1995), *Maritime Law*, Lloyd's of London Press, London.

Hill, C. W. L., Hwang, P. and Kim, W. C. (1990), 'An Eclectic Theory of the Choice of International Entry Mode', *Strategic Management Journal*, vol. 11, no. 2, pp. 117-128.

Hirsch, P. (1987), *Pack Your Own Parachute*, Addison-Wesley, Reading, MA.

Holmlund, M. and Kock, S. (1995), 'Buyer Perceived Service Quality in Industrial Networks', *Industrial Marketing Management*, vol. 24, pp. 109-121.

Hogg, M. K., Long, G., Hartley, M. and Angold, S. J. (1993), 'Touch Me, Hold Me, Squeeze Me, Freeze Me: Privacy - The Emerging Issue for Relationship Marketing in the 1990s', in M. Davies, S. Kirkup and J. Saunders (eds), *Emerging Issues in Marketing*, Proceedings of the 1993 Marketing Education Group Annual Conference, vol. 2. Loughborough University Business School, Loughborough, pp. 504-514.

Hood, N. and Young, S. (1979), *The Economics of Multinational Enterprise*, Longman, London.

Hopson, C. (1995), 'Vanguard and Navigo in Offshore Venture', *Lloyd's List*, Wednesday, December 13, p. 2.

Houston, F. S. and Gassenheimer, J. B. (1987), 'Marketing and Exchange', *Journal of Marketing*, vol. 51, October, pp. 3-18.

Huber, G. and Daft, R. (1987), 'The Information Environment and Organisations', in F. Jablin, L. L. Putnam, K. H. Roberts and L. W. Porter (eds), *Handbook of Organisational Communication: An Interdisciplinary Perspective*, Sage Publications, Newbury Park, pp. 130-164.

Hughes, C. N. (1989), *Shipping: A Technoeconomic Approach*, Lloyd's of London Press, London.

Hunt, S. D. (1976), 'The Nature and Scope of Marketing', *Journal of Marketing*, vol. 40, July, pp. 17-28.

Hunt, S. D. (1983), 'General Theories and the Fundamental Explananda of Marketing', *Journal of Marketing*, vol. 47, Fall, pp. 9-17.

Hunt, S. D. (1995), 'The Resource-Advantage Theory of Competition: Toward Explaining Productivity and Economic Growth', *Journal of Management Inquiry*, vol. 4, December, pp. 317-332.

Hunt, S. D. (1997a), 'Resource-Advantage Theory: An Evolutionary Theory of Competitive Firm Behaviour?', *The Journal of Economic Issues*, vol. 31, March, pp. 59-77.

Hunt, S. D. (1997b), 'Competing Through Relationships: Grounding Relationship Marketing in Resource-Advantage Theory', *Journal of Marketing Management*, vol. 13, no. 5, pp. 431-445.

Iacobucci, D. (1994), 'Toward Defining Relationship Marketing', in J. N. Sheth, and A. Parvatiyar (eds), *Relationship Marketing: Theory, Methods and Applications*, 1994 Research Conference Proceedings, Centre for Relationship Marketing, Emory University, Atlanta.

Ion, E. (1995), 'Malaysia Owner Moves to Expand into Japanese Shipmanagement', *Lloyd's List*, Monday, April 10, p. 1.

Iverson, R. and Deery, M. (1997), 'Turnover Culture in the Hospitality Industry', *Human Resource Management*, vol. 7, no. 4, pp. 71-82.

Jackson, B. B. (1985), 'Build Customer Relationships that Last', *Harvard Business Review*, vol. 63, no. 6, pp. 120-128.

Jaques, B. (1998), 'Versatility with Capital V', *Seatrade Review*, March, p. 89.

Jerman, R. E., Anderson, R. D. and Constantin, J. A. (1978), 'Shipper versus Carrier Perceptions of Carrier Selection Variables', *International Journal of Physical Distribution and Materials Management*, vol. 9, no. 1, pp. 29-38.

Johnston, R. and Lyth, D. (1991), 'Service Quality: Implementing the Integration of Customer Expectations and Operational Capability' in S. W. Brown, E. Gummesson, B. Edvardsson and B. Gustavsson (eds), *Service Quality: Multidisciplinary and Multinational Perspectives*, Lexington Books, Lexington, MA.

Judd, V. C. (1987), 'Differentiate with the 5th P: People', *Industrial Marketing Management*, vol. 16, pp. 241-247.

Juran, J. M. (1988), *Juran's Quality Control Handbook*, McGraw-Hill, New York.

Juran, J. M. (1992), *Juran on Quality by Design*, The Free Press, New York.

Kaplan, R. S. and Norton, D. P. (1992), 'The Balanced Scorecard – Measures that Drive Performance', *Harvard Business Review*, January-February, pp. 71-79.

Kendall, L. C. and Buckley, J. J. (1994), *The Business of Shipping*, 6th ed., Cornell Maritime Press, Centreville, Maryland.

Kent, R. A. (1986), 'Faith in Four Ps: An Alternative', *Journal of Marketing Management*, vol. 2, no. 2, pp. 145-154.

Kerr, P. (1996), 'Developing New Management Business', in *7th International Lloyd's Ship Manager Ship Management Conference*, Lloyd's of London Press, London.

Khandwalla, P. N. (1981), 'Properties of Competing Organisations', in P. C. Nystrom, and W. H. Starbuck (eds), *Handbook of Organisational Design*, vol. 1., Oxford University Press, Oxford, pp. 409-432.

King, G., Keohane, R. O. and Verba, S. (1994), *Designing Social Inquiry: Scientific Inference in Qualitative Research*, Princeton University Press, Princeton, NJ.

Kogut, B. (1988), 'Joint Ventures: Theoretical and Empirical Perspectives', *Strategic Management Journal*, vol. 9, pp. 319-332.

Kogut, B. and Zander, U. (1993), 'Knowledge of the Firm and the Evolutionary Theory of the Multinational Corporation', *Journal of International Business Studies*, vol. 24, no. 4, pp. 625-646.

Kotler, P. (1980), *Principles of Marketing*, Prentice-Hall Inc., Englewood Cliffs, NJ.

Kotler, P. (1994), *Marketing Management - Analysis, Planning, Implementation and Control*, 8th ed., Prentice-Hall, Englewood Cliffs, NJ.

Kotler, P. and Bloom, P. N. (1984), *Marketing Professional Services*, Prentice-Hall, Englewood Cliffs, NJ.

Kotler, P. and Conner, R. A. (1977), 'Marketing Professional Services', *Journal of Marketing*, vol. 41, January, pp. 71-76.

Kuei, C-H. (1999), 'Internal Service Quality – An Empirical Assessment', *International Journal of Quality & Reliability Management*, vol. 16, no. 8, pp. 783-791.

Lamont, B. T. and Anderson, C. R. (1985), 'Mode of Corporate Diversification and Economic Performance', *Academy of Management Journal*, vol. 28, pp. 926-934.

Lapierre, J. (1997), 'What Does Value Mean in Business-to-Business Professional Services?', *International Journal of Service Industry Management*, vol. 8, no. 5, pp. 377-397.

Lawford, H. (1989), 'Liability and the Ship Management Industry', in *International Ship Management: Profit or Loss from Shipping's Revival*, Lloyd's Ship Manager and Shipping News International Conference, Lloyd's of London Press, London.

Lawford, H. (1992), 'Management Liability: An Insurer's View', 2nd International Lloyd's Ship Manager Ship Management Conference 1991, Lloyd's of London Press, London, pp. 10-16.

LeCraw, D. J. (1984), 'Diversification Strategy and Performance', *Journal of Industrial Economics*, vol. 33, no. 2, pp. 179-198.

Leeson, J. (1983), 'Exploding the Myths on the Concept of Managing Ships', *Lloyd's List*, April 21, p. 7.

Lehmann, D. R. and O'Shaughnessy, J. (1974), 'Difference in Attribute Importance for Different Industrial Products', *Journal of Marketing*, vol. 38, April, pp. 36-42.

Leibenstein, H. (1976), *Beyond Economic Man*, Harvard University Press, Cambridge, MA.

Leontiades, M. (1986), *Managing the Unmanageable: Strategies for Success within the Conglomerate*, Addison-Wesley, Reading, MA.

Leszinski, R. and Marn, M. V. (1997), 'Setting Value, Not Price', *The McKinsey Quarterly*, vol. 1, pp. 99-115.

Levitt, T. (1983), 'After the Sale is Over', *Harvard Business Review*, vol. 61, no. 5, pp. 87-93.

Levy, H. and Sarnat, M. (1970), 'Diversification, Portfolio Analysis and the Uneasy Case for Conglomerate Mergers', *Journal of Finance*, vol. 25, September, 795-802.

Lilien, G. L. (1975), 'Model Relativism: A Situational Approach to Model Building', *Interfaces*, vol. 5, no. 3, pp. 11-18.

Lim, J. (1999), 'Singapore Benefits from Hong Kong's Problems', *Ship Management – Special Issue of the Baltic Magazine*, February, pp. 8-9.

Lippman, S. and Rumelt, R. P. (1982), 'Uncertain Imitability: An Analysis of Interfirm Differences in Efficiency under Competition', *The Bell Journal of Economics*, vol. 13, pp. 418-438.

Lloyd's Maritime Directory (1995), Lloyd's of London Press, London.

Lorenz, E. H. (1988), 'Neither Friends Nor Strangers: Informal Networks of Sub Contracting in French Industry', in D. Gambetta (ed), *Trust: Making and Breaking Co-operative Relations*, Basil Blackwell, London, pp. 194-210.

Lorenzoni, G. and Baden-Fuller, C. (1995), 'Creating a Strategic Centre to Manage a Web of Partners', *California Management Review*, vol. 37, no. 3, pp. 146-163.

Lorsch, J. (1986), 'Managing Culture: the Invisible Barrier to Strategic Change', *California Management Review*, vol. 28, pp. 95-109.

Lovelock, C. H. (1980), 'Towards a Classification of Services', in C. W. Lamb and P. M. Dunne (eds), *Theoretical Developments in Marketing*, Chicago, American Marketing Association, pp. 72-76.

Lovelock, C. H. (1981), 'Why Marketing Management Needs to be Different for Services', in J. H. Donnelly and W. R. George (eds), *Marketing of Services*, American Marketing Association, Chicago, IL., pp. 5-9.

Lovelock, C. H. (1983), 'Classifying Services to Gain Strategic Marketing Insights', *Journal of Marketing*, vol. 47, pp. 9-20.

Low, B. K. H. (1996), 'Long-term Relationship in Industrial Marketing: Reality or Rhetoric?', *Industrial Marketing Management*, vol. 25, pp. 23-35.

Lowry, N. (1997), 'Mare in Switch to Athens', *Lloyd's List*, Tuesday, November 25, p. 2.

Lu, C-S. and Marlow, P. (1999), 'Strategic Groups in Taiwanese Liner Shipping', *Maritime Policy and Management*, vol. 26, no. 1, pp. 1-26.

Lubatkin, M. H. (1987), 'Merger Strategies and Stockholder Value', *Strategic Management Journal*, vol. 8, no. 1, pp. 39-53.

Luffman, G. A. and Reed, R. (1982), 'Diversification in British Industry in the 1970's', *Strategic Management Journal*, vol. 3, no. 4, pp. 303-314.

Luffman, G. A. and Reed, R. (1984), *The Strategy and Performance of British Industry*, 1970-1980, St Martin's Press, New York.

Lustrin, R. E. (1999), 'Insights into United States Public Offerings', in *International Obtaining Finance for Shipping Seminar*, IBC UK Conferences, London.

Lyons, B. (1995), 'Specific Investment, Economies of Scale, and the Make-or-Buy Decision: a Test of Transaction Cost Theory', *Journal of Economic Behaviour and Organisation*, vol. 26, no. 3, pp. 431-443.

Madhok, A. (1998), 'The Nature of Multinational Firm Boundaries: Transaction Costs, Firm Capabilities and Foreign Market Entry Mode', *International Business Review*, vol. 7, pp. 259-290.

Mahoney, J. T. and Pandian, J. R. (1992), 'The Resource-Based View within the Conversation of Strategic Management', *Strategic Management Journal*, vol. 13, pp. 363-380.

Mariti, P. and Smiley, R. H. (1983), 'Co-Operative Agreements and the Organisation of Industry', *The Journal of Industrial Economics*, vol. 31, no. 4, pp. 437-451.

Markides, C. C. (1995), 'Diversification, Restructuring and Economic Performance, *Strategic Management Journal*, vol. 16, pp. 101-118.

Martilla, J. A. (1971), 'Word-of-Mouth Communication in the Industrial Adoption Process', *Journal of Marketing Research*, vol. 8, May, pp. 173-178.

Martyr, P. (1994), 'Room for Improvement', *Lloyd's Ship Manager,* February, p. 9.

Matear, S. M. and Gray, R. (1993), 'Factors Influencing Freight Service Choice for Shippers and Freight Suppliers', *International Journal of Physical Distribution and Logistics Management*, vol. 23, no. 2, pp. 25-35.

McCarthy, E. J. (1981), *Basic Marketing: A Managerial Approach*, Richard D. Irwin, Homewood, IL.

McFarlan, F. and Nolan, R. (1995), 'How to Manage an IS Outsourcing Alliance', *Sloan Management Review*, vol. 36, no. 2, pp. 9-23.

McFetridge, D. and Smith, D. (1998), *The Economics of Vertical Disintegration*, The Fraser Institute, Vancouver, B.C.

McGinnis, M. A. (1980), 'Shipper Attitudes Towards Freight Transportation Choice: A Factor Analytic Study', *International Journal of Physical Distribution and Materials Management*, vol. 10, no. 1, pp. 25-34.

McGrath, R. G., MacMillan, I. C. and Venkataraman, S. (1995), 'Defining and Developing Competence: A Strategic Process Paradigm', *Strategic Management Journal*, vol. 16, pp. 285-305.

McKelvey, B. (1978), 'Organisational Systematics: Taxonomic Lessons from Biology', *Management Science*, vol. 24, pp. 1428-1440.

McKinney, J. C. (1966), *Constructive Typology and Social Theory*, Appleton-Century-Crofts, New York.

MacNeil, I. R. (1978), 'Contracts: Adjustment of Long-Term Economic Relations Under Classical, Neo-Classical, and Relational Contract Law', *Northwestern University Law Review*, vol. 72, no. 6, pp. 854-905.

MacNeil, I. R. (1980), *The New Social Contract: An Inquiry into Modern Contractual Relations*, Yale University Press, New Haven, CT.

Mehra, A. (1994), 'Strategic Groups: A Resource-Based Approach', *The Journal of Socio-Economics*, vol. 23, no. 4, pp. 425-439.

Mersha, T. and Adlakha, V. (1991), 'A Location Choice Approach for Professional Service Firms', *Journal of Professional Services Marketing*, vol. 6, no. 2, pp. 59-67.

Meyer, J. (1992), 'Tomorrow's Training Requirements', in *Leading Developments in Ship Management,* 2nd International Lloyd's Ship Manager Ship Management Conference 1991, Lloyd's of London Press, London, pp. 93-96.

Michel, A. and Shaked, I. (1984), 'Does Business Diversification Affect Performance?', *Financial Management*, vol. 13, no. 4, pp. 18-25.

Midoro, R. and Pitto, A. (2000), 'A Critical Evaluation of Strategic Alliances in Liner Shipping', *Maritime Policy and Management*, vol. 27, no. 1, pp. 31-40.

Miles, R. H. (1982), *Coffin Nails and Corporate Strategies*, Prentice-Hall, Englewood Cliffs, NJ.

Miller, D. (1981), 'Toward a New Contingency Approach: The Search for Organisation Gestalts', *Journal of Management Studies*, vol. 18. pp. 1-26.

Mitas, D. K. (1992), 'Long-Term Potential of New Crew Sources', in *Leading Developments in Ship Management,* 2nd International Lloyd's Ship Manager

Ship Management Conference 1991, Lloyd's of London Press, London, pp. 88-92.

Mody, A. (1993), 'Learning through Alliances', *Journal of Economic Behaviour and Organisation*, vol. 20, pp. 151-170.

Mohr, J. J., Fisher, R. J. and Nevin, J. R. (1996), 'Collaborative Communication in Interfirm Relationships: Moderating Effects of Integration and Control', *Journal of Marketing*, vol. 60, July, pp. 103-115.

Mohr, J. J. and Nevin, J. R. (1990), 'Communication Strategies in Marketing Channels: A Theoretical Perspective', *Journal of Marketing*, vol. 54, October, pp. 36-51.

Montgomery, C. A. (1994), 'Corporate Diversification', *Journal of Economic Perspectives*, vol. 8, no. 3, pp. 163-178.

Monroe, K. B. (1990), *Pricing. Making Profitable Decisions*, 2nd ed., McGraw-Hill, London.

Moorman, C., Zaltman, G. and Deshpande, R. (1992), 'Relationships between Providers and Users of Market Research: The Dynamics of Trust Within and Between Organisations', *Journal of Marketing Research*, vol. 29, August, pp. 314-328.

Morel, G. (1994), 'The Role of the Ship Manager in Shipping Joint Ventures', in J. Abhyankar and S. I. Bijwadia (eds), *Maritime Joint Ventures*, ICC Publication, Paris, pp. 300-305.

Morgan, R. M. and Hunt, S. D. (1994), 'The Commitment-Trust Theory of Relationship Marketing', *Journal of Marketing*, vol. 58, July, pp. 20-38.

Moriarty, R. T., Kimball, R. C. and Gay, J. H. (1983), The Management of Corporate Banking Relationships', *Sloan Management Review*, vol. 24, no. 3, pp. 3-15.

MOU (1994), *Memorandum of Understanding on Port State Control*, Annual Report.

Mueller, D. C. (1969), 'A Theory of Conglomerate Mergers', *Quarterly Journal of Economics*, vol. 82, November, pp. 643-659.

Muller, M. J. (1994), 'Highlights of the Joint Venture Concept', in J. Abhyankar and S. I. Bijwadia (eds), *Maritime Joint Ventures*, ICC Publication, Paris, pp. 64-72.

Mulrenan, J. (1994), 'Vela to Take Control of its Tanker Fleet Management', *Lloyd's List*, Wednesday, October 12, p. 1.

Mummalaneni, V. (1987), *The Influence of a Close Personal Relationship Between the Buyer and the Seller on the Continued Stability of Their Role Relationship*, Unpublished Ph.D. dissertation, The Graduate School, College of Business Administration, The Pennsylvania State University.

Muris, T., Scheffman, D. and Spiller, P. (1992), 'Strategy and Transaction Costs: The Organisation of Distribution in the Carbonated Soft Drink Industry', *Journal of Economics and Management Strategy*, vol. 1, pp. 83-128.

Naert, P. A. and Leeflang, P. S. H. (1978), *Building Implementable Marketing Models*, Martinus Nijhoff Social Sciences Division, Leiden/Boston.

Nalebuff, B. J. and Brandenburger, A. M. (1997), *Co-opetition*, HarperCollins Business, London.

Neely, A. (1999), 'The Performance Measurement Revolution: Why Now and What Next', *International Journal of Operations & Production Management*, vol. 19, no. 2, pp. 205-228.

Ohmae, K. (1982), *The Mind of the Strategist*, McGraw-Hill, New York.

Oliver, C. (1990), 'Determinants of Interorganizational Relationships: Integration and Future Directions', *Academy of Management Review*, vol. 15, no. 2, pp. 241-265.

Osler, D. (1996), 'Welsh Shipmanager to Close', *Lloyd's List*, Wednesday, October 23, p. 12.

Osler, D. (1997), 'Bibby and Harrison Start Joint Venture', *Lloyd's List*, Wednesday, October 1, p. 2.

Osler, D. (1998), 'V Ships in Singapore Move', *Lloyd's List*, Tuesday, February 17, p. 12.

Osler, D. (1999a), 'European Shipmanagement: Sites of Global Excellence', *Lloyd's List*, Tuesday, June 8, p. 8.

Osler, D. (1999b), 'Acomarit Wins Canada Deal', *Lloyd's List*, September 22, p. 5.

Packard, W. V. (1978), *Voyage Estimating*, Fairplay, Surrey.

Packard, W. V. (1979), *Laytime Calculating*, Fairplay, Surrey.

Packard, W. V. (1980), *Timechartering*, Fairplay, Surrey.

Packard, W. V. (1986), *Sea-Trading 3–Trading*, Fairplay, Surrey.

Packard, W. V. (1988), *Sale and Purchase*, Fairplay, Surrey.

Palepu, K. (1985), 'Diversification Strategy, Profit Performance and the Entropy Measure', *Strategic Management Journal*, vol. 6, pp. 239-255.

Palmer, A. (1994), 'Relationship Marketing: Back to Basics?' *Journal of Marketing Management*, vol. 10, pp. 571-579.

Palmer, A. and Bejou, D. (1994), 'Buyer-Seller Relationships: A Conceptual Model and Empirical Investigation', *Journal of Marketing Management*, vol. 10, pp. 495-512.

Panayides, Ph. M. (1996), 'Profit from Relationship Marketing', in *7th International Lloyd's Ship Manager Ship Management Conference*, Lloyd's of London Press, London.

Panayides, Ph. M. (1999), *International Ship Management: Market Analysis and Strategic Opportunities*, International Institute of Research Publications, London.

Panayides, Ph. M. (2000), A Guide to the CREWMAN Standard Ship Management Agreement, in *The Nautical Institute on Command: A Practical Guide*, 2nd ed., chapter 24, The Nautical Institute, London, pp. 163-165.

Panayides, Ph. M. and Gray, R. (1997a), 'Marketing the Professional Ship Management Service', *Maritime Policy & Management*, vol. 24, no. 3, pp. 233-244.

Panayides, Ph. M. and Gray, R. (1997b), 'Perceptual Mapping in Relationship Marketing: The Case for Professional Ship Management Services', in

Marketing Without Borders, Proceedings of the Academy of Marketing/American Marketing Association Conference, Manchester Metropolitan University, Manchester, pp. 1443-1446.

Panayides, Ph. M. (1998), *A Relationship Approach to the Marketing of Professional Ship Management Services*, Unpublished Ph.D. Dissertation, Institute of Marine Studies, University of Plymouth, UK.

Panayides, Ph. M. and Gray, R. (1999a), 'An Empirical Assessment of Relational Competitive Advantage in Professional Ship Management', *Maritime Policy and Management*, vol. 26, no. 2, pp. 111-125.

Panayides, Ph. M. and Gray, R. (1999b), 'An Empirical Investigation of Professional Ship Manager-Client Relationships', in H. Meersman, E. Van De Voorde and W. Winkelmans (eds), *World Transport Research, Selected proceedings of the 8th World Conference on Transport Research, Transport Modes and Systems*, vol. 1, Pergamon, Oxford, pp. 29-42.

Parasuraman, A., Berry, L. L. and Zeithaml, V. (1990), *An Empirical Test of the Extended Gaps Model of Service Quality*, Marketing Science Institute Working Paper, No. 90-122.

Parasuraman, A., Berry, L. L. and Zeithaml, V. (1991), 'Refinement and Reassessment of the SERVQUAL Scale', *Journal of Retailing*, vol. 69, no. 1, pp. 140-147.

Parasuraman, A., Zeithaml, V. and Berry, L. L. (1985), 'A Conceptual Model of Service Quality and its Implications for Future Research', *Journal of Marketing*, vol. 49, pp. 41-50.

Parasuraman, A., Zeithaml, V. and Berry, L. L. (1988), 'SERVQUAL: A Multiple Item Scale for Measuring Consumer Perceptions of Service Quality', *Journal of Retailing*, vol. 64, no. 1, pp. 12-40.

Parasuraman, A., Zeithaml, V. and Berry, L. L. (1993), 'More on Improving Service Quality Measurement', *Journal of Retailing*, vol. 69, no. 1, pp. 140-147.

Parvatiyar, A. and Sheth, J. N. (1994), 'Paradigm Shift in Marketing Theory & Approach: The Emergence of Relationship Marketing', in J. N. Sheth and A. Parvatiyar (eds), *Relationship Marketing: Theory, Methods and Applications*, 1994 Research Conference Proceedings, Centre for Relationship Marketing, Emory University, Atlanta.

Pearson, R. (1980), *Containerline Performance and Service Quality*, University of Liverpool Marine Transport Centre, Liverpool.

Penrose, E. (1959), *The Theory of the Growth of the Firm*, Oxford University Press, Oxford.

Perrien, J., Filiatrault, P. and Ricard, L. (1992), 'Relationship Marketing and Commercial Banking: A Critical Analysis', *International Journal of Bank Marketing*, vol. 10, no. 7, pp. 25-29.

Perrien, J., Filiatrault, P. and Ricard, L. (1993), 'The Implementation of Relationship Marketing in Commercial Banking', *Industrial Marketing Management*, vol. 22, pp. 141-148.

Perry, G. (1994), 'The Right Place at the Right Price - Locations for Ship Management', in *International Ship Management-4,* 4th International Ship Management Conference, Lloyd's of London Press, London, pp. 43-48.

Peteraf, M. A. (1993), 'The Cornerstones of Competitive Advantage: A Resource-Based View', *Strategic Management Journal,* vol. 14, pp. 179-191.

Peteraf, M. (1993), 'Intra-industry Structure and Response toward Rivals', *Journal of Managerial and Decision Economics,* vol. 14, pp. 519-528.

Peterson, T. D. and Porges, K. S. (1991), 'Marketing and Communication Tools for Services Marketers', in C. A. Congram and M. L. Friedman (eds), *The AMA Handbook of Marketing for the Service Industries,* AMACOM, New York, pp. 345-365.

Pfau, B., Detzel, D. and Geller, A. (1991), 'Satisfy your Internal Customers', *Journal of Business Strategy,* November-December, pp. 9-13.

Pfeffer, J. and Leong, A. (1977), 'Resource Allocations in United Funds: Examination of Power and Dependence', *Social Forces,* vol. 55, pp. 775-790.

Pfeffer, J. and Salancik, G. R. (1978), *The External Control of Organisations: A Resource Dependence Perspective,* Harper & Row, New York.

Phillips, A. (1962), *Market Structure, Organisation and Performance,* Harvard University Press, Cambridge, MA.

Pitts, R. A. (1980), 'Towards a Contingency Theory of Multi-Business Organisation Design', *Academy of Management Journal,* vol. 5, pp. 203-210.

Porter, M. E. (1980), *Competitive Strategy: Techniques for Analysing Industries and Competitors,* The Free Press, New York.

Porter, M. E. (1985), *Competitive Advantage: Creating and Sustaining Superior Performance,* The Free Press, New York.

Porter, M. E. and Fuller, M. B. (1986), 'Coalitions and Global Strategy', in Porter, M. E. (ed), *Competition in Global Industries,* Harvard Business School, Boston, MA.

Prahalad, C. and Hamel, G. (1990), 'The Core Competence of the Corporation', *Harvard Business Review,* May-June, pp. 79-91.

Prescott, J. (1995), 'Independent Owners move to Fill Void Left by Oil Majors', *Lloyd's List,* Thursday, January 26, p. 5.

Proctor, T. (1997), 'Establishing a Strategic Direction: A Review', *Management Decision,* vol. 35, no. 2, pp. 143-154.

Pruit, D. (1981), *Negotiation Behaviour,* Academic Press, New York.

Ramanujam, V. and Varadarajan, P. (1989), 'Research on Corporate Diversification: A Synthesis', *Strategic Management Journal,* vol. 10, pp. 523-551.

Ravald, A. and Gronroos, C. (1996), 'The Value Concept and Relationship Marketing', *European Journal of Marketing,* vol. 30, no. 2, pp. 19-30.

Ravenscraft, D. and Scherer, F. (1988), 'Mergers and Managerial Performance', in J. Coffee, L. Lowenstein, and S. R. Ackerman (eds), *Knights, Raiders and Targets,* chapter 12, Oxford University Press, New York, pp. 194-210.

Ready, N. P. (1992), 'Second National Registers V. Open Registers', in *Leading Developments in Ship Management*, 2nd International Lloyd's Ship Manager Ship Management Conference 1991, Lloyd's of London Press, London, pp. 72-77.

Ready, N. P. (1994), *Ship Registration*, Lloyd's of London Press, London.

Reichelstein, S. (1995), 'Reliance Investment Under Negotiated Transfer Pricing: An Efficiency Result', *The Accounting Review*, vol. 70, no. 2, pp. 275-291.

Redman, T. and Mathews, B. P. (1998), 'Service Quality and Human Resource Management: A Review and Research Agenda', *Personnel Review*, vol. 27, no. 1, pp. 57-77.

Reece, J. S. and Cool, W. R. (1978), 'Measuring Investment Centre Performance', *Harvard Business Review*, vol. 56, no. 3, pp. 28-46.

Reed, R. and Luffman, G. A. (1986), 'Diversification: The Growing Confusion', *Strategic Management Journal*, vol. 7, pp. 29-35.

Reichelstein, S. (1995), 'Reliance Investment under Negotiated Transfer Pricing: An Efficiency Result', *The Accounting Review*, vol. 70, no. 2, pp. 275-291.

Reichheld, F. F. and Sasser, W. E. (1990), 'Zero Defections: Quality Comes to Services', *Harvard Business Review*, vol. 68, no. 5, pp. 105-111.

Reichold, F. (1993), 'Loyalty-Based Management', *Harvard Business Review*, March-April, pp. 64-73.

Reynolds, F. M. B. (1985), *Bowstead on Agency*, 15th ed., Sweet & Maxwell, London.

Ricardo, D. (1891), *Principles of Political Economy and Taxation*, G. Bell, London.

Rich, P. (1992), 'The Organisational Taxonomy: Definition and Design', *Academy of Management Review*, vol. 17, no. 4, pp. 758-781.

Richardson, A. J., Ampt, E. S. and Meyburg, A. H. (1995), *Survey Methods for Transport Planning*, Eucalyptus Press, Parkville, Australia.

Richardson, P. (1995a), 'European Shipmanagement: Ugland and Interocean in Tie-Up', *Lloyd's List*, Wednesday, June 28, p. 8.

Richardson, P. (1995b), 'Barber Relocates HK Business to Malaysia', *Lloyd's List*, Tuesday, August 8, p. 1.

Richardson, P. (1995c), 'Hanseatic Wins Crew Deal from Sea-Land', *Lloyd's List*, Monday, August 21, p. 1.

Richardson, P. (1995d), 'New Ship Management Company Takes on Two Norasia Vessels', *Lloyd's List*, Thursday, October 26, p. 10.

Richardson, P. (1995e), 'New Ship Management Agenda', *Lloyd's List*, Saturday, July 8, p. 3.

Roberts, E. B. and Berry, C. A. (1985), 'Entering New Businesses: Selecting Strategies for Success', *Sloan Management Review*, vol. 27, no. 3, pp. 57-71.

Robicheaux, R. A. and El-Ansary, A. I. (1976), 'A General Model for Understanding Channel Member Behaviour', *Journal of Retailing*, vol. 52, no. 4, pp. 13-30, 93-94.

Rodger, D. A. (1989), 'What Level of Management Fees can Ship Managers Justify?', in *International Ship Management: Profit or Loss from Shipping's Revival*, Lloyd's Ship Manager and Shipping News International Conference, Lloyd's of London Press, London.

Rodger, D. A. (1993), 'Overview of an Industry at the Crossroads', in *International Ship Management: The Right Product at the Right Price*, 3rd International Lloyd's Ship Management Conference 1992, Lloyd's of London Press, London, pp. 3-13.

Root, F. R. (1987), *Foreign Market Entry Strategies*, AMACOM, New York.

Rugman, A. M. (1986), 'New Theories of the Multinational Enterprise: An Assessment of Internalisation Theory', *Bulletin of Economic Research*, vol. 38, no. 2, pp. 101-118.

Rumelt, R. P. (1974), *Strategy, Structure and Economic Performance*, Division of Research, Harvard Business School, Boston, MA.

Rumelt, R. P. (1982), 'Diversification Strategy and Profitability', *Strategic Management Journal*, vol. 3, pp. 359-369.

Rumelt, R. P., Schendel, D. E. and Teece, D. J. (1994), 'Fundamental Issues in Strategy', in R. P. Rumelt, D. E. Schendel and D. J. Teece (eds), *Fundamental Issues in Strategy*, Harvard Business School, Boston, MA., chapter 1, pp. 9-47.

Ryoo, D. K. and Thanopoulou, H. A. (1999), 'Liner Alliances in the Globalisation Era: A Strategic Tool for Asian Container Carriers', *Maritime Policy and Management*, vol. 26, no. 4, pp. 349-367.

Saleh, F. and Lalonde, B. J. (1972), 'Industrial Buyer Behaviour and the Motor Carrier Selection Decision', *Journal of Purchasing*, vol. 8, no. 1, pp. 18-33.

Salter, M. S. and Weinhold, W. S. (1978), 'Diversification Via Acquisitions: Creating Value', *Harvard Business Review*, vol. 56, no. 4, pp. 166-176.

Saporta, B. (1989), *Industrial Marketing*, Eyrolles Management.

Sasser, W. E., Olsen, R. P. and Wyckoff, D. D. (1978), *Management of Service Operations*, Boston, MA., Allyn & Bacon.

Scanzoni, J. (1979), Social Exchange And Behavioural Interdependence, in R. L. Burgess and T. L. Huston (eds), *Social Exchange in Developing Relationships*, Academic Press Inc., New York, pp. 61-98.

Schlesinger, L. A. and Heskett, J.L. (1991), 'Breaking the Cycle of Failure in Services', *Sloan Management Review*, vol. 32, no. 3, pp. 17-28.

Schonberger, R. J. (1994), 'Human Resource Management Lessons from a Decade of Total Quality Management and Reengineering', *California Management Review*, vol. 36, no. 4, pp. 109-123.

Scott, D. R. and Shieff, D. S. (1993), 'Service Quality Components and Group Criteria in Local Government', *International Journal of Service Industry Management*, vol. 4, pp. 41-53.

Scott, D. R. and van der Walt, N. T. (1995), 'Choice Criteria in the Selection of International Accounting Firms', *European Journal of Marketing*, vol. 29, no. 1, pp. 27-39.

Shanley, M. T. (1994), 'Determinants and Consequences of Post-Acquisition Change', in G. Von Krogh, A. Sinatra and H. Singh (eds), *The Management of Corporate Acquisitions*, The Macmillan Press, London, pp. 391-413.

Shemwell, D. J., Cronin, J. J. and Bullard, W. R. (1994), 'Relational Exchange in Services: An Empirical Investigation of Ongoing Customer Service-Provider Relationships', *International Journal of Service Industry Management*, vol. 5, no. 3, pp. 57-68.

Shleifer, A. and Vishny, R. W. (1991), 'Takeovers in the '60s and '80s: Evidence and Implications', *Strategic Management Journal*, vol. 12, Winter, pp. 51-59.

Shostack, G. L. (1977), 'Breaking Free from Product Marketing', *Journal of Marketing*, vol. 41, pp. 73-80.

Shostack, G. L. (1984), 'A Framework for Service Marketing', S. W. Brown and R. P. Fisk, *Marketing Theory: Distinguished Contributions*, John Wiley & Sons, New York, pp. 250-261.

Shostack, G. L. (1987), 'Service Positioning through Structural Change', *Journal of Marketing*, vol. 51, January, pp. 34-43.

Singh, H. and Montgomery, C. A. (1987), 'Corporate Acquisition Strategies and Economic Performance', *Strategic Management Journal*, vol. 8, July-August, pp. 377-386.

Skinner, W. (1974), 'The Decline, Fall and Renewal of Manufacturing', *Industrial Engineering*, October, pp. 32-38.

Skinner, S. J., Gassenheimer, J. B. and Kelley, S. W. (1992), 'Co-operation in Supplier-Dealer Relations', *Journal of Retailing*, vol. 68, no. 2, pp. 174-193.

Sletmo, G. K. (1986), 'The Transformation of Shipping and the Role of Ship Management', in *Proceedings of the World Conference on Transport Research*, vol. 1, pp. 734-746.

Sletmo, G. K. (1989), 'Shipping's Fourth Wave: Ship Management and Vernon's Trade Cycles', *Maritime Policy & Management*, vol. 16, no. 4, pp. 293-303.

Sletmo, G. K. and Holste, S. (1993), 'Shipping and the Competitive Advantage of Nations: The Role of International Ship Registers', *Maritime Policy & Management*, vol. 20, no. 3, pp. 243-255.

Sokal, R. R. and Sneath, P. H. A. (1963), *Principles of Numerical Taxonomy*, Freeman, San Francisco, CA.

Solomon, M. R., Suprenant, C., Czepiel, J. A. and Gutman, E. G. (1985), 'A Role Theory Perspective on Dyadic Interactions: The Service Encounter', *Journal of Marketing*, vol. 49, Winter, pp. 99-111.

Sonnenberg, F. K. (1988), 'Relationship Management is more than Wining and Dining', *Journal of Business Strategy*, vol. 9, May-June, pp. 60-63.

Spekman, R. E. and Johnston, W. J. (1986), 'Relationship Management: Managing the Selling and the Buying Interface', *Journal of Business Research*, vol. 14, pp. 519-531.

Spruyt, J. (1990), *Ship Management*, Lloyd's of London Press, London.

Spruyt, J. (1994), *Ship Management*, 2nd ed., LLP Limited, London.

Stalk, G., Evans, P. and Shulman, L. E. (1992), 'Competing on Capabilities: The New Rules of Corporate Strategy', *Harvard Business Review*, March-April, pp. 57-69.

Stansell, S. R., Harper, C. P. and Wilder, R. P. (1984), 'The Effects of Advertising Expenditures: Evidence from an Analysis of Major Advertisers', *Review of Business and Economic Research*, Fall, pp. 86-95.

Steiner, G. A. (1969), *Top Management Planning*, Macmillan, New York.

Stephens, T., Suprenant, C., English, M. and Gillet, T. (1987), 'Customers Speak out About Value', in C. Suprenant (ed), *Add Value to Your Service*, AMA, Chicago, IL., pp. 5-6.

Stern, L. W. and Reve, T. (1980), 'Distribution Channels as Political Economies: A Framework for Comparative Analysis', *Journal of Marketing*, vol. 44, Summer, pp. 52-64.

Stock, J. R. and Zinszer, P. H. (1987), 'The Industrial Purchase Decision for Professional Services', *Journal of Business Research*, vol. 15, pp. 1-16.

Stohl, C. and Redding, W. C. (1987), 'Messages and Message Exchange Processes', in F. M. Jablin, L. L. Putnam, K. H. Roberts and L. W. Porter (eds), *Handbook of Organisational Communication: An Interdisciplinary Perspective*, Sage Publications, Newbury Park, CA., pp. 451-502.

Stokes, P. (1992), *Ship Finance*, Lloyd's of London Press, London.

Stokes, P. (1997), *Ship Finance*, 2nd ed, LLP Limited, London.

Stone, M. and Woodcock, N. (1995), *Relationship Marketing*, Kogan Page, London.

Stopford, M. (1997), *Maritime Economics*, 2ild ed, Routledge, London.

Suprenant, C. F. and Solomon, M. R. (1987), 'Predictability and Personalisation in the Service Encounter', *Journal of Marketing*, vol. 51, April, pp. 73-80.

Tallman, S. B. (1991), 'Strategic Management Models and Resource-Based Strategies Among MNEs in a Host Market', *Strategic Management Journal*, vol. 12, pp. 69-82.

Teece, D. J. (1980), 'Economies of Scope and Scope of the Enterprise', *Journal of Economic Behaviour and Organisation*, vol. 1, pp. 233-247.

Teece, D. J. (1982), 'Toward an Economic Theory of the Multiproduct Firm', *Journal of Economic Behaviour and Organisation*, vol. 3, pp. 39-63.

Terpstra, V. and Yu, C-M. (1988), 'Determinants of Foreign Investment of US Advertising Agencies', *Journal of International Business Studies*, Spring, pp. 33-46.

The Rochdale Report (1970), *Report by the Committee of Inquiry into Shipping*, Her Majesty's Stationery Office, London.

The Shipmanagers' Register (1994), Ocean Press and Publishing, London.

The Shipmanagers' Register (1999), Spring/Summer, IRR Publications, London.

Thorpe, A. (1996), 'British Firm to Manage 30 Vessels from Jebel Ali: Acomarit Wins Saudi Fleet Deal', *Lloyd's List*, Friday, December 6, p. 1.

Tolofari, S. R. (1989), *Open Registry Shipping - A Comparative Study of Costs and Freight Rates*, Gordon and Breach Science Publishers, New York.

Turbin, M. S. and Rosse, J. G. (1990), 'Staffing Issues in the High Technology Industry', in L. Gomez-Meija, and M. Lawless (eds), *Organisational Issues in High Technology Management*, JAI Press, Greenwich, CT.

Turnbull, P. W. and Gibbs, M. L. (1987), 'Marketing Bank Services to Corporate Customers: The Importance of Relationships', *International Journal of Bank Marketing*, vol. 5, no. 1, pp. 19-26.

Turney, P. B. B. and Anderson, B. (1989), 'Accounting for Continuous Improvement', *Sloan Management Review*, vol. 30, no. 2, pp. 37-48.

Twomey, D. (1974), *Power, Trust and Inter-organisational Conflict Resolution*, Unpublished Doctoral Dissertation, Kent State University Graduate School.

Underwood, D. (1988), 'Ship Management: International, Not Foreign', *Fairplay*, 17th November, pp. 22-28.

Underwood, D. (1989), 'A Personal Perspective on the Growth of the Ship Management Industry Over the Past Thirty Years', in *International Ship Management: Profit or Loss from Shipping's Revival*, Lloyd's Ship Manager and Shipping News International Conference, Lloyd's of London Press, London.

Urban, G. L. and Star, S. H. (1991), *Advanced Marketing Strategy, Phenomenon, Analysis and Decisions*, Prentice-Hall, Inc., Englewood Cliffs, NJ.

Varadarajan, P. R. and Ramanujam, V. (1987), 'Diversification and Performance: A Re-Examination Using Two-Dimensional Conceptualisation of Diversity in Firms', *Academy of Management Journal*, vol. 30, no. 2, pp. 380-393.

Verma, V. B. (1993), 'Personnel and Technical Ship Management', *Maritime Transport International*, Sterling Publications, London.

Vikoren, D. (1992), 'Norwegian Tax Reform-What are the Implications for Norwegian Shipping?' in *Leading Developments in Ship Finance,* 4th International Lloyd's Shipping Economist Shipping Finance Conference 1991, Lloyd's of London Press, London, pp. 35-43.

Vining, A. and Globerman, S. (1999), 'A Conceptual Framework for Understanding the Outsourcing Decision', *European Management Journal*, vol. 17, no. 6, pp. 645-654.

Walker, D. (1990), *Customer First: A Strategy for Quality Service*, Gower, Aldershot.

Walker, G. and Weber, D. (1987), 'Supplier Competition, Uncertainty, and Make-or-Buy Decisions', *Academy of Management Journal*, vol. 30, no. 3, pp. 589-596.

Wansley, J., Lane, W. and Yang, H. (1983), 'Abnormal Returns to Acquired Firms by Type of Acquisition and Method of Payment', *Financial Management*, vol. 12, Autumn, 16-22.

Watson, E. J. (1986), 'Managing the Relationships with Corporate Customers', *International Journal of Bank Marketing*, vol. 4, no. 1, pp. 19-34.

Webster, F. E. (1970), 'Informal Communication in Industrial Markets', *Journal of Marketing Research*, vol. 7, May, pp. 186-189.

Weinstein, A. K. (1977), 'Foreign Investments by Service Firms: The Case of Multinational Advertising Agencies', *Journal of International Business Studies*, Spring/Summer, pp. 83-91.

Wernerfelt, B. (1984), 'A Resource Based View of the Firm', *Strategic Management Journal*, vol. 5, pp. 171-180.

Whyte, J. L. (1993), 'The Freight Transport Market: Buyer-Seller Relationships and Selection Criteria', *International Journal of Physical Distribution and Logistics Management*, vol. 23, no. 3, pp. 29-37.

Withley, M. J. and Cooper, W. H. (1989), 'Predicting Exit, Voice, Loyalty and Neglect', *Administrative Science Quarterly*, vol. 34, no. 4, pp. 521-539.

Wikstrom, S. and Normann, R. (1994), *Knowledge and Value: A New Perspective on Corporate Transformation*, Routledge, London.

Wilkinson, A., Marchington, M., Ackers, P. and Goodman, J. (1992), 'Total Quality Management and Employee Involvement', *Human Resource Management Journal*, vol. 2, no. 4, pp. 1-20.

Wilkinson, A. and Witcher, B. (1991), 'Quality Concerns for Managers', *International Journal of Quality & Reliability Management*, vol. 9, no. 2, pp. 64-67.

Williams, G. (1993), 'The Ship Management Market – Developments in the Industry Structure', *Putteridge Papers*, vol. 1, no. 1, pp. 18-25.

Williams, J. (1992), 'How Sustainable is your Competitive Advantage', *California Management Review*, vol. 33, pp. 29-51.

Williamson, O. E. (1975), *Markets and Hierarchies: Analysis and Antitrust Implications*, The Free Press, New York.

Williamson, O. E. (1979), 'Transaction Cost Economics: The Governance of Contractual Relations', *Journal of Law and Economics*, vol. 22, pp. 233-262.

Williamson, O. E. (1981), 'The Economics of Organisation: The Transaction Cost Approach', *American Journal of Sociology*, vol. 87, pp. 548-577.

Williamson, O. E. (1985), *The Economic Institutions of Capitalism*, The Free Press, New York.

Willingale, M. (1992), 'Do the Risks Outweigh the Rewards?' in *Leading Developments in Ship Management*, 2nd International LSM Ship Management Conference Proceedings, London, Lloyd's of London Press, pp. 29-33.

Willingale, M. (1998), *Ship Management*, LLP Limited, London.

Wilson, A. (1972), *The Marketing of Professional Services*, McGraw-Hill, London.

Wilson, D. T. and Mummalaneni, V. (1986), 'Bonding and Commitment in Buyer-Seller Relationships: a Preliminary Conceptualisation', *Industrial Marketing & Purchasing*, vol. 1, no. 3, pp. 44-58.

Wilson, D. T. and Mummalaneni, V. (1988), *Modelling and Measuring Buyer-Seller Relationships*, Working paper, Report 3-1988, Institute for the Study of Business Markets, College of Business Administration, The Pennsylvania State University.

Wind, Y. and Perlmutter, H. V. (1977), 'On the Identification of the Frontier Issues in International Marketing', *Columbia Journal of World Business*, vol. 12, pp. 131-139.

Wittreich, W. J. (1966), 'How to Buy/Sell Professional Services', *Harvard Business Review*, March-April, pp. 127-138.

Yip, G. S. (1982), 'Diversification Entry: Internal Development versus Acquisition', *Strategic Management Journal*, vol. 3, pp. 331-345.

Young, L. C. and Wilkinson, I. F. (1989), 'The Role of Trust and Co-operation in Marketing Channels: A Preliminary Study', *European Journal of Marketing*, vol. 23, no. 2, pp. 109-122.

Yuchtman, E. and Seashore, S. (1967), 'A System Resource Approach to Organisational Effectiveness', *American Sociological Review*, vol. 32, December, pp. 891-902.

Zeithaml, V. A. (1981), 'How Consumer Evaluation Processes Differ Between Goods and Services, in J. H. Donnelly and W. R. George (eds), *Marketing of Services*, American Marketing Association, Chicago, Ill, pp. 18-27.